the STUFF

the STUFF

Unlock Your Power to Overcome Challenges, Soar, and Succeed

DR. SAMPSON DAVIS
AND SHARLEE JETER
WITH MARCUS BROTHERTON

GALLERY BOOKS

JETER PUBLISHING

New York   London   Toronto   Sydney   New Delhi

Gallery Books / Jeter Publishing
An Imprint of Simon & Schuster, Inc.
1230 Avenue of the Americas
New York, NY 10020

First Gallery Books hardcover edition May 2018

GALLERY BOOKS and colophon are registered trademarks
of Simon & Schuster, Inc.

For information about special discounts for bulk purchases,
please contact Simon & Schuster Special Sales at 1-866-506-1949
or business@simonandschuster.com.

The Simon & Schuster Speakers Bureau can bring authors
to your live event. For more information or to book an event,
contact the Simon & Schuster Speakers Bureau at 1-866-248-3049
or visit our website at www.simonspeakers.com.

Interior design by Davina Mock-Maniscalco

Illustration on page 111 © Tom Booth

Manufactured in the United States of America

10   9   8   7   6   5   4   3   2   1

Library of Congress Cataloging-in-Publication Data is available.

ISBN 978-1-5011-7515-2
ISBN 978-1-5011-7517-6 (ebook)

For Jalen and Bella,
may you always live a life dedicated
to helping others find their Stuff.
—Sharlee

For my sons, Jaxson and Luke.
Always do your best.
—Sampson

the Stuff: [*stuhf*] noun:
a cultivatable inner fortitude used by people
to overcome obstacles, soar, and succeed

Contents

FOREWORD
by Derek Jeter

My younger sister, Sharlee, the coauthor of this book, is one of the strongest people I've ever known. When she was just twenty years old and still in college, she was diagnosed with cancer. But instead of giving up, my sister fought back. Sharlee and I have always been close, but sometimes the people you know best can still surprise you. When she got sick, I saw something in her I hadn't realized was there—an incredible well of perseverance and courage she used to overcome her life's toughest challenge. As I was then, I'm still inspired by her story and know she's not alone in finding the Stuff within her during an immense personal trial.

Although Sharlee was the one truly suffering, my parents and I were also sick with worry and disbelief. It was among the most trying times of our lives, but we drew strength from her resilience. Seeing her determination made us stronger, too. We knew we had to be to provide her the quality of support she deserved. But even when I just wanted to drop everything and head home to be with her—talking to her or teasing her or holding her hand through all those treatments—I had to press forward and keep living my day-to-day life. My entire family had to keep going, even though it was hard to do.

Watching my parents find the Stuff within themselves and use it to remain confident that Sharlee was going to be okay was also inspiring. We believed she was going to beat this thing. And she did. Seeing her dig deep inside herself to access an inner power to prevail was amazing. I think she even surprised herself. Sharlee indeed had the Stuff.

I first met Dr. Sampson Davis at a high school leadership conference my Turn 2 Foundation hosted in Chicago. Since then, he's become close friends with my sister and a steady supporter of our foundation's efforts and participants. Sampson's story has been an inspiration to others for many years. His journey—growing up in Newark, New Jersey, and becoming a successful doctor and motivational speaker—is one we showcase to the young people we serve. He's got the Stuff, too.

Both my sister and Sampson have faced tremendous challenges, and not only did they come out on the other side as stronger individuals, but they've also both made it their mission to help others realize their own potential. They have a passion for giving back and sharing what they've learned and experienced—a quality I admire in every courageous person with a motivational story to tell.

The individuals profiled in this book are incredible, and how they overcame seemingly insurmountable obstacles, stayed so hopeful, kept charge of their lives, and remained resilient in the face of trauma and tragedy can provide all of us with tremendous insight. Stories of triumph energize us to become better people. I hope reading this book arms you with the tools you need to tackle whatever hurdles stand in your way and that it will newly inspire you to believe in yourself and what you're capable of achieving. Dive into any chapter and you will be moved by the stories you read. These people might not be world-famous athletes or celebrities, but they are true heroes. This book shows us that, just like them, we are going to have good days and bad ones, and life may hit us hard at one point or another. But, just like them, we're going to keep pushing forward, discover the best parts of who we are, and do amazing things for ourselves and our families, for our communities, and for the whole world around us.

We've got the Stuff, and we always will.

the STUFF

CHAPTER **ONE**

The Question Everybody Asks

In the depth of winter, I found there was,
within me, an invincible summer.
—Albert Camus

1

When Sharlee Asked the Question

EARLY SPRING 2001

Britney and I are speeding in her car on the back roads from Spelman College to the Atlanta airport. It's the second Thursday of the month, right on schedule, and we're late for my plane. The music is blasting and all the windows of the car are rolled down and we're both singing along with Alanis Morissette at the top of our lungs and we're both terrible singers. Britney has a whole head full of long, long braids, and as she drives her braids dance in the wind. My hair is patchy and shorter, and I'm trying hard to think of an excuse to miss my flight. An idea dawns on me, and I smile.

"Britney!" I yell.

She stops singing long enough to glance in my direction. "Yeah?"

"I need to stop."

"What for?"

"Water."

"Water?"

"There's a gas station just ahead. Please stop. I gotta get a bottle of water."

I'm still smiling.

Britney signals, begins to pull over, and says, "Okay, Sharlee. But if you miss this flight, it's not going to be because of me."

She screeches to a stop and we both run inside. We're superlate now, but I take my time in front of the glass doors of the cooler, examining all the different brands of water to see what's what. Water is water and I know that, but I'm trying to get to that place where missing my plane won't look like it's my fault. I can imagine me on the phone with my mother. *Whoops, missed my flight. Yeah, we needed to stop. What am I going to do?*

Britney is my closest friend, and she's by my side now at the cooler, nudging me to hurry up and pick a bottle so we can get going. Her voice adopts a motherly tone. "Sharlee, I am *not* talking to your parents for you. I *am* getting you to this airport. The choice is yours, but you need to decide you can do it. You need to get better. You need to get on the plane."

I let out a deep sigh. Britney's right. *Of course* Britney is right. She understands why I don't want to go back, but she's being the strength she knows I need right now. She's part of my team, part of my support network—and I'm beyond grateful for her, although I don't always tell her. I grab a bottle and pay for my water and shuffle back to the car and we both climb inside. Britney starts the engine and we roar off down the road. The windows are still rolled down and Alanis is still cranked and Britney starts singing again, but I'm not singing anymore. I'm deep in thought. And I'm aching. I mean, literally aching. Every joint in my body hurts. My arms hurt. My legs hurt. My hips hurt. My knees hurt.

That all-over achiness is a constant reminder that I have Hodgkin's lymphoma, and the thought of it gnaws at my mind just as the achiness nags at my body. I wrestle with the injustice of life. *You are not supposed to get a life-threatening disease when you're only twenty-one and a senior in college. You are not supposed to have to put your life on hold when you've nearly finished your degree and your whole life stretches out before you. You are not supposed to be having chemo treatments when you have big dreams for your future and you want an awesome career and you want to get married someday and you want to have a baby someday and the cancer messes with all that boundless possibility. No, cancer isn't part of the plan. It most definitely isn't supposed to happen.*

I glance at the road and we're nearing the airport now. Britney stops singing and we are both quiet. I think back to months ago, when I first felt a lump on the side of my neck, when I first heard the news that I had lymphoma. After the initial shock wore off, pragmatic decisions needed to be made. It was my decision to return to school despite the need to go through chemo. My parents are firm believers in getting a college education, but they wanted me to sit out a semester, maybe a full year—whatever it took for me to get better. They even prepared a little apartment for me in their basement at their house in West Orange, New Jersey, so I could live with them and still retain some independence while being close to Memorial Sloan Kettering Cancer Center in New York for my treatments.

It would have been easy for me to sit at home. But I didn't want to quit college. Not even for a semester. I didn't want to put my life's plans on hold. My oncologist, Dr. Stephen Nimer, assured me that both school and treatments could be done simultaneously. "We don't need to stop her life for her to get through this," he told us all. "As long as she listens to her body and makes good decisions, she can do both." To my surprise, my parents respected my decision and let me go back to Spelman for the spring semester, just after my treatments had begun. I was a math major, and my final semester was filled with tough courses. My life became a roller coaster of sickness and studying, sickness and studying.

Britney and I pass the rental-car return, and I see the sign for Departures. *You wanted to do this, Sharlee*, I remind myself. *It was your decision to do both*. I call my mom on my cell phone. I say hello, and she jumps in with questions.

"Are you at the airport yet?" Mom always knows my schedule. She has a habit of checking weather reports. Flight times. She's a walking Wikipedia of travel information. Particularly when the travel plans pertain to my treatments.

"Yeah, we're almost there, Mom. But I don't want to come home." I blurt the words out. An avalanche of emotion is within me.

"You need to, Sharlee." She says it matter-of-factly. We have had similar conversations before.

"No, really." A tear rolls down my cheek. "I feel better. I don't think I have cancer anymore. I'm all cured. You know I don't want to come home. Please don't make me. Mom, please—" I'm fully crying now. The tears are genuine.

Mom starts to say something, but there's a pause in her sentence and I know she's crying, too. I hear some static and the phone bumps as she hands it to my dad. He's got his PhD in sociology and is a counselor by profession. His voice is calm and understanding. "I know, Sharlee," he says. "I know. But you *need* to come home—and you know that. You only have a little more time when you need to do this. Let's just do it. Okay?"

They know what's ahead for me.

They know.

Every other Thursday after classes are over for me at Spelman, I fly from Atlanta to Newark. My parents and I have dinner that evening, and maybe I'll do something fun that night in the city. A movie or a show with friends. One last hurrah. Early the next morning, my parents and I drive over to Sloan Kettering, where I'm pumped full of chemo. It takes all of the morning and into the early afternoon.

Then the treatment will be over and the toxic cocktail of cancer-killing drugs will slosh through my veins. My stomach will heave and waves of nausea will roll over me and all I'll want to do is close my eyes and lie down. I'll go back to my parents' house and sleep for the night. The next morning I'll get back on a plane and fly back to Atlanta. I'll feel absolutely miserable on the flight and Britney will pick me up at the airport because she's the best friend ever. I'll go back to the apartment we share off campus and my stomach will heave again and I'll want to lie down again. For the next week I'll feel sick every morning. Every afternoon. Every evening. Every middle of the night. Every darkest hour before the dawn. I'll battle through the sickness and attend classes and write papers and do my homework and feel totally horrible. Then the nausea will lift and I'll have a few glorious days when I'll feel okay again. One day of normalcy. Two days. Three. Then, all too quickly, it'll be time to go back to New Jersey for another round of chemo. Another round of feeling horrible. Each round feeling worse than the last.

Britney has stopped the car at the curb in front of the airport. I unlock the door and glance at my hand before I step out. My fingernails have dark black streaks running through them. My toenails, too. Common reactions from the chemo. I need to give myself daily shots in my legs, and they're a mass of bruises. I'm on steroids and I've gained a lot of weight, which I hate. To receive the treatments, you can get a port put into your chest, but I don't want to have a big scar, so I chose another option: injections through my veins. That's riskier, because you can burn out your veins, and if that happens, then you'll need to have a port put in after all—plus your veins will be shot. The nurses at Sloan Kettering are some of the best in the world, but my veins aren't easy to find in the first place. After each treatment, my veins become harder and harder to find, and I feel like a pincushion; my arms are bruised all over. The treatments themselves burn. During chemo, I put ice bags all over my arms to cool the heat. And when each treatment is over, I feel as though I have metal in my mouth. All foods make me nauseous. Even my favorites. Pizza? *Barf.* Steak? *Yuck.* Ice cream? *Gross.* It's a severe sort of nausea, too, where every taste and even the smell of food bother me. I am afraid to eat. Not to mention my hair has been falling out in clumps.

I am standing on the sidewalk now in front of the airport. My carry-on bag is with me. Britney whisks around the front of the car to me and gives me a hug. No need to pay for parking. We both know the routine.

"See ya soon, honey," she says. "Hurry back, okay?"

I nod into her shirt collar. Then she's back in the car and driving away. I'm all alone at Departures and I glance at my watch and a thought runs through my mind: *What would happen if I just didn't show up?* I'm still wrestling with myself, and I quickly brush away the thought. *I can't do that to my parents. If they came to meet me at the airport back in New Jersey and I wasn't there—that would really let them down. I don't want to disappoint them. They have my back already, and this is hard enough for them.*

My bag feels heavy and I begin to walk, but I'm still dragging my feet. Altogether, I have been prescribed somewhere between thirty and forty medications. Each does something positive, but each comes with side effects. Some medications battle only the side effects of other medications. One medication makes me constipated. One makes me go to the bathroom. Another gives me migraines. Another takes away the migraines. I never take all my medications. I don't like having that much in my system.

Another thought shoots through my mind: *I could just get into a taxi and leave. Go back to Spelman. Forget treatments. I'm done. I'm cured. I don't need the chemo anymore.* But then reality sets in. *I'm broke. I have no money for a taxi. College is a thirty-minute drive away. I am stuck at the airport. I can only go forward.*

I sigh, square my shoulders, and head toward the check-in counter. This time I'm walking a little faster. Altogether, I'm scheduled for six months of chemo. Twelve treatments total. One treatment every other Friday. With each treatment, even though I have a brief reprieve toward the end of each cycle, I feel progressively sicker and sicker.

I get my boarding pass, navigate through security, and hurry toward my gate. One final thought hits me as I walk onto the plane and find my seat: *I am only halfway done—and I am not sure I'm going to make it.*

The question I'm asking is: *Do I have the Stuff?*

2
_____

When Sampson Asked the Question

MIDSUMMER 1990

'm only seventeen, but already I like to think of myself as a young man who knows the streets. I'm walking with my older sister, Fellease, up the hard concrete steps of the police department in Newark, and my heart thumps like a shoe in a clothes dryer, but I'm feeling strangely peaceful, too. Fellease is fourteen years older and knows the system. She's assured me this is what needs to happen. I'll confess my part in the crime. Then I'll get a notice to appear before a judge. That will be it—I'll be home by suppertime, wolfing down Mom's homemade mac and cheese.

We are inside the front door of the police station, and I explain my story at the front desk. The walls feel cold, they're painted brick, and we are led to a back room with no windows and told to sit. A table squats in the middle. A police officer walks around the table and sits on the other side. He's in his fifties and sports a mustache and reminds me of my father. His tone is encouraging, comforting, but serious, too. He means business.

"So you came here to turn yourself in?" he asks.

"Yeah," I say. "I mean, *yes, sir.* My car was impounded, so I figured my car would get traced back to me. That's why I'm here."

"You were involved in the crime, then?"

"No, not really." I try to minimize my part as I tell him the rest of the story. I was hanging out with two older guys and one younger guy and we decided to become the Robin Hoods of Newark. Our plan was to steal from rich drug dealers and give to the poor, which is *us,* of course. So my three friends robbed some teens on a corner who looked like drug dealers while I was behind the wheel of the getaway car. In the midst of the theft, I heard the cops coming and took off. My friends all got arrested. I got away but left my car at the scene. Fellease and I both figured the law would go easier on me if I came in on my own initiative.

A story such as mine wasn't unheard of in my neighborhood. Life had never been easy for anyone I ever knew. My parents divorced when I was ten. Dad moved out, and money was always tight, although Mom found new ways to stretch a meal. Most of my friends came from similar broken family structures. I did well in school, but most of my friends enjoyed hanging out on street corners, stealing cars, getting into fights, and strutting around as the bad boys of the neighborhood. In that low-income, drug-infested inner-city environment, a young man is considered either all good or all bad. If you're good, then your friends make fun of you. If you're bad, then you're respected. You're admired. You're the Man. That's what I had to live up to.

My story is told to the police officer and it feels like we are finishing up, so Fellease says, "Can I sign him out now and take him home?"

"Oh, no," says the police officer. He looks almost surprised at the question. "Since there were guns involved, that won't be happening today. He'll be in juvenile detention until his court date."

The news hits me like a load of bricks. I am stunned. Speechless. The police officer walks around the table, tells me to stand up, and snaps handcuffs on my wrists. Hey, I didn't sign up for this nightmare. He walks me out of the precinct and into a holding area, where I'm told to wait for transportation. My sister is crying, and I quickly decide to steel myself and look tough. On the outside, my face shows all the emotion of the Marlboro man. But inside, I'm crumbling.

They put me into a white van with blue lettering on the side. Me and a couple other guys. The van has windows, but there's metal fencing over them. We are transported about ten miles away to the juvenile facility in downtown Newark. On the street, it's known to be the toughest juvenile facility in the state of New Jersey. When we get there, we drive through an underground tunnel to reach the entry door. The van stops, and we are taken inside.

I'm in a line of young men now. We are each fingerprinted. The guard orders us to strip for our body-cavity search. I lift my testicles. I bend over and cough. They search me thoroughly. After that they look inside my mouth. Anywhere I might hide drugs or a weapon. The search over, I am still naked. I walk forward to get my new detention clothes: a blue jump shirt and blue worker pants. I feel completely vulnerable. Open to attack. I'm allowed to keep my own sneakers.

They escort me through the hallways to Unit A, the toughest unit in the toughest facility. The older teens are here. The ones who've done the most serious crimes. It's an old building. Same cold brick walls as the police station. Some missing tiles on the floor. A faint smell of mildew and ammonia in the air. It's July, and there's no air-conditioning. It's stifling hot, and sweat rolls down my face. There are windows here and there and the windows are open, but the windows have bars. I can hear people outside the facility. Kids like me. They're laughing. Chattering. Free in summertime. I shake my head in anger, disgust, shame. It's my own doing, and I'm actually in jail.

Jail!

The room I'm led to is open, like a big cafeteria. Teenage guys dressed in detention clothes are everywhere in the room. About a hundred youths in all. The teens are oversized. Overgrown. Many have facial hair. Some play cards. Some watch TV. A guard known as a "counselor" sits behind a desk, but he doesn't seem to be doing much. All types of chaos surround the guard. Teens are throwing paper. Arguing. Yelling. Cursing. The guard ignores the commotion. He's not paying attention at all.

I feel the focus turn toward me and the other new guys. We are released into the room, and I recognize a couple of guys from my neighborhood and go over to them and nod. No one says much. I learn later that no one asks you what you're in for. No one cares. The other teens are all sizing you up at first, trying to see who's weak and who's strong. I spend the rest of the afternoon sitting in a chair watching TV. Out of the corners of my eyes, I study the other inmates. Trying to figure out my next move.

We are fed supper. A baloney sandwich on white bread. Then I'm taken to my cell. It's small, maybe seven by nine feet, with one metal-frame bed inside. Teens are not housed with cellmates. The bedsprings are rusty, and on top is a thin mattress stained with urine. A bottom sheet and top sheet are provided but no pillow. A pillow is a privilege. A community bathroom is down the hallway, but there's no toilet in my cell. If you need to go at night, you cross your legs and hang on until morning.

The guard locks me in my cell. The lights are turned off. It's nine o'clock, and I hear other inmates yelling, shouting. The noise goes on throughout the night. It grows cold in my cell despite the July heat, and I wrap myself in my top sheet in an effort to protect myself. From exactly what, I don't know. I don't sleep a wink.

At six the next morning the lights snap on. The start of a new day. I am led to a communal shower. I don't know what will happen and keep a close lookout. I'm in survival mode, and all I can think about is making it through this day. Shower over, I dry myself and dress in my detention clothes and am led to breakfast. Dry toast. Cereal. Rejected food from a supermarket. We are led back to the open area, and the day of waiting begins. All that's left to do now is kill time.

I learn the names of two guys. The first is "Champ." Nearly eighteen years old, he's the lion of the bunch. Six feet, three inches tall. Solid muscle. The king of juvenile detention. The story about Champ is he is a repeat offender. For what, I'm not told. But by the way he carries himself with a swagger, I figure he knows he's going to be in the system a long time. Champ acts like he has nothing to lose.

The second is Champ's sidekick. "Pissy Pillow" is his name, or at least that's what I call him in my mind. He spends his days paying homage to Champ. He's about fifteen, small-framed, and witty. He doesn't have the size or strength to survive inside detention, but he's a wordsmith. He survives by making other guys laugh.

"Hey, Marshall," he says to me one day, calling me by my middle name, which I often go by. "I got a pillow for you. Mine. But I gotta be honest with you. I wet my bed every night, so there's pee on the pillow. And after I finish playing with myself, I use my pillow to dry off. But you can have it. It's yours." All the guys around him laugh.

I mutter in a low voice, "I don't think I want that pillow."

One afternoon I am in the open room playing cards with another guy. I don't know him very well. Champ comes up to us. He's staring hard at me, his eyes locked on mine, but quicker than anything he hauls back and bashes the other guy with his fist. One punch. The guy is knocked out and falls to the floor. No explanation is given. Nothing is spoken. Champ just walks away. That's why he's called Champ. He does whatever he wants.

Pissy Pillow is quick on the draw. In a voice like Howard Cosell's he offers commentary on the fight: "Oh, man! Champ just knocked him out. He's on the ground. He's stunned. It's a complete and total victory."

The guards don't do anything. When the other guy comes to, he's transferred to another unit.

I hate where I am. I hate this place of bars and cruelty. Other guys act as though they're proud to be in juvenile detention, but not me. One afternoon a repeat offender is led in by a guard and all his friends gather around him, welcoming him back. I learn that for some kids, this is how it goes. Every year they spend their school year outside and their summers in detention. Year after year after year.

I'm from the streets, too. I am no different from these kids. But I am not comfortable with being in jail, and I never get comfortable with it. The facility feels like an allergy to me. Jail is like having hives. I'm itching. Scratching. Aching to get out.

But I don't know if I ever will. My court date is changed twice and eventually set for four weeks from the time those detention doors first locked behind me. My folks put aside their marital differences, pool their money, and hire me a five-hundred-dollar lawyer, one step up from a public defender. My lawyer comes to my cell and explains that he's been talking deals with the prosecutor. The best he can get is a ten-year sentence where I'll need to serve the first three in jail.

Three years in jail.

That thought sinks in hard. I'm not going to fight the charges or the sentencing. What do I know about the law? If that's the best my lawyer can get me, then I'll do the time. But my vow is this: if the prison system depends on me to stay in business, they're going to go broke. I don't have the blueprint or the formula to figure out the way forward. Not yet. I'm desperate. I'm hoping. I'm praying that God will show me mercy. But somehow, some way, I'll do my time, get out, and never come back.

One day—and it feels so far away I can hardly envision it—I'm going to truly make something of my life. Won't I?

The question I'm asking is: *Do I have the Stuff?*

3

The Conversation That Led to a Book

SOMEWHERE BETWEEN TAMPA AND NEW YORK, 2015

Sharlee explains: It's early evening, almost dark, and the drone of the airplane engines provides a wall of white noise so our conversation feels secluded. Sampson and I are sitting side by side, and the passengers around us are engrossed in movies and books.

Years have passed since my cancer scare and Sampson's brush with the law. I beat cancer, finished my degree, and eventually became president of the Turn 2 Foundation, which promotes healthy lifestyles, leadership development, and community service among thousands of young people nationwide. Many of the people we help live below the poverty line and often in challenging environments. I'm the proud mother of an energetic four-year-old boy. Life has not become perfect for me, but in many ways I'm living my dreams.

Sampson powered his way out of the drug- and crime-infested area of Newark, New Jersey, where he had been raised, and went on to become one of the top emergency-room physicians in the state. He's also a *New York Times* bestselling author, an in-demand public speaker, a frequent television and radio guest, and a cofounder of the Three Doctors Foundation, an organization that promotes health, education, and community leadership. He's an amazing father of two boys. Life isn't perfect for Sampson, either, but in many ways he's living his maximized life, too.

The airplane cabin is dimly lit. I always bring work with me on flights, and stacks of papers sit on the tray table in front of me along with my ever-present highlighters and tabs. Sampson is reading a magazine article and sipping fresh coffee while I'm already on my second cup. He sets down his magazine and raises an eyebrow like he's been thinking big thoughts and wants me to listen. I'm always up for a deep conversation, and Sampson has a ton of good thoughts. But he also knows I'll give him a tough time if his ideas are too loaded with medical jargon, which they sometimes are. (You lost me at frontal lobe, Sam. Just give it to me in layman's terms, *please.*) Sampson clears his throat.

"So I've got this idea for a book," he says.

I chuckle. *Oh boy, here we go again!*

We've known each other for about two years now and have become good friends and colleagues along the way—almost like brother and sister. We joke around and trash-talk each other, but there's also a lot of camaraderie and support that's developed in our friendship. We first met when Sampson's foundation honored me with an award for my community work. I was like, "Thanks very much, but who are you, again?" So before the fund-raiser, I picked up a copy of the book Sampson wrote with his two friends, *The Pact*, and read it straight through. Wow! I liked it so much I ended up getting copies for all my students in my Jeter's Leaders program. His memoir clearly showed how a young man overcame big obstacles, but in a way that was easy to understand, entertaining, and relatable. It also provided real-life proof to my students that they could do the same. After the event, I asked Sampson and his friends, known as "the Three Doctors," to speak at a Jeter's Leaders Leadership Conference, and things took off like a rocket from there. This year, Sampson has spoken at three of the baseball clinics I run. So even though I give him a hard time, I have the utmost respect for this man.

I set down my highlighter and say, "Okay, what's your big idea, Sam?"

He launches right in. "So I've been thinking about obstacles and how some people are defeated by their obstacles but others overcome their obstacles in big ways. Obstacles can even redefine someone's life. Like Magic Johnson. Remember right before the summer Olympics in 1992, when Magic first announced he was HIV positive? Everybody figured HIV was a death sentence back then. But Magic looked straight at the camera with this stone-cold face and told the whole world he was going to beat the disease. I remember *exactly* where I was at that moment. Don't you?"

"Nope. You're way older than me, Sam. I know about Magic's story, but I was just a kid when that happened."

Sam laughs. "Well, he's accomplished that. He's a successful businessman today, alive and healthy, and not only has he smashed the obstacle he faced, but he's redefined his life's purpose by it. And there are lots of people like that. Take Rick and Dick Hoyt, the father-and-son marathon-running team. The son has cerebral palsy, and his father pushes him in a wheelchair. The father reached deep into himself and redefined his life's purpose around his son's special needs. That's what I'm talking about. I want to figure out what that quality is."

I can see Sampson's onto something. My brain shifts into high gear, and immediately I remember a similar story about my older brother, Derek.

"One day Derek called me over to his apartment with this really urgent tone in his voice, and it turned out he wanted me to watch this TV special with him. Derek had already watched it three times. It was about Katie Piper, a model from England. An abusive ex-boyfriend attacked Katie and threw acid in her face, and Derek was completely blown away by the story. But what really captivated him was Katie's demeanor: totally upbeat and optimistic. She'd healed from the attack, although she's still got scars today, and she'd started a foundation that helps other people who've been hurt. When the show finished, Derek said to me, 'Sharlee, if that was me, there is no way I would handle it that way. I'd be finished. How do you even go on after something like that?' I'd never seen Derek so moved by a TV show before, and I said, 'Well, I understand. Katie is amazing, but I am sure you would be just fine, Derek. Why would you say you wouldn't be able to?' I've always known that my big brother can accomplish anything he puts his mind to. But Derek kept insisting that if something that difficult happened to him, he would be so angry and deflated and there'd be no way he would handle things as well as Katie."

(If you're unfamiliar with Derek, he played twenty seasons for the New York Yankees before retiring in 2014. He's a fourteen-time All-Star and a five-time World Series champion. He also has a supportive family who wouldn't allow much to defeat him.)

Sampson nods. "That's exactly why this book is needed—everyone has had that moment, a moment when they've heard a story or met someone who's inspired them and done something that they can't fathom going through themselves. These people are so motivating that they have this unique impact on our lives. We are moved by them, and we become fixated on them and what they've accomplished."

I add, "Derek said that Katie Piper was someone he would absolutely love to meet. And that rocked me to my core, Sam. Derek's accomplished what few people have and could pretty much meet anyone he'd like—and he wanted to meet Katie Piper. This is who he was in awe of. Not another sports star. Not a high-powered business or political leader. But Katie. It was such a powerful moment for me. And we've all been there! We all have that one story. But what was even crazier to me is that Derek can beat anything that comes in his way. He's the most competitive person I know. Yet he also believes that if faced with this battle, he wouldn't be as successful."

Sam gives me a look like he knows he has me hooked, undoubtedly part of his master plan, and says, "Sharlee, you and I both know that Derek is capable of getting through this. He could overcome this challenge and any other obstacle. Too often, people grasp at reasons why they feel unable to push through difficulties. They say things like 'Well, Magic's got a lot of money, so he can buy his way out of HIV.' Or 'Katie Piper's a model, so she has resources I don't have.' Or 'That's way too hard, I could never do that.' Derek's reaction shows we're all in the same boat. He's got talent, money, resources, and a supportive family, and you and I are both looking at Derek, saying, 'But of course you could overcome that.' But Derek doesn't believe he would. That's the exact position so many people are in. We don't believe *we* can overcome obstacles, and we think the people who overcome have something extra that we don't have."

"I agree. When I was going through cancer and decided to go back to college in the midst of my treatments, my mom told me that if this had been my brother's fight, he would've stayed home and gone through his treatments, then returned to school afterward. There's nothing wrong with that approach. Yet what intrigued me was to hear that maybe I had handled this situation differently and in a way that would be admired by my brother."

"Anyone can overcome an obstacle if they want it badly enough—right?" Sampson asks. "Derek has the ability to overcome any obstacle, and so do you, Sharlee."

"Nah, this conversation isn't about me. I just think it's interesting how people can excel or be the best in their craft in one aspect of their lives but then insist they wouldn't be able to overcome a different obstacle. I'd say that as a whole, people are stronger and more capable than they think."

"True." Sampson takes another sip of coffee. "We can usually see this quality in other people, but it's difficult to see it in ourselves. Derek can see it in Katie. I can see it in you. If people are not able to recognize it in themselves, it is very tough for them to believe they already have the ability to overcome anything that may come their way."

"I don't know, Sam. I truly just wanted to go back to college and be with my friends. It was my senior year, and everyone was preparing to graduate. I didn't want to miss that. My decision had nothing to do with my being able to overcome huge obstacles—"

"Sure it did! Do you realize how crazy that is? You were battling cancer at twenty-one and refused to let that stop you. You had plans, and you said, 'Cancer isn't part of those plans.' So you went back to school and finished what you were doing."

I wave off Sam's words. "Well, I can't wait to read your book now, because you need to tell me exactly what I tapped into when I was in college, so in the future I can use it when I have to face other obstacles or challenges in my life!"

Sam laughs. He can see his idea starting to come together, and his eyes sparkle with excitement. "So maybe there's this gene that all people who overcome major obstacles share. If I can find out what that is—"

"Sam, Sam, Sam . . . you just lost me. You know I'll support anything that you do, and I know you'll write an amazing book, but please don't make me read a medical book! I don't want to have to do any research to understand what you're telling me. If you can find the qualities and common thread that link all of these people, you'll have done something amazing. I don't want to read a book that confuses me or makes me feel like I have to be a rocket scientist to figure it out. Just tell me what I need to do. What traits do I need to embody? You're a doctor who's great at explaining things to people in a way they're able to understand. Do that. Find a group of people from all different walks of life—people readers can't make excuses for—and tell their stories and see if you can figure this out."

"You're right," Sampson says. "The book needs to be clear, not complex. Far too many people face an obstacle and get stuck. They let their obstacle swallow them whole. Their negative situation defines the rest of their life. If done right, this book has the potential to help a lot of people."

It's a lightbulb moment for me. For the next several hours we talk nonstop, and I become more and more excited about Sampson's book idea. We both get off the plane with a sense of new energy and excitement.

Numerous conversations follow that first plane ride, and anytime the two of us discuss Sam's book idea while other people are in the room, they immediately have their own stories to share about someone who inspired them. The same questions are raised: How did they do it? What strengths did they tap into to succeed?

But Sampson gets the last laugh one day when he says, "Hey, you need to help me write this book, Sharlee. Let's do the project together. It'll be great!"

My brain starts to tick like a hamster on a wheel. "Me? I've never written a book before."

"Just think—we can both go on this journey. Let's find the common thread, and then you can discover what you had in college that you didn't know you had. Think about it. If we figure this out, do you know how many of your kids in your programs would benefit from this? How many people would benefit everywhere? I'm just saying!"

In the end, Sampson always finds a way to win. This is why I want to strangle him sometimes but also why I admire him. He always knows we have one common bond, and it's finding a way to help change the lives of the people we come into contact with.

We started coming up with plans to put this book into motion. We took notes, researching stories and people from all over. We set out to help people live their maximized lives and equip them with the tools to conquer the obstacles that come their way.

4
___

Your Story, Your Question

*S*ampson explains: Fairly early on, we came up with a name for this common thread: the Stuff. Like, *That person really has the Stuff.*

Defined in practical terms, the Stuff is the necessary mental, emotional, physical, and spiritual outlook and actions that any one of us can use to face and overcome difficulty, adversity, temptation, and even lethal danger. Think of the Stuff as true grit, resilience, an unshakable inner strength. It's that "invincible summer" within you that Camus talked about in the quote at the top of this chapter.

We quickly discovered the encouraging foundation of research that kept propelling us forward: that fortitude is a shared human quality. We've all got the Stuff. We just need to know how to turn it on.

A pioneering researcher, Dr. Hugh Crichton-Miller, studied fortitude extensively in 1940 as his country, Great Britain, was in the throes of the Second World War and concluded that "fortitude is available to all."[1] The Stuff isn't just for "extraordinary" people. Everybody is able to overcome obstacles regardless of race, socioeconomic background, or circumstances. It's the Stuff that binds us as people across the world.

In the present day, the behavioral researcher James Clear sums it up this way: "Mental toughness is like a muscle. It needs to be worked to grow and develop. It's the individual choices that we make on a daily basis that build our mental toughness muscle."[2]

This means that the Stuff requires discovery and development—

yet the Stuff is already there. It's an inner engine that needs to be started and fine-tuned, which is what this book is all about. All of us are capable of overcoming obstacles. None of us is forced to stay stuck. Each person can live his or her maximized life.

Our encouragement to you is to keep this in mind as you go through this book, because you might be tempted to read certain stories and say to yourself, "Well, that's fine for that guy, but I'm never going to climb Mount Everest, so I clearly don't have the Stuff." And maybe that's true about you and extreme mountain climbing. But you can climb your own "Mount Everest"—whatever form that takes. None of the people featured in this book described themselves as extraordinary. These are stories of "regular" people who have overcome big obstacles. The same can be true of you.

Let's face it: challenges happen in life. Period. When obstacles occur, you're asking the same big question that Sharlee and I asked ourselves—*Do I have the Stuff?*—and perhaps you're not positive that you do. Maybe you're confronting not just one but a series of painful situations, one right after the other. Allow yourself to see victory on the horizon. On the other side of those obstacles lies a good opportunity, a new path ahead, if only you can make it through to the other side.

You're in good company. We're all confronted with situations that call for us to step up. These situations provoke fear, anger, anxiety, depression, disappointment, conflict, and self-doubt, and when an obstacle stares us in the face, we have a choice: either we can fall apart or we can face that obstacle with courage. That's our invitation to you: choose to face your obstacle.

In the pages ahead, you'll read about the actions and mind-sets of real people who have faced and overcome their obstacles. We'll tell their stories, reveal their secrets, show core discoveries about fortitude, and even tell you about some of the surprises we encountered along the way. Ultimately we'll point you toward your own pathway of success.

This is not meant to be a step-by-step guide. We don't want to give formulaic answers, because we know life is too messy and nuanced for that. But we want to point you in the right directions, acknowledging the honest journey of discovery that happened in us, too. Our findings take the tone of "pathways toward answers" that you can discover and develop and then apply to your own individual situation. Ultimately the message of this book is straightforward: no matter how big the obstacle in front of you, you can overcome it. If you cultivate the necessary elements that make up the Stuff, your obstacles realistically don't need to stand in your way.

Sharlee and I add the caveat of "realistically" because we don't want to puff up our message, as helpful as we've discovered it is. If you're fifty years old, your dream of becoming an Olympic gold-medal sprinter is behind you. So our encouragement is always to consider the reality of your situation as you face and tackle your obstacles, but to challenge and even broaden that reality, too (as we'll talk about in a chapter to come). Because the good news is that much can be accomplished—often far more than we initially think. No one needs to be stuck in a defeated or less than fulfilling life.

This book doesn't sugarcoat the issues. Overcoming your obstacles won't be easy. You'll be challenged to dig deep, summon up the inner fortitude that's already inside you, develop it, and then cultivate whatever else might be needed. You'll need to work toward developing your resolve to go forward. And then you'll need to take action. You'll need to set out on your way and persevere.

The obstacle in front of you never needs to become your final destiny. There's big hope ahead—and that's our promise to you in this book. By coming along on this journey of discovery with us, you'll be able to sort through the qualities and actions of fortitude and gain a greater sense of what the Stuff is and how it works. By the end of the book you'll have the skills and inspiration to step toward developing what's needed so you can move forward in your own journey. You'll be able to pull out the Stuff and use it for greater strength and benefit whenever you wish.

If that all sounds good to you, we invite you to turn the page and take another step toward living a better, more fulfilling, maximized life. Hopefully along the way you'll have some fun, too.

And I'll work on toning down the medical terms and explanations, as long as Sharlee agrees to cut me some slack.

CHAPTER TWO

Choose to Hope

"Only when it is dark enough, can you see the stars."
—Martin Luther King, Jr.

1

The Little Boy and the Gas Can

JANUARY 17, 1987

SATURDAY MORNING, ABOUT 7:30 A.M.

John O'Leary is nine years old and dreams of pitching in the big leagues someday. When he closes his eyes, he can almost hear St. Louis Cardinals announcer Jack Buck call his name. But on this particular Saturday morning John is seeking a different sort of adrenaline rush.

He grabs the handle of the red gas can, the five-gallon one his dad keeps for the riding lawn mower, and tugs with one hand and feels the scrape of metal on the cement floor of his parents' garage. *Mmph. Too heavy.* With two arms, John bear-hugs the can to his chest, lifts it, and slowly tips it toward a scrap of lit cardboard on the garage floor a foot away. The tiny flame on the cardboard is almost out. *Gotta hurry*, he thinks. *This is going to be so cool.*

Just normal boyhood hijinks. Earlier in the week John watched some older neighborhood boys in the quiet suburb of St. Louis as they sprinkled some gas on the sidewalk and sparked it to life. This morning he plans to tip out a few drops of gas onto the lit cardboard and hear a gratifying *whoosh*. He believes the fire will jump a foot or so and then die. What he doesn't know is just how flammable gasoline vapors can be.

Mom and Dad are both out of the house this Saturday morning. Dad, an attorney, is busy at his office, preparing for a trial next week. Mom has taken his two-year-old sister, Laura, and fifteen-year-old sister, Cadey, to Cadey's singing lesson. Still asleep in the house are John's seventeen-year-old brother, Jim; eleven-year-old sister, Amy; and seven-year-old sister, Susan.

It is winter, and the overhead garage doors are shut tight. John struggles to control the unwieldy gas can. The spout is inches away from the tiny flame and moving closer. The fumes sniff the flame and beckon it in. In a flash, the flame is sucked up the spout and into the can itself.

KA-BOOM!

John hurtles through the air. Slams against the far wall. Collapses to the concrete. Smoke detectors blare throughout the house, and his ears ring. His head pounds like someone's striking it with a hammer. His body is wet all over, and he stinks of gas. He notices the metal can is split in two. He sees all that in a heartbeat and shakes his head, confused, tearless at first, taking stock of his wounds. In front of his eyes he sees a mass of carroty orange flames, red and yellow licks of color. Smoky blue-black billows of haze cloud his vision. Then it dawns on him. He is on fire.

A shriek of horror erupts from John's lips. He sprints across the garage, yanks open the side door to the house, and tumbles inside, through the kitchen and into the front hall. In every direction he's surrounded by the fire that clings to him. Flames leap three feet off his body. He shouts, sobs, prays, pleads for help. John's sisters Susan and Amy are awakened into a living nightmare. They're screaming, crying, panicking. His older brother, Jim, is up from his basement bedroom and sprinting toward him. In an instant the bigger boy scoops up a throw rug and blankets his younger brother with it. He collapses John in a tackle, beats down the flames, and rolls himself and the boy on the floor. The flames disappear, only to reignite instantly. Jim yells to his sisters to call 911. He opens the front door and heaves John outside into the wet snow. He runs after him and rolls him in the slush to douse the flames.

The fire on John's body is out at last. Amy rushes into the front yard, gathers John in her arms, and hugs him close. Her little brother feels strangely hot. Charred. Bits of skin hang from him. Pieces of clothes have become enmeshed with his flesh. She releases him, thinking she's only compounding his pain, because John is screaming actual words now, begging to die. Susan grabs a glass of cold water from the kitchen on her way out. She throws the water onto John's face, runs back inside, fills another glass, and does the same thing. The dog tumbles out of the house and barks his head off.

Everyone is outside now. Dazed. There's nothing to do but wait for the ambulance. The fire has spread through the rafters into the rest of the house. John is nearly naked. He stops screaming, stands, and stares at his family's burning home. Only he's hunched over. His arms and legs won't straighten fully. He worries what the neighbors must think. He has no idea of the extent of his injuries. All that runs through his mind is *I just set our house on fire. There's no way I'm talking myself out of this one.*

The fire station is less than a mile away. Seventeen houses away, to be precise. In mere minutes a fire truck and an ambulance hurtle down the street and screech to a stop. A paramedic jumps out, takes one look at John, and sets him inside the back of the ambulance. Jim tries to climb inside, too, but the paramedic shakes his head. John hears Jim say, "Please, I have to go with him. He's my little brother."

The paramedic is already focused on John, already uncapping a cooling solution, already cradling the phone to the hospital to his ear.

"Where does it hurt?" the paramedic asks. A voice on the phone crackles.

"Everywhere," John says.

The paramedic drops the phone and pours the cooling solution all over John, eases him onto the stretcher, and helps him lie down. John looks at the roof of the ambulance as the vehicle starts up and accelerates down the road. John glances through the rear window. The last thing he sees growing smaller in the distance is the look of utter alarm on his older brother's face.

2

The Incredible Power of Hope

I t's hard for anyone to fully grasp the level of damage done to little John O'Leary's body. A photograph taken at the hospital's burn unit shows a little boy lying on a blue gurney. The boy has a tube taped to his nose. His hair is gone, not missing as much as singed close to his scalp. His face, one arm, and one shoulder are visible. The boy's skin is a mass of white, red, and black lesions. His skin is bubbled up. Scalded. Seared. It looks like the rawness underneath a scab that's been picked away. The boy's eyes are closed, and he still has his eyelashes, eyebrows, lips, nose, chin, and forehead. But the fingers of the hand that's visible are welded together.

All told, some 87 percent of John's body is covered in third-degree burns. Most of his skin is damaged so badly it will never grow back. It's been burned through to the muscle, in spots even to the bone. In places it's completely gone. The remaining 13 percent of John's body is covered in second-degree burns, like a terrible sunburn, where the skin blisters, pops, and bleeds but eventually heals.

John's lungs are damaged. He can barely breathe. The likelihood of infection is deemed sky high. His heart races up to 200 beats per minute in a frantic attempt to push blood where it's needed. But his body is leaking fluids everywhere. The skin is the body's largest organ, and John's skin is damaged so severely the fluids can hardly stay inside him. To arrive at a mortality prognosis, doctors take the percentage of a body that's burned and add the age of the patient.

John's mortality rate is 109 percent. That means there is no chance of survival.

Absolutely *zero*.

He's a little boy in his last, agonizing stage of life. Almost immediately he will enter into a series of emergency surgeries. One Hail Mary after another. Before it begins, his parents are allowed to see him one final time.

John hears a familiar voice from down the hallway. It's his dad asking "Where's my son?" A nurse brings the father to the burn unit and pulls the curtain. The father tries to put on a brave face. He grins and asks, "John, what did you do?" John thinks, *Clearly no one has told my dad what happened. He doesn't know I blew up the house. Maybe I'll get away with this after all.* Already it's time for John's dad to leave. The father's face falls from a grin and he says, "I'm so proud of you" and then murmurs three times, "I love you. I love you. I love you." Then the father is ushered out.

John's mother is still racing to the hospital. The family is Catholic, and the mother is so distraught she can repeat only one word as a prayer all the way to the hospital: *Jesus. Jesus. Jesus.* Minutes later she arrives and is rushed to the burn unit where John is lying. John has been hurt before. Stitches. Twisted ankle. That type of thing. John, still unaware of the severity of his injuries, thinks his mother will give him a cuddle and tell him he'll be fine. If he braves up for the medicine, maybe she'll take him through Steak 'n Shake on the way home for a cheeseburger and fries. But this time she looks into his eyes deeply. Strangely. Unnervingly. It's enough to shake the boy.

"Mom, am I going to die?" John asks. He croaks out the words.

She takes a deep breath and asks one question: "Baby, do you *want* to die?"

John is confused. Unsure how to answer except "No, Mom, I don't want to die. I want to live."

She pats the top of his head—the part that's the least burned—lightly, lovingly, reassuringly. Then her voice grows direct again. "Good. Then look at me, baby. Because you need to take the hand of God, and you need to walk this journey with him, and you need to fight like you've never fought before. You fight for your life! Your father and I will be with you at every step of the journey, but, John, you need to fight now. You need to *want* to live."

John nods and whispers, "Okay, Mommy."

John lives through that day and night. Then another day and night. His odds of survival are upped to half of 1 percent. The burn unit at St. John's Hospital is nationally acclaimed. Its chief surgeon, Dr. Vatche Ayvazian, is one of the best in the world. But John is far from better. His body will eventually double in size from the swelling. His eyes will close tight and stay closed. A tracheotomy is the only thing that will enable him to breathe.

But he won't stop fighting.

Over the next five months he will undergo thirty surgeries. The enormity of the fight he puts up is almost unbelievable. His entire body is basically one open wound. Skin grafts from donors aren't an option, so the only place where the surgeons can take grafts is from the top of his head. A person's scalp heals within about five days, so each Monday they take a skin graft from John's scalp; then, each Tuesday, they must shave the graft to keep infection away. The pain is excruciating. Each day for two hours, John has his bandages changed in a tub of water. The pain is unbearable. He's bandaged and rebandaged from head to toe. He throws up repeatedly from all the medicines.

But he won't stop fighting.

As soon as the doctors are able, they start John on physical and occupational therapy, pushing and pulling against his fragile skin so his body doesn't lock up. The therapy lasts for three torturous hours every day. John screams so loudly that the therapists put a towel in his mouth so he won't disturb the other patients. As he screams he weeps. The therapists weep along with him. Pushing through the pain is the only way he can ever hope to move again. But it isn't just one joint that's damaged and needs therapy. John's whole body needs stretching. Knees. Hips. Ankles. Elbows. Wrists. Shoulders. Waist. Torso. Neck. Everything.

But he won't stop fighting.

Through a friend of a friend, the Cardinals' announcer, Jack Buck, hears about John's fight and comes to visit the little boy in the hospital. Buck is a larger-than-life personality who walks into John's room in the dim light and declares, "Kid, wake up—you are going to live! You are going to survive. Keep fighting. We're going to have a John O'Leary Day at the ballpark. See you soon."

Jack Buck comes back for more visits. He brings professional baseball players with him. Hockey players. Football players. Coaches. Teachers. John's story takes on a life of its own. Letters of encouragement pour in by the box load from around the country, around the world. The president writes John a get-well letter. Even the pope says hello.

Trying to heal never becomes easy. John wakes up from a surgery one day to find all his fingers gone. They'd turned gangrenous and needed to be amputated. His dreams of playing in the big leagues are over. A surgeon keeps hope alive with some tough but sweet love when he says, "John, it's true you'll never pitch for the Cardinals. But someday you might manage the Cardinals. You might not be a court-room reporter, but you can become a judge. You might not become a carpenter, but you can become a general contractor. Your life hasn't been taken from you. It's been given back to you."

And the little boy refuses to die.

Keep that image with you, will you? A little boy refuses to die. His family, friends, and medical staff are there for him at each agonizing step of the way. A community rallies around him. Just hold that image in your soul and don't let it out. Because we all need what's wrapped around that image. The wrapping is an integral component of the Stuff.

And it goes by a familiar name. Hope. It's that simple. That basic. That *needed*.

3
___

Your Point of Choice

(SAMPSON AND SHARLEE)

Let's face it: obstacles are thrown at all of us. Severity is relative. Sometimes life feels like you're standing in your front yard, staring in shock at your burning house. You're overwhelmed and have no idea how to go forward. You feel pain, dismay, and bewilderment. At other times an obstacle will present itself not in your own life but in the lives of people you love. Someone you care for is deeply troubled or experiencing sorrow, confusion, or fear, and you're wondering how—even if—you can help.

We've come to call this realization the POINT OF CHOICE. It's when you haven't sorted out a plan of attack yet and a solution might still be far away. But you see that you're at a starting line. You have a race in front of you, and the finish line is some distance away. You must decide now whether to step forward and begin. Your POINT OF CHOICE happens when you see that something is not the way it's supposed to be. You've faced, felt, identified, and articulated that an obstacle or challenge is in front of you, and now you have a decision to make. Your POINT OF CHOICE might have been a long time coming. You might come to this realization gradually, over a season, even over years. Or this realization might happen fast—in a moment of chaos or turbulence. Either way, the realization itself is significant, because it signals that a decision must be made. Remember what John O'Leary's mother asked him? *John, do you want to live?*

That's a POINT OF CHOICE. In a hospital, when you've just been handed a 109 percent mortality rate, hope needs to be strong, and love needs to be tough. You can't look at your obstacle and coddle the situation. You have to fight. And your fight begins with an unlikely weapon.

It's your choice to hope.

That's what John did that day while lying on the gurney. He chose to answer his mom's question "Yes." He chose hope.

Hope is not the final remedy. Hope is not the sum of all that will be needed. John still needed surgeons and nurses and therapists and modern medicine and a good insurance plan to pay the hospital bills and much more. There might be a thousand more steps of light needed in your journey toward victory. But at the very beginning, you simply need to declare that a 109 percent mortality rate is just bad math. If you accept the bad math, you will wither and die. Yet somewhere, perhaps buried under a lot of layers, hope still breathes. The hope you have might not look like much at first. But you know the hope is there because you can at least croak out the same response John O'Leary did. You might croak it out in a quiet rasp, but you croak it out in boldness of spirit.

Yes.

I hope.

I choose to fight.

When we were researching this book, this hopefulness, even the specific action of choosing to hope, was something we saw in every person we interviewed. The participants articulated their decisions in different ways, and it came at different times in their stories, but all of them said that somewhere along the line they deliberately chose to go forward. They made a calculated decision that their obstacle wouldn't get the better of them. Yes, hope wasn't the final remedy. Yes, action needed to follow the hope. But hope was the starting place. Hope was the point from which their journey forward began.

What exactly is hope? Picture yourself on the way to a baseball game. You're going to root for your favorite team. Or maybe you're going to play in the game yourself. Can you feel the excitement inside yourself? The sense of anticipation within? You *hope* your team will win. That's the embryo of this action and character trait. It's a feeling that better things are ahead.

Yet hope is much more than a feeling. If hope is only a feeling, then that feeling can come and go, and we're at the whim of an emotion. Hope might buoy us when it's present, but hope will leave us despairing in its absence. So hope must be more than a feeling.

Fortunately, research shows that hope is actually a mixture of things. The psychologist and author Dr. Shane J. Lopez described how hope is certainly an emotion, but is also far more than that. Hope actually mixes a variety of emotions such as joy, awe, and excitement, and those emotions combine two important forces: the ethereal power of our hearts and the rational calculations of our heads. Lopez pictured hope as "the golden mean between euphoria and fear . . . a feeling where transcendence meets reason and caution meets passion."[1]

Reason and passion—those are the two key words. Reason means your head is involved. You choose to hope. It's a deliberate decision, a matter of will. Passion means your heart is involved, too. And you can't ignore either. That's what we all must discover for ourselves, because the research doesn't lie.

- People with chronic medical conditions have been proven to get healthier—and healthier *faster*—when they choose to hope.[2]

- Students have been proven to do better on exams when they combine study with the decision to hope and then walk into an exam room feeling hopeful.[3]

- Employees who choose to feel hopeful produce one more entire day's worth of work each week than employees who don't feel hopeful. That means more promotions, raises, and rewards.[4]

Lopez put it succinctly: "We can't live without hope"[5]—even when the situation is so dire that hope is all a person has.

4
___

The Smallest Scrap of Hope

LIBERIA, AFRICA
JUNE 2003

A teenager named Mercy wakes up in the darkness, her heart pounding. She hears shouts. Cries. Screams. Gunshots. Her first thought is of her two younger brothers, David and James, and her younger sister, Teta, sleeping in other rooms in the orphanage. She throws on her clothes and rushes to find them. There is confusion at first. Orders. More gunshots. More crying.

Big men, strong men, are ordering everyone to leave the compound. They are militia loyal to the warlord-turned-Liberian-president Charles Taylor, and the buildings belong to the rebels now. Their hostility is almost unsurprising. The civil war in Liberia has gone on forever. The orphans are forced to leave.

They walk through the darkness, one mile. Two. The children

haven't been allowed to take anything with them. It begins to rain. Mercy is nearly fifteen years old, one of the oldest in the orphanage. She carries a little girl strapped on her back, about four years old. Her little brothers and sister and another little girl she's watching grab hold of Mercy and hang on any way they can. A hand. The hem of her shirt. Three miles. Four. Mercy fears the worst. She is afraid of their all getting shot. Slaughtered. Raped. Five miles. Six. The rain turns from a drizzle into a downpour. Their thin clothes are plastered to their bodies. She spots a log on the ground. It looks out of place. Jumbled. She realizes it's not a log and shudders. It's a dead body. She marches on.

The orphans are hungry and exhausted. After staggering ten miles, the children reach a place of relative safety where they can spend the night. A vacant school building. At least they can stop walking for a while. Mercy tends to the younger children as they try to get settled, try to get warm in their damp clothes, try to sleep. She smooths the hair of one. She sings softly to another. Her eyes close for what seems like only a minute, and then it's morning. The orphans get up and walk another seven miles, then board a bus to Monrovia, the capital city of Liberia. Rumors are there's a vacant warehouse available there where the children will be able to stay for a while.

On the bus ride, Mercy thinks back over her young life. She and her siblings were so small when they were first brought to the orphanage. An aunt took them there after both parents died. The aunt was poor and couldn't take care of them herself. The children's lives had never been great. When Mercy's parents were alive, the family had never even had a shelter of their own. Night after night, they slept at the homes of different relatives. Their mother tried to do whatever she could. Most days she sold water on the street. Then she got sick and died. Their father was someone the children hardly knew. He was killed in the war.

At the new site in Monrovia, the children settle in and go back to school, but it's never much of an education. Life develops a new routine. They do chores. They wash clothes. Mercy looks after the little ones. Braids the girls' hair. Plays simple games. Sings them songs. That is her life. And her future? Well, there's not much hope an orphan can cling to when she's in the midst of a fourteen-year-long civil war.

Sure, there's adoption. Mercy can barely breathe out the word— it's such a long shot. Particularly for a teenage orphan who knows her adoption clock is ticking. By law, Liberian children must be adopted before they turn sixteen. Most of the older girls Mercy knows who've left the orphanage are struggling to provide for themselves. Even if adoption is an option, no way could all four of Mercy's siblings ever be adopted into the same family. The odds of that happening are staggering. Maybe one chance in a million. Maybe less.

Still, Mercy hopes.

In fact, all she has is the smallest scrap of hope.

Life continues, and somehow a choir is cobbled together with the best of the children's voices. A bit of money is raised, and twelve boys from the orphanage are to be sent to the United States for an entire year. It's actually a fund-raising strategy. The boys will tour various cities and towns, raising awareness of the plight of the orphans back home. The boys will also be available for adoption. One boy picked for the trip is Mercy's younger brother David, age thirteen. Mercy will miss her brother greatly, but she's overjoyed he will have the experience. Food is scarce in the orphanage. Two meals a day at most. She hopes David will eat better on tour. The boys leave for the United States.

It just so happens that one Wednesday evening a North Carolina empty nester named Debbie Alexander hears the boys sing. She doesn't even know where Liberia is on a map, but she feels a spiritual tap on her shoulder. *Wouldn't it be great*, she thinks after hearing about their plight, *if someone were to adopt some of the children right here, right now*. She looks around the room, wondering if such a thing could ever happen.

Her husband, David, wishes he could attend that evening, but he is working late. David and Debbie Alexander have already raised two sons of their own. Their biological children—Josh, nineteen, and Matt, twenty-one—are both in college. David and Debbie are both looking forward to the next stage of their lives, expecting it to be a quiet season.

After the choir performance, Debbie connects the dots. The tapping on the shoulder. The ache in her heart. Debbie goes home and has a series of long talks with her husband. They decide to take the plunge together. Fairly soon, they adopt Mercy's little brother David and another orphan from the choir named Seeboe.

Back in Liberia, Mercy is overjoyed when she hears the news. Sure, she's worried she'll never see her brother again, but mostly she is happy for him. She knows there is so little for him to come back to, and now at least he has a chance.

In North Carolina, life at the Alexanders' house soon settles into a new routine. The two adopted boys are happy and begin to adjust to their new family, but as weeks pass and the Christmas season arrives, both boys become withdrawn, even sad. One day their new father asks why.

"It's because we miss our brothers and sisters back at the orphanage," they say. It's the first the Alexanders have heard of other siblings. Never would they have separated brothers and sisters had they known.

The possibility of their adopting four more children is slim. Talk about hoping for the impossible.

The Alexanders make sure the boys are able to call home to Liberia to speak to their siblings, which proves to be very difficult for both of them. During one phone call, Mercy asks to speak to Debbie. "Mom, we are so happy that David has a home! Thank you for taking care of him. We love you so much for adopting our brother. I want you to know that I pray for you every night."

That's all that transpires during this phone call. There are no hints. No pressure. No requests. No offers. But Debbie is quietly blown away. There's not a hint of jealousy or duplicity in the girl. Mercy is genuinely happy and appreciative that the two boys are being cared for.

A new decision is solidified for the Alexanders.

Mercy remembers the day well, not long after, when the father, David, flies to Liberia and visits the orphanage in person, along with his older biological son, Matt. David takes Mercy into a side room so they can talk in private. The words from the man she's just met are straightforward. "We would like to adopt you all," he says.

All.

Six orphans adopted by one family. Mercy. David. Teta. James. Plus Seeboe and his brother, Joe. The children are aged eight to fifteen.

That first night, after hearing the news, Mercy cries in her bunk. A friend asks her why. "I have hoped every night for a family," she replies. "I've hoped for so long. At last I have one."

It takes a while for all the legal work to be completed, but Mercy makes it over the line and is adopted just before her sixteenth birthday. The children fly to the United States by themselves. They carry no luggage. Everything they own has been left back at the orphanage.

Mercy has only spoken to her new mother on the phone and seen pictures of her, but she is so excited to meet her new family, she can hardly wait. All the children are bubbling over with excitement. Mercy sees her new mother from a distance in the airport and recognizes her immediately. They run to close the distance, embrace, and hold on to each other, both of them sobbing.

The Alexanders fall in love with their new children and the children with their new parents, but it's not all easy for the new family in the United States. The children test at a kindergarten level academically—even Mercy—so the Alexanders arrange for tutors and a private school to bring the children up to speed. The children must work to overcome cultural differences. They must learn a new language. But there are benefits, too. The children marvel at hot running water, television remote controls, and elevator rides. Mostly they marvel that they're all together. Loved by new parents. Loved by family. The odds were a million to one.

5

Your Decision to Hope

(SAMPSON AND SHARLEE)

When we traveled to Memphis to meet with Mercy Alexander and her parents, we coordinated the meeting less than a week prior to our trip. A concern we both had was being prepared for the interview but also making sure we would be respectful of the family's time. The minute we sat down, we knew we were going to experience something amazing. We connected with them instantly and listened spellbound to their story. On the plane ride back home, we could not stop talking about how humble Mercy was. We also discussed the reality of how not every orphan's story will end with the same positive outcome. Life doesn't always work that way, sure. Yet there is something we just love so much about how the small scrap of hope that Mercy clung to was never lost, how it turned into something big and life-changing. How Mercy's life today is becoming a beacon of hope for others. Her story is something that all of us can remember and point to in our own journeys of overcoming obstacles. Hope may be a very small thing indeed. But if the tiniest flicker of hope is there, then hope is never to be underestimated.

Years have passed since the adoption, and Mercy graduated with honors, on time, from Brewton-Parker College with a degree in psychology. She's in her twenties now and heading on to get her master's degree in counseling. She owns her own car, has a job at a preschool, and lives with three housemates in the city. The other children, too, have done well with their academics and adjustment. The future continues to look bright. Why has Mercy chosen a future in counseling?

"Because I can identify with people going through a hard spot," she says. "I want to help people overcome their own obstacles. I'd tell anyone to never let an obstacle define who you are. Keep hoping. Keep trusting, no matter what you're going through. Always believe that things can get better."

And how does John O'Leary's story turn out?

He never quits fighting. After months in the hospital and countless hours of therapy, John is finally able to go home. He's in a wheelchair at first when he starts school again, but soon he learns to walk again. Jack Buck stays true to his word and organizes a John O'Leary Day at Busch Stadium. It's an evening of great celebration, the Cardinals beat the Padres in ten innings, and John is overjoyed. With the help of tutors and summer school he's able to stay with his same class at school. A year later he's back on the soccer field, taking it easy but scoring his first goal in a penalty kick. By the next year, his surgeries and therapies are all finished, finally behind him for good.

Today John is a college graduate. He's married with four beautiful children. After college he worked as a general contractor for nine years, then became an author and speaker. To date, he's told his inspiring story in all fifty states and more than twenty countries. It's a story of love and courage, and it points to the ability to do more with our lives, even when something bad comes our way.

John's body is still scarred from the fire, but his face has healed remarkably well, perhaps due in part to the two glasses of cool water his little sister splashed on his face the day of the trauma. Today John water-skis and snow skis and plays piano and loves to shoot baskets with his kids. He gives a wry chuckle when he says he has "a great life, in part because the therapists put a towel in my mouth and demanded that I stretch."

He also chuckles at the recollection of the events the first evening he arrived home from the hospital. His mom makes him his favorite meal. The only problem is John doesn't have fingers. So his younger sister Amy grabs a fork, scoops up some chicken, and guides the fork toward John's mouth. But Mom stops any special treatment right then and there: "Amy, drop the fork! If John's hungry, then John will feed himself." No excuses are allowed, and John describes how that day marked the first day of his life slowly returning to normal.

Surely hope is made up of little decisions and actions of head and heart. The choice to eat chicken by yourself. The choice to believe that someday you might actually be adopted. If you can nurture even a tiny bit of hope, it enables you to move forward and create bigger and bigger chunks. What we've learned is never to discount even those tiny initial shreds of hope.

Dr. Susie Sympson, a psychologist with the University of Kansas, describes the decision to hope this way: "Any improvements that are attained can stimulate the process of reclaiming hope: the ability to see future returns, and with that, meaningful personal goals and the belief in one's ability to attain these goals as well as the strategies for doing so. The steps may be slow and cumbersome, but the trip is worth the effort for those who are willing to take the first step."[6]

Which is to say that hope breeds hope. Hope is not a transitory emotional state but a choice—one to which we need to recommit each and every day of our lives. It's where our journey toward overcoming begins. It's all part of discovering and developing the Stuff.

That's good news, but there's another step involved. Hope doesn't do too much for us unless it's actually articulated. We need to put a voice to hope and combine it with action. One of the best ways we can do that is when we actually put hope into a memorable and repeatable sentence, as we'll see next.

CHAPTER THREE

Forge Your Motivation Statement

The only thing worse than being blind
is having sight but no vision.
—Helen Keller

1

When the World Says You Can't

Shortly after Rich Ruffalo turns four years old, his parents notice he consistently cocks his head sideways to look at things. They take him for an eye test, and the optician fits him with thick-framed, thick-lensed spectacles. These glasses are two-tone specials—black on the upper half of the lens, clear on the lower half—and Rich feels like a four-eyed goofball. No other kid he knows wears glasses. His parents hope his eyesight will gradually stabilize and improve. But things aren't looking good.

Rich is a skinny kid in kindergarten, a bookworm of a boy, always picked last when choosing teams for dodgeball. With his thick glasses, he becomes a target for all his world's bullies. Two bigger kids choose Rich as their special project; each day they rough him up and make him cry. Plus the bullies eat Rich's cookies, a fate that to Rich feels even worse than being roughed up. Week after week goes by, and the harassment continues. Rich consults his mother.

"Did you tell them to stop?" his mom asks.

"Yeah, but they don't," Rich says.

"Then tell them again."

The bullying continues. Again he asks his mom what to do.

"Did you tell the teacher?" she asks.

"I'm no snitch," Rich says under his breath.

He doesn't tell the teacher, and the two bullies only increase their torture. They stick his nose in the dirt. They bend the frames of his glasses. They continue to devour his cookies. Rich has had enough. Right about then he finds a motivation statement for life. He doesn't remember where it came from. He can't recall today if he generated it himself or heard it somewhere. But this becomes his motto: "When the world says, 'You can't,' champions say, 'Watch me!'"

There's no simple way Rich can make the bullies stop. There's no way Rich can quit being a skinny kindergartner with glasses. One day at recess, the two bullies sidle up to him and begin to throw him around. As usual. They tell him he looks like a nerd. As usual. They push him. They tell him he can't have his cookies today.

When he hears the word *can't*, a spark ignites in Rich's heart. It catches the end of his internal fuse and rushes down the wick until it hits the stick of dynamite and explodes with a huge *ka-boom!* Rich says, "Watch me." He grabs one of the bullies and throws him to the ground. He grabs the other and throws him on top of the first. He jumps on the pile of bullies and pretends he's on a trampoline. *Boing! Boing! Boing!*

The playground monitor, already familiar with the two aggressive bullies, actually turns her head to look the other way. Rich isn't trying to provide the future politically correct world with a primer on how to handle bullies. He's simply declaring in his five-year-old soul that enough is enough. After he does the job, he brushes the dust off his hands and goes and eats his cookies, making sure both bullies see him enjoying every morsel. From that day forward, the bullies never bother Rich again.

Rich has learned a much larger lesson—one he will need to relearn as years go by. It's life's fundamental mandate that you must stand up for yourself. You must not allow the aggressive voices of the world to define what you can and can't do. That basic mandate evolves into an imperative to drive for your dream with all you've got. Your dream might need some reshaping along the way, but never let anyone tell you that you "can't."

Time goes on, and Rich turns out to be a fast runner. He adds bulk and muscle, and by the time he enters high school he's become a solid athlete. He dreams of playing basketball for the school team, and in summer he shoots hoops in the driveway day after day. He dreams of someday getting a varsity letter.

But four days before basketball tryouts, he's playing sandlot football with the neighborhood kids on the funeral parlor lawn. Rich makes a great tackle, but a kid falls hard on Rich's leg. Everyone hears a loud *snap!* Turns out Rich's leg has broken in seven places. It takes a year for his leg to heal, and he walks with a limp for a while after that. Though he still tries out, he's never able to make the high school basketball team. The coach tells him, "Sorry, but you can't be a basketball player. Not even third string."

Rich tells himself he's an athlete anyway—messed-up leg and all. He plays intramural basketball. He plays summer Watermelon League baseball and bats .300. He gets a part-time job at sixteen unloading trucks at the supermarket. All day long Rich lifts heavy boxes. He grows bigger and stronger from the work, tries out for the track team, and finds he has a knack for throwing the javelin. He practices until his hands are blistered and raw. His senior year, he earns a varsity letter in track and field.

Silently, he repeats his motto: "When the world says, 'You can't,' champions say, 'Watch me!'"

Rich goes to college at Montclair State, dreaming of becoming a biology teacher and a coach someday. He's six foot two and 210 pounds, goes out for track again, and earns a varsity letter in javelin all four years, qualifying for the nationals in his junior and senior years. He has overcome the athletic hurdle.

As each year passes, however, his eyesight problem grows worse and worse. He goes from doctor to doctor, but all they can do is keep giving him stronger lenses. He can hardly see the blackboard anymore, even when sitting in the front row of the classroom. His grades drop from As to Bs. Rich drives his car, but each trip is a white-knuckle experience.

Doctors' tests show nothing. But Rich can feel his eyes going downhill. His field of vision is diminishing. Where he should see things, he has blank spots. His eyes constantly hurt from the light. He squints to keep the light out and his pupils dilate, straining to let more light in. His vision turns from clear to translucent.

Still he doesn't stop.

Rich graduates and gets a job teaching at an inner-city school. He coaches basketball and loves the kids he works with—once spending his whole year's basketball stipend on a team dinner out—but the school is rough. A female teacher is pushed down a flight of stairs. Another teacher is beaten over the head with a telephone. One day four students jump Rich in the hallway. They push him into his classroom and open up their aggression, hitting, punching, kicking. Rich fights back and wrestles each kid to the ground. The kids respect him after that and start to call him "Mr. Ruff." It's short for "Mr. Ruffalo," but it's also an overt term of respect in that age group. To them, his nickname connotes a teacher who can handle everything any student might throw at him. To them, his name is really spelled "Mr. Rough."

The next year he's hired to teach biology, electronics, and environmental science in a different location, Belleville High School, and also becomes head coach for the cross-country and track teams. He keeps his nickname, but he's still going forward, living his dream, working with students in academics and athletics. He starts his master's degree at Montclair State, his eyesight still on the decline. By now he can barely read his mail, much less a graduate-level textbook. He gets into a traffic accident because he can't see well enough. He has a hard time seeing students' faces in the classroom.

Rich goes to the Board of Education's eye doctor, who examines his eyes and shakes his head. "I can't believe that you can teach with such little functional vision," the doctor says.

"Just lay it on the line for me," Rich says. "I can take it. Will my eyes ever improve?"

The doctor pauses, then shakes his head again. "No. I'm sorry. It's just a matter of time. You're going blind."

Blind.

2

Champions Say, "Watch Me!"

t turns out that Rich has retinitis pigmentosa, an inherited eye disease. There is no treatment, no cure. His eyesight gradually morphs from translucent to opaque. He needs to make some drastic changes in his life, likely quit his vocation, but he doesn't want to admit it. How will he ever teach public school as a blind man? How will he ever continue to coach if he can't see?

For a season, Rich simply wallows in self-pity. He quits driving and feels angry. Disheartened. Abandoned. He drinks too much in an attempt to quell his pain. He finishes his master's degree in biology, but by now he can barely see through a microscope. He marries, but with the pressures of his job and his impending blindness, the marriage unravels and the couple soon divorces. Rich is thirty years old and feels washed up. Afraid for his job, he tells no one at his school about his condition. All the while his vision grows dimmer and dimmer.

One day at school, Rich reaches the bottom. It's a few years before the protections and awareness brought about by the Americans with Disabilities Act of 1990 will come to fruition. He's struggling in the classroom. Struggling in his personal life. Losing hope. That day he's in the teachers' lounge, and his supervisor, the department chairperson, sees tears in his eyes. This isn't normal for Mr. Ruff, but the supervisor says with a scowl, "I don't know what you're trying to prove. Everybody knows. Why don't you just quit?"

Quitting is not Rich's style, but he knows he can't keep his near blindness under wraps anymore. With his resignation letter in his pocket, he heads down to the principal's office, squinting as he goes. It feels like the last walk on death row, and he hands the principal his letter and tells him the truth.

"I can't see the pages of the textbook," Rich says. "I can't grade papers. It's over. Everybody knows it. I'm blind."

The principal scans the letter, crumples it up, and throws it into the wastepaper basket. "Listen, Richard, I'm not accepting this," he says firmly. "I've watched you teach, and I've never heard a bad word about you from parents, students, or anyone in this city. You're an excellent teacher. We'll get you a classroom aide. Whatever you need to succeed. Now get out of my office and go teach."

With this display of support, Rich is encouraged but not yet convinced. He's beginning to sense support and acceptance—real teamwork—but before it sinks in, there's another audience he needs to face: his students. His next class is general biology, a mixed class of tenth through twelfth graders, one of his more difficult classes. He describes the students as "the *Welcome Back, Kotter* kids—misfits, mischief makers, fun-loving gum poppers—kids other teachers gave up on."

His emotions running high, Rich walks into the classroom with tears still in his eyes. The bell rings, and it's time to call the classroom to order, but he can't pull himself together. Usually he greets his students with a smile and a joke, then goes straight from bell to bell with academics.

"Mr. Ruff, why are you crying?" a student asks.

Rich doesn't respond.

Another student asks tentatively, "Did . . . did someone die?"

The students are all silent now. All watching him. Rich decides to come clean. "I've never said this out loud to any students," he says. "But I'm losing my eyesight, and I'm just about completely blind. I know you guys know that. I don't think I can do this anymore."

"What do you mean?" says a student in the front row, fired up, indignant. "You're not going to quit?!"

"No way!" says another. "You can't leave. We don't want you to go! We love you, Mr. Ruff. What can we do to help?"

Rich says quietly, "But I can't read the textbook."

Another student stands, her voice nearly a shout. "We'll read it to you, then. We'll read it, and you explain it to us."

The whole class comes to life, voices mixing in agreement. "We don't ever want to lose you," says one student. "Don't even think about quitting," says another.

And Rich remembers his motto: "When the world says, 'You can't,' champions say, 'Watch me!'"

From that point onward, Rich vows to be the absolutely best teacher, coach, and role model he can be. He pours himself into his vocation with renewed vigor. He memorizes seating charts and even entire textbooks. He teaches with a new attitude that spills over and nourishes his students: *If I can do this, then you have no excuses. I will succeed, and you will succeed with me.*

And the awards flow in.

He's voted his school's teacher of the year.

He wins Princeton University's Distinguished Secondary School Teaching Award.

He's voted state teacher of the year.

He's inducted into the National Teachers Hall of Fame—as of 2017, one of only 130 teachers.

He wins the Walt Disney Company McDonald's American Teacher Award for both outstanding coach and outstanding teacher of the year. The vice president of the United States presents the award to him on national television. After that award, Rich returns to school for another day of teaching. As he walks through the front door, someone grabs his arm. He's led to the auditorium, where 1,500 students rise to their feet, clapping and cheering. Full standing ovation. It's a surprise assembly in honor of Mr. Ruff.

One day a woman observes his classroom. Rich teaches as normal. He's memorized his textbook and mentally turns pages. He knows where all the students sit, knows each name, and knows the content cold. He throws in humor and infuses his students' learning experience with clarity, joy, and fun. The woman observes four straight classes. When Rich finishes the day's last lesson, he leaves the classroom, trailing his hand on the wall en route to the teachers' lounge. The observer asks him what he's doing.

"Trying to find the door," Rich says. "Didn't you realize I'm blind?"

The observer takes a deep breath and says, "I had no idea. I want you to know I'm recommending you for an award. Not because you're blind. But because you're a great teacher."

3

Your Powerful Motivation Statement

(SAMPSON AND SHARLEE)

There's something key for us to note in Rich's story—it's a component of the Stuff that we saw being lived out in nearly every person we interviewed. A motto.

That idea sounds so simple—that you can craft your own motivation statement, then remind yourself of it again and again, and somehow propel yourself forward by it. Yet a motto plays a surprisingly big part in overcoming obstacles.

"Motivation statement" is a term we like to use, and requires some explanation both in concept and in practice. Countless books and articles have been published that teach how to create personal vision and mission statements. But a motivation statement isn't the same as either one.

Let's say you're on a road trip toward overcoming your obstacles, heading toward a good destination. Your car is your mission statement: it's where you are right now and what you're about. Your road map or GPS is your vision statement: it pinpoints the destination and tracks how you'll reach your good opportunity. The gas in your tank is your motivational statement: it's what keeps you going and why.

We won't give away all the motivation statements we discovered just yet, but here are three we encountered in our interviews.

- Mindee Hardin's motto (see chapter 4) is "Listen for the whisper." It's an encouragement to set aside tomorrow's worry and yesterday's taunting and be fully alive in the moment that's happening right now, today.

- Glenn and Cara O'Neill's motto (see chapter 5) is "Hope is a nice word, but we need action." In other words, you need to keep going. You need to *do*. Hope is the starting place, but you must work hard to achieve your goals.

- Austin Hatch's motto (see chapter 9) is a faith-based phrase: "I can do all things through Christ, who strengthens me."

Although not interviewed for this book, a surprising number of public figures show the same pattern, such as:

- Staff Sergeant Travis Mills is one of only five soldiers in the history of modern warfare to survive quadruple amputee injuries. He developed his motto on the grueling road to recovery: "Never give up. Never quit."[1]

- Phil Hansen is an artist whose career was nearly destroyed when he developed a tremor in his hand. Then he learned how to "Embrace the shake,"[2] meaning: stop fighting the limitation. Embrace a restraint, use it, and even transcend it. He went on to great success using new and unique art forms.

- Derrick Coleman, Jr., Super Bowl champion with the Seattle Seahawks in 2014, is the first legally deaf athlete to play offense in the NFL. The obstacles he encountered on this quest were enormous. Yet he decided there would be "no excuses"[3] for fulfilling his dreams, a phrase he reminded himself about and lived by, again and again.

The act of forging a motivation statement—and then truly living by it—can provide an ongoing source of renewal when your internal resources are depleted. Your motto might be as simple as "I can, and I will." Yet that motivation statement can yield big rewards, serving as fuel in the tank to help you overcome.

It sounds so simple, yet there's more to this plan than appears at first glance. Being mentally prepared for a tough road ahead is essential—especially when you feel least able to access your inner strength. As we saw in the last chapter, choosing to hope establishes a baseline mind-set for overcoming obstacles. Yet hope alone won't hold off the darkness. People with the Stuff gird themselves for this absence of light by forging a statement that motivates them forward—and then articulating this statement to themselves again and again. They develop a goal-oriented mantra that continually points them toward success.

Possibly one of the most famous motivational statements is found in a speech made by the British prime minister Winston Churchill on May 13, 1940, when his country was losing the war against the Nazis. All Churchill had to offer his countrymen was "blood, toil, tears and sweat," a quartet of concepts that seems depressing, even antimotivational.

But the endgame held out by that quartet of words contained a much more triumphant note. The endgame was this: "Victory, victory at all costs, victory in spite of all terror, victory, however long and hard the road may be; for without victory, there is no survival."[4] The British people embraced Churchill's motivation statement as a call to victory. They were energized by his eloquent and inspirational speeches, including "We shall fight on the beaches, we shall fight on the landing grounds, we shall fight in the fields and in the streets, we shall fight in the hills; we shall never surrender."[5]

Likely there were many in the nation who had been thinking, at least secretly, *This war is too costly; we might as well just give in. How bad could life be under the Nazis?* But Churchill provided the motivation to keep going with something as simple as words. His determination to claim victory for the survival of a free world was what energized a whole nation to "never surrender." They and their allies went on to spend the "blood, toil, tears and sweat" to make it happen. So how can you discover the choice words that will energize you?

It helps to think of a motivation statement as a motto or mantra, a simple word group that you can remember and repeat until the statement becomes part of you. But don't think of this statement and what you'll do with it as mindless repetition. Rather, it's a statement that engages your mind, your emotions, and your will.

Remember Churchill's "We shall never surrender." That statement undoubtedly fueled a trembling young soldier to rise up from a foxhole and go over the top despite the danger, or helped a mother who saw her bombed-out home reduced to rubble to put one foot in front of the other and move on. It echoed another British wartime mantra, which first appeared on posters issued by the Ministry of Information: "Keep calm and carry on."[6] You might see this motivation statement on T-shirts or wall plaques today. People around the world still quote this bit of self-talk to keep going.

Recent research points to why a few choice words work so well to keep us going in our chosen directions. These studies confirm a link between short, repetitive speech practices and slower breathing patterns, quieted brain function, and ultimately psychological calm, an essential component of the Stuff.

A group of Israeli researchers enlisted twenty-three people who had never practiced meditation techniques and had them choose a calming word and repeat it until they felt rested. Meanwhile, they measured the subjects' breathing and brain activity by measuring their cerebral blood flow using blood oxygen level dependent (BOLD) contrast imaging, a kind of functional magnetic resonance imaging (fMRI).

Researchers found that after the participants repeated their words for an average of eight minutes, the participants experienced a measurable reduction in BOLD signals, meaning that their brains were in a more restful state. They were indeed calmed. And all they had done was repeat a word. The researchers concluded, "The triggering of a global inhibition by the minimally demanding repetitive speech may account for the long-established psychological calming effect associated with commonly practiced Mantra-related meditative practices."[7]

Too much research for you? Think of it this way: We conduct a form of this kind of test whenever we attempt to soothe a crying baby. We repeat a motion, such as rocking a cradle back and forth or gently patting a baby's back. Or we sing or chant calming words. Notice how repetitive lullabies are. The best ones repeat simple sounds or words: "Hush-a-bye" . . . "Rock-a-bye, baby" . . . "Twinkle,

twinkle, little star" . . . Before you know it, your crying baby is calm and hopefully even asleep.

Of course, we don't want to put ourselves to sleep with our motivation statement. We want it to energize us and help us reach our goal. So the value for us in repeating a motivation statement is that it causes us to focus. This reduces unimportant thoughts and calms the wild chatter in our heads that can so easily lead us on irrelevant tangents.

Twyla Tharp, a dancer and choreographer, recommends role rituals or pregame routines for anybody seeking success. She describes a set of repeated actions that keep her in her own personal fitness routine: she wakes up at the same time, puts on workout clothes, walks outside, hails a taxi, and tells the driver where to go. Her simple ritual, repeated, has created a positive habit. That pregame habit cuts the chances of skipping her exercise routine, and she doesn't even have to think about it.[8] Her motivational statement could be articulated as simply: "Stay on schedule."

There's no secret formula to writing your own motivation statement. It must be short enough to remember, clear enough that you know what it means, and able to inspire you to move forward. That's the whole point. You can borrow someone else's statement or create your own. Tinker with it all you need to so it fits your circumstances. Then, when you're happy with your motivational statement, do one more thing: share it with somebody who will be on your side, not on your back. Somebody who can be part of your personal support team, which we'll talk about in chapter 5.

4
––––––

A Big Bag of Optimism

SAMPSON'S MOTIVATION STATEMENT

ampson explains: It's Christmastime and I'm eleven years old and I still hold out a faint hope that Santa Claus might actually exist, although I'd never admit that to my friends at school.

Our home is just across the street from the projects in Newark, and as a child I don't realize the full dynamics of our struggle. *Poor* is not a word we use in our home, but I can see on our tiny black-and-white TV that Ricky Schroder, the star of *Silver Spoons*, has all the video games he could ever want. I don't have what Ricky Schroder has, but with my brothers we make games out of anything within reach. We fight each other with pillows. We play hide-and-seek; red light, green light. We are rich in imagination. In the togetherness, we feel as family.

My father is gone. It is Christmastime, and it's just Mom at home with me and my brothers. We check a neighbor's *TV Guide* and see that *A Charlie Brown Christmas* will be broadcast Wednesday night at eight. That's our big treat to look forward to. VCRs have been invented, but VCRs are only for Ricky Schroder's family, so we gather around the TV at the scheduled time, and the picture is just fuzzy enough on the thirteen-inch screen that Snoopy looks a little gray, Linus looks a little unclear, and Pigpen's ever-present cloud of dust looks a bit bigger than it actually is. But we don't care. We have Lucy and her five-cent psychiatric help on TV, we know exactly what Sally means when she writes Santa and asks for "tens and twenties," and we dance along to the jazzy Vince Guaraldi score in the Christmas play rehearsal scene. A few days pass, and now it's Christmas Eve, and we all go to sleep early, dreaming of the gifts Santa is sure to bring tomorrow morning.

We are all up early. We don't have a tree. Trees cost money. Mom has taken three shoe boxes and put nuts and fruit into them. One box each for me and my two brothers. An orange. An apple. A handful of walnuts. These are our Christmas presents. The shoe boxes aren't wrapped. Wrapping paper costs money.

Mom says with a jaunty grin, "Look, if you don't have anything else, at least you have food."

And we all grin back at her.

Sure, there's a promise she will get us something later. Something when the child-support check comes, although we aren't fully aware of the dynamic. There's no way we can be upset with Mom, because we can see her furrowed brow, the pain of not being able to provide. Even at my young age, I can recognize this. And none of us is going to give Mom a hard time. Mom is our first love. Our family situation isn't going to change anytime soon, this struggle we're in, and maybe we could get angry, but what's the point? None of us cry over our shoe boxes or even feel disappointed, at least that we communicate to one another. We peel our oranges and carefully eat each juicy slice, then munch on our walnuts, then bite into our fresh apples and finish them to the core. Then we go play with the toys in our room. We aren't destroyed, no.

This Christmas only puts a fire into me.

In the bigger picture of my life, this background, this context of poverty, eventually leads to my brush with the law as a teenager. But it also fuels an uncommon quest to truly make something of myself.

Later in high school, I make an unconventional promise with two of my friends, Rameck and George. I'll describe this pact in more detail in chapter 4, but basically what we did was chart our course to pursue something considered impossible for a person from our socioeconomic situation and unfathomable for three of us to achieve as a collective.

Later, during college and medical school, this pursuit will often give me difficult moments, and that's when I chant my mantra. I call it the "Three Ds," and I write out the words—*Dedication, Determination, Discipline*—on notes and place the notes on my college desktop, on the door frame of my dorm room, on the bathroom mirror.

"Dedication, Determination, Discipline" is the ironclad mantra that prevents negative thoughts from sinking in and growing into my soul. It allows me to change direction if thoughts of surrender ever enter my mind. It prompts me to dig deeper than ever before in pursuit of my dreams. I can't prevent a negative thought from entering my mind or a negative circumstance from entering my life, but I can certainly shape my response.

Like toward the end of my second year of medical school. I fail an important exam by one point.

One lousy point.

It means I won't move up with the rest of my class from academics into clinical rotations.

I've been weathering the academic storms until now. But failing this exam rocks my foundations. I feel gutted, exhausted, completely worn through. So much of the last few years of my young life has been devoted to education. I've sacrificed family life. Outside hobbies. Girlfriends. You can imagine sitting in a big, drafty university library reading books all day long. Every. Single. Day. Picture doing this year after year. This is my life.

The dean sits me down and says, "You can take another stab at it. Don't worry—you're going to get through this." But all I can focus on is his crazy-colored sweater vest. We stand up, and he actually gives me a hug, and I walk out of his office, holding myself together as tightly as I can muster. I don't want to break down in front of this man I respect so much. All I feel now is numb. I drive down Highway 295 back to the apartment I share with two roommates and sit on our old sofa staring off into space. My roommates are in the same program as I am but passed the exam. I don't know what to do. I don't know whom to call.

In six weeks I will take the exam again. *Dedication, Determination, Discipline.*

There's nothing to do but prepare for the retake. I crack my first book and begin to read. The hours blend together, and I enter a zone of studying, sleeping a few hours, and getting up to study again. This is all I do, day after day after day, for the next forty-two days. I barely eat. I don't go outside to look at the sky. *Dedication, Determination, Discipline.*

One night I wake, my heart pounding, and think of the exam, my mind racing. If I fail the exam again, I'll need to sit out a whole year. The next night the same fearful waking happens. Then the night after that. And the night after that. *Dedication, Determination, Discipline.*

You hear statistics. Out of a hundred and fifty biology majors who start their freshman year of college, only a handful—maybe forty or fifty—are still biology majors when they graduate four years later. Out of those forty or fifty, only a handful go on to medical school. Maybe ten or fifteen. That handful joins other handfuls from other colleges, and by the time they finish medical school, there are very few left who started together.

That's me. I fear I am going to be that statistic—one of the dropped.

Sure, I pray. I meditate. I visualize the exam room. I try to ram positive thoughts into my head. Then, on those nights I can't sleep, I come back to the Three Ds.

Dedication. Growing up, the only real thing of value any kid in my neighborhood owned was loyalty. You pledge your loyalty to someone or something, and that's better than a bag of gold, more significant than signing a contract. I am loyal to this life direction. I have pledged my steadfastness to this road.

Discipline. If I'm not the smartest in my class (and I know I'm not), then I am certainly willing to work the hardest. If twenty-four hours of study is needed in a single day, then that's what I will put in.

Determination. I didn't know Rich Ruffalo back then, but our mantras have a similar theme. You can't tell me I *can't* do something. I may need to come in by the side entrance, not the front door, but I'll find a way forward, whatever it takes. I have been told "You can't" so many times that the words have lost meaning for me. I ignore the words. They simply don't enter into my vocabulary anymore.

Dedication, Determination, Discipline. I repeat my mantra out loud. I repeat it in my mind. I close my eyes and see the Three Ds in big handwriting scrawled on every wall. The mantra resets my negativity button. My mantra battles with the dark moments in my mind, the negativity that tells me to quit.

The day of the makeup exam dawns early and bright. I walk into the test room with two number 2 pencils and a big bag of optimism. In my hand, I hold two Hershey chocolates and set them on my desktop in front of me as rewards. The test, in two sections, will take eight hours, and I will reward myself with one Hershey chocolate at the end of each section.

And I crush it.

I completely crush it. My grade comes back, and I am so way over the line this time in the "pass" direction that it's not even a question. In my soul I feel pure exuberance. The day after the exam, I go straight into clinical rotations. It will take me a while to heal, to regain my confidence, not to feel like a statistic anymore. But I am on my way. The future looks bright, and I am not stopping.

5

Rich's New Motto

R ich Ruffalo lives his dream in academics, even as a blind man. But how does he do in sports?

He coaches high school sports for years, sometimes as an assistant, sometimes as a consultant. He coaches for the United States Organization for Disabled Athletes, the International Pan Am Youth Games, the United States Association of Blind Athletes, and the Paralympic Training Camps, Teams, and World Championship Teams. Along the way, he continues to pursue athletic endeavors of his own.

At the national championships at St. Louis University with the

United States Association of Blind Athletes, Rich has qualified for the association's international team and goes to take the required eye exam before his event. There are three categories of blindness: B1, fully blind, up to B3, partially blind. Rich believes he's a level B2 athlete, but the doctor performs the test and informs Rich that he's now B1. Totally blind.

"What makes you so certain?" Rich asks.

"Well, just now I almost punched you in the eye three times and you didn't even flinch," the doctor says.

This news kills Rich inside, and he leaves the exam room feeling sorry for himself.

In this particular meet, Rich is scheduled to throw the javelin, and officials have announced that each competitor will be able to throw only three times. Rich wants to lift his spirits. He wants to win the gold medal for himself. He wants to prove to the man in the now unseen mirror that he's still okay.

A large crowd has gathered around the javelin pit. Rich takes his mark, his coach runs down the field and claps his hands to signal the direction, and Rich throws with a mighty heave. The javelin lands, and Rich hears the call "Foul!" All throwers hate that word. His first effort has gone to the right, out of bounds. When you're a thrower, you want to land your first throw inbounds, which takes the pressure off the second and third throws. But now, with the first bad throw, the pressure mounts.

Rich is positioned in a group of athletes—he has several competitors—and while the next guys throw, he grows angry. He pulls up grass and throws it. He can't believe what a rotten day he's having.

During Rich's second throw, he's thinking too much. He pulls down on the back of the javelin as it leaves his hand, and the spear pancakes. The nose goes up and catches air; the tail goes down. It's a dud. Garbage. Rich can hear it land with a clang. Again he's angry. He goes to the sideline and paces furiously. He has one throw left. Sweat runs off his brow.

Rich is called to the on-deck circle. He's set to throw next. And right when he's on deck, a woman approaches him and says, "Mr. Ruffalo, may I speak to you for a minute?"

"Sorry," Rich says, "I'm getting ready to throw."

But she's undaunted. Politely persistent. She introduces herself as a teacher from a nearby school for blind children. The children she works with have all been blind from birth, and they'd really like to meet him. Can he take just a moment?

Rich sighs.

The woman leads Rich over to the children and introduces him. Rich gets down on one knee so he can be on their level, and they find his hand and shake it. They have different levels of personal space, and they feel his arms, his shoulders, his biceps, and all say *Wow*.

It's a moving moment. The children are nothing but beautiful. And in that nanosecond, Rich is humbled. He reminds himself that he's almost thirty-three years old and he's had the privilege of seeing before. He's had the gift of sight. But these children have never been able to see—ever. Rich counts his blessings. He has an education. A job he loves. A career he's always dreamed about. So what if he's just been declared totally blind? He tells himself to snap out of it.

Just then the announcer calls, "Ruffalo up."

Rich walks over to the circle, grabs the javelin, and takes his position. Then he pauses, because he knows what he needs to do next. In this moment, he needs to change his life's direction. He needs to adjust the reasons for doing what he does. Instead of winning this meet to lift himself out of a pit, he changes his focus so it's on other people. No longer is his performance about me, myself, and I. In this moment, Rich decides to do his very best for the benefit of others. He chooses to become—in his word—*unselfish*. He realizes his destiny is to show people that being disabled does not mean losing courage and determination. And he develops a new motto to help him remember: "Do it for all the people who think they can't."

Rich looks up into the sky and calls out a prayer—in a voice loud enough for all the people to hear. Spectators. Other competitors. The teacher from the blind school. The blind children. "Dear Lord, give me the strength to do this for these children who've never seen and for all the people who think they can't!"

Then he runs down the runway and throws.

It feels just right. Awesome, actually.

He can tell it's a great throw because the crowd erupts into applause as soon as it leaves his hand. And when the javelin lands and sticks, the crowd goes nuts.

Rich has beaten the world record for B1 athletes. By forty feet!

In the course of his career, Rich goes on to win four different world titles in shot put, discus, javelin, and power lifting. He breaks nine world records and earns seventeen international gold medals, thirty-two national titles, and thirteen USA Track & Field state titles against sighted competitors. In 1988, the United States Olympic Committee names him Disabled Athlete of the Year. Today he's in seven different athletic halls of fame, including being inducted in 2009 into the inaugural class of the United States Association of Blind Athletes Hall of Fame. On a personal level, he's remarried to a wonderful woman and they have a beautiful daughter together.

And that's only the short list of what he's accomplished.

Rich's story shows someone who used the Stuff in different circumstances and time periods of his life. He started with one motivational statement, then came up with a new one as he entered a different phase. Similarly, successful individuals have found that forging a motivation statement (or several motivation statements) is a vital component of the Stuff. The road toward victory begins with a few choice words—the statement we're talking about. Remember, it's the gas in your tank; it's what keeps you going and why.

But having hope and a motivation statement to wrap it around are only two of the components of the Stuff. Somewhere along the line you need to step forward. You must launch, as we'll see next.

CHAPTER FOUR

You Must Launch

A journey of a thousand miles begins with a single step.
—Lao-tzu

1

A Laptop on the Kitchen Counter

Mindee Hardin is looking out the window, wondering how she got here.

Here, so blessed, in the home she shares with her husband. Here, with their four-year-old son and eight-month-old sweet pea daughter. Here, the owner and operator of her very own part-time business—a growing and successful trade show called "The Northwest Women's Show." Here, busy every day, yet still with a smidgeon of time and energy left to garden, scrapbook, send cards to friends, exercise, rest from work on weekends, have Sunday-night dinner at her parents' house, take vacations, volunteer, and spend time with her husband.

How can one woman be so lucky?

But why does it feel as though something's missing? Mindee wonders about a strange, unsettled feeling that comes to her unbidden. She can barely whisper this restlessness to herself—and she's not sure she even wants to. It's this: In spite of all these good things in her life, she feels held back. Cornered. Even grumpy. What does she want? Well, amid all the goodness, she's also experiencing the hard kind of daily grind that can sometimes feel so unrewarding—the grind of doing laundry, walking the dog, doing the dishes—and she wants to do something more with her life than change diapers and run her trade show on the side.

Back in college, Mindee studied marketing. For ten years, she worked for corporate giants: Nike, the McDonald's corporation, and Procter & Gamble. She misses her old life, and part of her wants it back. She misses taking business trips, pumping up the cash flow, and being promoted and applauded. Mindee is a busy working mom—just like so many mothers—and she's striving to find balance on the work-home continuum, all the while feeling as though she needs to be doing *more*.

The unlikely catalyst that helps her facilitate her wish hits one day when her baby is sniffling with a cold.

Achoo!

It's one of those nasty, crusty, snot-filled colds, and Mindee wants to put some saline solution on her baby's nose, because saline can sterilize an area, dissolve snot, and help lessen cold symptoms. But Baby squirms and screams, bobs and weaves. Mindee wishes for more hands. In a moment of quick thinking, she grabs a diaper wipe, sprays saline drops on it, and takes a calculated swipe at Baby's nose. Baby pauses her squirming and gives the tiniest flutter of a smile. *Hey, that felt good.* It's not a dry, rough tissue. It's not a scary nose-sucking syringe.

The next time Mindee's at the store, she looks for a saline wipes product specially designed for little kids. The idea sounds so simple, so helpful, surely someone has thought of it before. She goes from store to store but finds none—and that's her lightbulb moment. Mindee has never invented or marketed her own product before. She doesn't have all her variables covered or her questions answered. Yet she decides to create and sell the product herself. She simply decides to *launch*.

So she goes to work. She whips up a chemistry lab in her kitchen, interviews manufacturers, learns how to file a patent, designs a logo, and quickly transforms her idea into a business. The booger business. The name for the product emerges right away. Her son, like so many other little kids, has always called boogers "boogies," so Mindee knows that the name of her product will be funny, funky, and easy for consumers to say and remember. Enter Boogie Wipes, a product designed to care for kids with stuffy noses. She has no idea of the size and scope and complications of the total picture she's getting into, but she knows that little kids get lots of colds and this product can help a lot of little noses. Sure, her dream is to make it big as an entrepreneur, and undoubtedly some sacrifices will be necessary to see her product soar, but her overall vision is to sacrifice now so her family will be financially flush down the road. She tells herself the sacrifices will be worth it.

Mindee and a friend become business partners, and each puts $7,500 into the kitty; they hire a manufacturing company and get a garage full of Boogie Wipes in return. They begin slowly, by selling Boogie Wipes to local stores. It soon proves to be a good product at a good price with a memorable name, and the business takes off fast. The more product they sell, the more money they need to buy more product, so they enlist the help of family and friends. Then they hit the distribution jackpot—the mother lode of stores that attract bargain-seeking moms with babies in tow: Walmart.

Landing the Walmart account changes everything. Mindee and her business partner quickly hire employees. They must raise more money to create more product, so they sell a third of their company to investors, and the influx of fresh cash helps the company launch into the highly competitive world of mass-market retail. The business soars like an elevator to the top of a skyscraper.

It's not planned, but right about this time Mindee becomes pregnant with her third child. Her husband is a pilot and often away from home, so the parents hire a nanny to care for their kids. Mindee sells her trade show business and is able to take a salary from her new company. She buys power suits and an ultracool minivan with all the bells and whistles. For about two years life is good, although the hours are crazy. Sixty hours a week at the office, minimum. All-nighters are often necessary. She seldom sees her kids or her husband and has no time to herself. But her nutty schedule is only temporary, she tells herself, and her business partner has older children and a more established marriage, so being at the office all the time isn't such a big deal for her. Mindee needs to pull the same weight.

Mindee handles the company's marketing and product development. Word gets around, and the company starts receiving attention from big media. It's an inspiring story. Mindee—the mom turned inventor—is successful. Camera crews follow her. She's featured on national TV shows. Most days, the work itself feels glorious.

But she's working at an unsustainable pace, and she doesn't feel she can ever turn the work off. Even when she's home, her laptop is always on the kitchen counter, always demanding attention. Her marriage grows strained. Sometimes the children refer to the nanny as "Mommy," which Mindee hates. After the third child is born, Mindee's emotions and schedule take another hit. She experiences postpartum depression, and it's the beginning of the end. One domino falls; then the rest quickly collapse.

She develops an eating disorder in an attempt to cope with her stress. She drifts in her faith, which she's always previously enjoyed and found to be a source of strength and inspiration. One night after the kids are in bed she grabs her laptop but drops it. She bends over to pick it up but feels so exhausted. So completely wiped out. She hopes her laptop is broken so she has a legitimate excuse not to work that night. With this realization, the dam inside her breaks. She collapses to the floor and begins to sob. Not cry. Sob.

Mindee knows she needs to make radical adjustments. She tells her business partner she needs a vacation, and for the first time in years takes several weeks off. Mindee spends one week by herself at her parents' house, listening to music, reading, writing, perusing old letters she wrote, filling up a journal with raw emotions—trying to get in touch with her original hopes and dreams. She goes to counseling and slowly begins to heal her heart and body. But it's not an easy way forward.

As a matter of first importance, she knows she must cut her work hours. No laptop at home. No emails on weekends. Her new hours become 8:30 a.m. to 3:30 p.m. But other people at work already have high expectations of her, and nobody at the office is too happy with her new schedule. Mistakes in communication occur. Tensions rise. Conflict is left unresolved.

Life at home is no easier. Mindee and her husband try to hang on to their relationship, but more mistakes are made. The distance between them grows wider. The couple separates, and a divorce is set in motion.

Frustrations continue to boil over at work. Mindee's partner gathers the investors and board members and makes a difficult decision.

Mindee is fired.

2

The Long Road to Balance

M indee Hardin is looking out another window, wondering how she got here.

Here, in the lobby of a lawyer's office on the twenty-second floor of a high-rise office building, waiting for her first meeting with her attorney. Waiting for papers to be prepared to sue her business partner.

Here, fired from a multimillion-dollar company she cofounded, the distributor of a product she invented.

Here, miserable, broke, nearly split from her husband of twelve years, seeing her kids sob at the back-and-forth game between homes, her house in foreclosure as part of the divorce proceedings.

Here, barely remembering her former life. The life where she had snippets of time left to garden, scrapbook, send cards to friends, exercise—to do all the things she loved. None of that fun stuff happens anymore.

Mindee wants to keep her job with the company she founded, but the vote to terminate her remains final. Her attorney is able to negotiate a severance package of one full year's salary, while Mindee drops the lawsuit and keeps her share of the company: 33 percent. She finds her company email shut off and her belongings boxed up and set outside the office door. Locks changed. She and her mom arrange a way to go back inside and get a large ficus plant that's been in her family for four generations. *There's no way they're keeping the ficus!*

The money from the year of severance pay dwindles quickly. Mindee rents a tiny house and reconnects with her children, now as a single mother. She's not sure what she'll do for income once her severance pay ends, but she's not worried. There's strong talk that the company will be sold soon. Thanks to the shares she still holds, her payout will be enormous. After all, it's the product she invented—and the company is now selling just under $15 million in Boogie Wipes annually. Wow, that's a lot of runny noses.

Sure enough, a buyer comes along. It's a fantastic company with great ethics, mission, and morals. The deal is put together. Everything is set.

The day of the sale dawns beautifully. It's springtime, and Mindee is at her rental house on the phone, talking to the board of directors. She can see through the sliding glass door that cherry blossoms are out. Squirrels scamper on the back lawn. The business is sold, and Mindee hangs up the phone, happy. The deal isn't quite what was hoped for, but she can still live comfortably for several years on the return.

But then the phone rings again. She picks up and hears her attorney on the other end. He clears his throat, pauses, and says, "Well, I'm sorry . . ."

The next words rush at her in a blur. The attorney rattles off a bunch of business lingo about common stock versus preferred stock. It seems that the investor has exercised some sort of contractual privilege to all the rights of the initial sale, which means the company needs to pay Mindee only if the company performs at some magical projected level agreed upon only at the very close of the sale. In simplest terms, her take has been relegated to unicorn land.

The attorney talks and talks and talks, and Mindee asks him to repeat this information several times. It becomes clear that she's the victim of a loophole in the contract. It's all right there in the fine print. All legal. The bottom line feels like a fist hitting her chin.

Mindee will get *zero*.

She'll receive a big fat *nothing* from the multimillion-dollar company that she cofounded and owned 33.33 percent of. All that work, all gone. She's absolutely broke. She's always a talker and wants to speak, but no sound emerges. Seconds pass while tears fall. Mindee loses it. She slams down the phone and screams, shouts, swears, throws things, paces around the room. She feels so hurt, so angry, so stupid, so taken advantage of. One huge thought that runs around in her mind is this: *Wait a minute! I traded all that time away from my kids and husband because I was supposed to be setting us up for some great success down the road—and now there's no money! I can't get that time back, and now all my sacrifices are for nothing?! Here I am, lonely, lost, divorced, living in a rental, recovering from an eating disorder, estranged from family and friends—and now I'm broke?! The "I'm broke" is the last straw!*

She's never been one to lose her temper, but she rants for ten solid minutes. Then she notices her nine-year-old son standing in the doorway of the room. His chin trembles, and he asks in a hushed voice, "Mom, who *are* you?"

Her son's comment pulls her back into the moment. She collects herself, hugs and reassures her son, ushers him out of the room, and closes the door.

Then she takes a deep breath.

For a while—completely alone—she lies in the fetal position, thinking, praying, crying, wondering what to do next. She needs to go forward, but she's not sure how.

Mindee's mom, the backbone of her team, is here at the house, helping take care of the kids, and Mindee and her mom talk for a while about how Mindee needs to be strong for the kids. Then a man Mindee has just started dating, another part of her team, comes over, and offers his support. Mindee calls her children's father to fill him in. The next morning she calls her attorney back.

Then she takes action.

A lawsuit for $1.3 million is drafted against Mindee's partner and the company's investor. It'll take a while for the suit to go through, and in the meantime, Mindee looks for a job. Somehow she has to pay the rent.

Time passes, and all the lawsuit needs is her signature, but the more she examines the documents and rolls them around in her soul, the more she wants nothing to do with an intense legal battle that could span the next several years. She's a hard-driving business-person, yet she's a hugger by nature, not a fighter, and somehow she feels deep within herself that everything is going to be okay if she just lets go. She listens to the voices in her mind that describe the right choices for her, to the whispers about what she hopes her children will think about her someday, and to the self-talk about what kind of impact she wants to have on the world. She doesn't want to be known forever as the mom who invented Boogie Wipes and then sued the people who had once been close to her. She just wants to be remembered as the mom who invented Boogie Wipes—a cool product with a quirky name that ultimately helps people.

So she chooses to take a higher road and puts the experience behind her. She refuses to waste her time bemoaning the state of her affairs. She chooses instead to go forward and overcome. Once her decision is made, she feels a giant weight lifted from her shoulders.

She drops the lawsuit.

It's certainly not an easy or overnight decision. She's deeply in debt. She has no income. The alimony is just kicking in, only enough to pay half the rent and the children's medical insurance. She applies for food stamps and eventually declares bankruptcy. Her ultracool minivan is repossessed.

She does a lot of soul-searching. A lot of redefining what's truly important to her. Then she gathers herself—and launches *again*.

Ever the entrepreneur, Mindee starts a brand-new business called Juicebox Consulting that offers business advice to enterprise-savvy moms. There's a ton of "mompreneurs" out there, and Mindee knows she now has some hard-won good advice to offer—about both what to do and what *not* to do. This time, her hours are deliberately way fewer. Her work email is separate from her personal email. She refuses to take on so much work that she falls back into her old patterns. She builds the business to the point where she has a steady income, then strategically levels it off to a sustainable pace. She also begins to develop a different saline product for adults called BlessYouz, although she's doing it on different terms now—her own.

Along the way, she develops a motivation statement: "Listen for the whisper."

It means listen for what life is telling you to do. Listen to the voices of integrity and intuition, and then do what you know to be true. She tells the moms she works with, "Maybe a whisper comes in a moment when you're falling asleep at night and you realize you haven't kissed your husband good night. Maybe you're mad at him, but you hear that whisper in your own heart, so you roll over and say, 'I love you.' The whispers are those moments when you think you should call your mom even though you're really busy, but you do it anyway and tell her you love her. The whispers are when your kids come home from school, and they're chattering about the day's events, and you choose to listen to the chatter, and engage in it, because you know you ultimately care for your kids more than words can describe. The whisper is the magic of invested presence."

Today, several years after her first company was sold, Mindee is happily remarried (to the same guy who supported her through her rock-bottom moment). She speaks, writes, and consults, telling her story of epic success and epic failure and what it means to pick oneself up and launch again. She purposely invests much more time in her children. And, no, she's never received a dime in payout money from her first company.

How would Mindee describe her message today? "Let's face it, work and parenting are exhausting," she says, "and if you're not tired, then you're probably not doing it right. When we're tired, it's so easy to reach for whatever feels good right now—whatever's easy. We reach for another piece of chocolate or another glass of wine or for our phones so we can endlessly scroll through social media posts. But when we're tired, the relationships around us are still worth investing in. Listen: my message is not 'Don't work.' And it's not 'You need to work from home.' And it's not even 'Live with less.' It's 'Be wise about life.' People think life is a buffet, but it's not. Life is a menu, and nobody gets to order everything from the menu. When you order one thing, it means you don't order something else. Ultimately that's hopeful, because it spurs us toward fulfillment. My message is also an encouragement that it's never too late to reframe our lives. We all make mistakes, but our mistakes don't need to define us forever. So my encouragement to anyone today is 'Slow down and breathe' and 'Deeply invest in the people you love' and 'Be fully alive in the moment that's happening around you right now, today.'"

3

The Necessity of Taking Action

(SAMPSON AND SHARLEE)

When we first heard Mindee Hardin's story, we were completely blown away. We were initially impressed that she took action to invent a product and start her own company. Lots of people are business-oriented and start companies, but she launched in such a big way—and from fairly humble beginnings. Sure, she had an education in marketing and some strong experience in the workplace, yet she didn't launch with anybody's help except that of her family, friends, and business partner. There was no corporate seed money provided to her, no grants given to her for her bright invention. She simply came up with a unique idea that would help a lot of people and went forward and took action on her dream. She could have sat around and chewed on her idea for twenty years, but she pushed her idea out of the conceptual realm and turned it into a reality. She *launched*. That action of going forward is so important, yet many people don't realize how necessary it is.

Even more remarkable to us is how Mindee launched a second time. After she was fired, her marriage fell apart, and she got nothing from the sale of her business—she launched *again*. Her story is such a great example of how setbacks don't need to stifle our launch codes. If we launch and fail, then we launch again, undoubtedly wiser and more experienced. Far too many people would have given up the second time around. Yet Mindee didn't. When she was at rock bottom, she grabbed hold of the Stuff she had inside her and went forward again, creating a new, amazing balance between her work and home life—something we can all identify with wanting. Wow!

The action of launching is an important part of the journey toward overcoming obstacles. The ability to launch is a component of the Stuff to seek out inside ourselves, discover, and develop. We found this pattern of launching in every person we interviewed for this book. John O'Leary launched by doing his physical therapy as he was supposed to. Mercy Alexander launched by helping her brother get ready for his trip to the United States. Rich Ruffalo launched when he chose to enter his first track-and-field meet after going blind.

When you develop this piece of the Stuff, it means that when an obstacle is in front of you, you don't sit idle—at least not forever. Patience and planning are part of the process, but somewhere along the way you must draw a line in the sand and then step over the line. You must start the process of going forward, then build and grow and learn as you go. Excuses and reasons to delay the process will always exist, but you must never allow those excuses to get in the way of your progress, growth, and ambitions. Give yourself a launch deadline, a definite date to begin. You can do this yourself, or you can allow a deadline to be set by your surroundings or circumstances. And then go.

Gregg Krech, an authority on psychology in Japan, describes how the psychology of action teaches us how to turn a plan into reality. His "taking action" program makes use of such concepts as prioritizing tasks and recognizing the power of small actions. He points out that when we face huge changes, taking small and seemingly unspectacular steps can help us move past our internal impasses. In other words, even before we have all the variables figured out and the questions answered, we launch. We go forward. We make the decision to move.[1]

How exactly does setting a deadline or a launch date factor into helping us move forward? It's because the albatross of simple old procrastination often holds us back. Strangely enough, even researchers on procrastination find themselves hitting the brick wall of—what else?—procrastination.

Dan Ariely and Klaus Wertenbroch researched and wrote a study titled "Procrastination, Deadlines, and Performance: Self-Control by Precommitment," yet ironically admitted that they themselves had struggled with the very same problem of procrastination while writing the article.[2] They wanted to know whether setting deadlines actually works to break through the wall. So they did a pilot study at the Massachusetts Institute of Technology in which they divided students into two groups and told the students in both groups to each write three research papers. Half of the students were given evenly spaced deadlines for turning in their papers. The other half could turn their papers in any old time they wanted—but they needed to set deadlines for themselves and then communicate those deadlines to the professor. If they missed their self-imposed deadlines, they lost grade points.

After a complex plan of scoring was set in place and implemented, Ariely and Wertenbroch learned that the temptation to procrastinate is real, and pretty much everybody feels it. To combat procrastination, self-imposed deadlines are good, yet even better are deadlines that people or circumstances set for us.[3]

Let's illustrate by putting their findings into relational terms. Say a boyfriend asks his girlfriend to marry him and she says yes. That's a good first step in going forward relationally, but if the initial proposal is all that ever happens, then the couple will never actually get married. They can languish in perpetual engagement for the rest of their lives. What's needed is a self-imposed deadline, a launch date.

So the couple marks a big bright red X on the calendar over the first Saturday in June. Good, they've set a date. Research shows they're much more likely to actually get married once they've set a date. Again, they continue to go forward. So they book the chapel and reception hall and hire the minister and send out wedding invitations and select a cake and register for a china pattern and buy a dress and rent tuxedos and fly in their groomsmen and bridesmaids from all over the country—and all those actions collectively lead up to the external deadline, a launch date that other people and circumstances now hold the couple to. Research shows that a wedding stands the strongest likelihood of happening once all these factors are in place. In fact, other research shows that the longer people procrastinate about making a decision or taking action on a decision, the more stress it actually causes them.[4]

Maybe this all sounds good to you, but you're still struggling with one key question: *when* to launch. How do you really know when it's time? For instance, when you look at the circumstances of Mindee Hardin's business collapsing, you may conclude that Mindee launched too soon. If only Mindee had done more homework, maybe developed a business team to oversee her contracts or taken a course in time management skills, then she could have avoided a lot of pain.

Maybe. But maybe not. Why? Because it's okay to launch and fail and launch again, just as she did. An initial failure can actually be good for us, because it sands off our rough edges, fine-tunes our engines, and develops resiliency and grit—all of which help us go forward and ultimately succeed.

Go ahead and launch. You can't study a thing forever. You can't tweak endlessly. You have to let the baby grow up, walk out the door, and face a tough world.

4

The Power of Launching

ampson explains: I've launched several times and in many ways. I launched as a high school junior when I began to spend more time with my friends who didn't get into trouble and refused to follow the pathway of crime. I launched when I decided to become a doctor. And I launched when, very early in the process, I decided that I would be a lifelong philanthropist.

When I was still a sophomore in college, I formed a nonprofit organization with my two friends Rameck and George for the sole purpose of giving back. Later in life the three of us started a different nonprofit organization called the Three Doctors Foundation, which continues today—but the first organization happened several years earlier. We called the first one Ujima. The name was taken from one of the principles of the African harvest festival of Kwanzaa, and the word stands for commitment to collective work and responsibility.

Ujima started organically, even before we had a name for it. The three of us knew we'd been given a lot already, so we wanted to give back. At first we looked at several clubs and organizations around Seton Hall and explored what they did, with the idea that maybe we'd just join something that was already up and running. We knew we wanted to do something altruistic, with an educational component, and hopefully something that would give back to the community. No existing club or organization quite fit what we were looking for, so we began exploring the idea of starting our own nonprofit group.

We wanted to connect with high school students who were in the same position we'd been in back in high school and then help introduce them to college. We wanted to show kids that there were possibilities ahead. Later we coined a phrase that defined our mission for the Three Doctors Foundation: "Our children cannot aspire to be what they cannot see." Our thought was that if we could just show high school students what college was like, then maybe we could help them aspire to attend.

We knew we needed to raise money to make this happen, so we held our own parties, called Ujima-jams, to generate capital. We invited everybody, and everybody came. Even the star basketball players came to the parties. Our team wasn't in the Final Four at the time, but they'd made it to the NCAA tournament as well as the Elite 8 and Sweet 16 in 1991–92 and 1992–93, so having all the students there, plus the presence of the basketball players, helped Ujima-jams eventually become epic parties. We raised enough money to hire buses to bring kids from nearby Newark neighborhoods to Seton Hall. We held orientation sessions to explain what college was like, how the students could apply and be accepted, and what potential careers awaited them. We toured the campus with them to show them all the beauty that existed in college life.

Ujima ran for two years before we disbanded it out of scheduling necessity after we graduated with our undergrad degrees and went on to medical school. Even then, we continued forward with various volunteer efforts. During medical school we tutored kids in high school and volunteered at a free outpatient clinic organized by medical staff and supervised by a seasoned doctor.

After the three of us completed medical school, the Newark *Star-Ledger* did a story on our graduating as doctors. We didn't think much about it at the time—after eight long years we were all just happy to finally be out of school and looking forward to beginning our residencies. But it felt surreal for me when the story came out. Smack-dab on the front page of the newspaper was a big picture of us above the fold, with the headline "The Start of Something Big." The story took the angle that the three of us had succeeded as individuals, yet the community as a whole had also succeeded because we'd come together and collectively achieved something special. We'd helped pave the way for more good things to come.

Once that story came out, things really started to snowball, and a new chapter in our lives opened up, one we'd never planned. The city of Newark gave us an award. The mayor invited us to his office, and we were given the key to our beloved city. A church group called and asked us to do a talk. We did a few more speaking events, and pretty soon we'd accumulated about $1,000. We all still had big student loans. We often joke that we were the only philanthropists we knew who had student loans. I rented a room in a house and drove an old, beat-up car. But we agreed not to use the cash for ourselves. With that money we established the Three Doctors Foundation. The process of getting the legal documents lasted about six months, and it took all of our $1,000 to do it. A law firm in New Jersey did much of the work pro bono.

With the Three Doctors Foundation, we held health summits, put together mentorship programs, and gave free health screenings. We did holiday giveaways for communities in New Jersey, providing toys and clothing for children and families in need. During the first part of this new season of our lives, the story from the *Star-Ledger* was picked up by the wire. The *Washington Post* did a bigger spread on us, and it was picked up by all the major newspapers. *Essence* magazine did a feature on us, and later we were honored at the *Essence* televised awards program along with Michael Jordan and Danny Glover. Oprah Winfrey hosted the awards show. Afterward, we were connected with a literary agent, and our first book deal was put together in just a few weeks. About a year and a half later the book came out, Oprah had us on her show, and our story took off from there.

We'd never planned for any of this exposure or publicity or opportunity. All we'd done initially was try to better our lives. Along the way we'd decided to give back, even when we didn't have much to give. Our story was about showing others that success is possible.

As Mindee Hardin said, "I just started."

That's launching: you're faced with a new initiative, a new problem to overcome, even a new opportunity to try—as we did with our first foundation. So you move forward. You focus your intention and clarify what you want to accomplish. You face your fears and push toward your goal. You might need to get training either before you begin or along the way. You might need to do research, take a class, hire a coach, talk with a counselor, or seek treatment or medical help. Along the way, you strengthen your weaknesses. You kick your perfectionism to the curb and know that failing and launching again can be an important part of the process. And you keep making adjustments as you go.[5]

The point of this chapter isn't to encourage you specifically to start a business or a nonprofit organization. We're encouraging you to live out your own story of success, to live your own truth—whatever that looks like, whatever your opportunities are. Don't sit idle. Start the process, and build as you go. There will always be reasons to delay, but never allow these excuses to get in the way of your growth, your ambitions, and your ability to reach your goals.

We're encouraging you to *launch*.

The good news is that when you launch, you seldom launch alone. You walk the road with a team. And teamwork is an essential component of the Stuff.

CHAPTER FIVE

Develop Your Team

*No man is an island entire of itself; every man is a
piece of the continent, a part of the main.*
—John Donne

1

We Need Others

COLUMBIA, SOUTH CAROLINA

In the beginning they are just like any other young family.

There are the dad and mom, Glenn and Cara O'Neill. Glenn is a business consultant. Cara is a pediatrician.

There's big brother Beckham, age six and a half. He's a healthy, fun-filled little guy who loves playing soccer, jumping on his bed, and playing at the beach. Beckham adores his little sister, Eliza.

Eliza is three and a half. She says the alphabet, sings her favorite songs, and loves riding her little bike with the training wheels. Eliza particularly loves hats. She owns a cowboy hat with a gold sheriff's star, a festive Santa Claus hat that's bright red and white, and a jaunty yellow-and-black bumblebee hat. Eliza tries them all on in front of the mirror, one after another, tufts of blond hair sticking out wild and crazy from underneath the brims.

In the beginning, life for Eliza and her family is good.

Glenn and Cara have always wanted a daughter along with a son. After Beckham is born, the couple miscarry. Then miscarry again. Then Cara finds out she's pregnant again, and the couple deliberately chooses not to find out the baby's gender until birth. Boys run in the extended family, and Glenn is one of five boys in his family, so they think the baby will be another boy. But then Eliza emerges. *Surprise!* Glenn and Cara just grin.

From the get-go, Eliza has a few complications. It's hard for her to breathe, and she spends a few days in the neonatal intensive care unit at the hospital. Everything's soon cleared up, and the family goes home. At six months old, Eliza starts day care and has lots of ear infections. Her mom's concerned, but kids get colds, right? Two years pass and Eliza starts talking and has a few speech issues, but nothing major. Sometimes her speech is slow, so she goes to speech therapy, and sometimes her big brother does the talking for her, but what big brother doesn't? At age three, Eliza "should be evaluated," says a day care staff member, because "things look just a bit different." Glenn and Cara take Eliza in for a number of routine tests. Nobody is even sure what they're looking for. One practitioner thinks Eliza might be autistic. An MRI shows some differences in Eliza's upper spine. A friend recommends a screening test for a specific group of diseases. The parents don't think much about it at first. They just want to cross the screening off their list.

Cara takes Eliza to the screening test. It's with a geneticist, a colleague, and later, when the results are back, as soon as the specialist walks into the room, Cara senses something's off.

The genetic counselor clears his throat and says, "Cara, I'm not going to beat around the bush. Eliza has Sanfilippo syndrome."

"Wait," Cara says. "I need to call Glenn. We need to hear the rest of this together."

There's silence while she texts Glenn: "You have to come over here, right now. Not good."

Cara is familiar with the group of illnesses that Sanfilippo is a part of, although she doesn't yet know all the details. In her medical practice, she's never seen anyone with it, but she knows enough to know it's one of the worst things a family can face. Eliza is in the geneticist's room, waiting for her dad to arrive, and she's acting hyper by this point, bouncing around, getting into bins, ransacking the room. Glenn arrives and they try to calm Eliza, and Glenn and Cara hear the specifics together, as much as they can handle at this point.

Sanfilippo is a rare genetic disorder in which the body doesn't have enough of the necessary enzymes to break down long chains of sugar molecules called glycosaminoglycans. The disease is inherited and progressive; it acts like Alzheimer's disease for little children, except worse. Children with Sanfilippo don't show any signs of the disease at birth. They learn to walk, talk, and feed themselves, and everything in their development looks normal. But then the disease hits. Soon it will tear through Eliza's body. In three years from now, by age six, Eliza will stop speaking and walking. She'll become hyperactive, have seizures, and lose her hearing and vision. She'll experience dementia. Her hands, wrists, and other joints will become stiff and twist up, and she'll be in a lot of pain. By age ten, she'll be in a wheelchair and need around-the-clock care. Worse yet? The disease is always fatal. Life expectancy is fifteen years.

Glenn whips out his smartphone in the geneticist's office and in panic mode begins researching the disease, doing the math in his head. Cara sits stunned. There's no gradually getting used to this news, and the severity of the facts hits them like a tidal wave: Sanfilippo is a rapidly degenerative disease—and unbeknownst to the family, the disease has been building up in Eliza since birth. Glenn and Cara are both fighters, but this news feels like more than they can bear. They leave the geneticist's office, strap Eliza into her car seat, and stand outside the car, sobbing and holding each other. Already they feel like they're out of time.

They don't tell anyone at first. Not grandparents. Not friends or coworkers. It's a Thursday when they hear the news, and the parents ditch work and take the children to the beach for the weekend. Reality presses down on them, but they need to go away as a family and try for one last weekend of normalcy while they work to get their heads around the bad news. They splash in the surf, play in the sun, and pretend life is okay. As parents, it's hard to talk. A dark cloud has invaded their minds, and now, knowing the diagnosis, they are able to see the effects of the disease already in Eliza. Children with Sanfilippo don't have a sense of danger. Sometimes Eliza will just run and run on the beach and not listen when her father shouts at her to come back. Glenn catches up and runs with her, hand in hand. He doesn't want to turn around. He just wants to keep running down the beach and pretend that they don't need to come back.

The weekend ends, they go home, and Cara and Glenn have a series of long talks. They're both on the same wavelength. They plan to enjoy every moment they have left with their daughter. They'll give her the best care they can. They'll fight the disease with all they have. They will do anything and everything they need to do.

They dig into research. Cara's medical background helps. With cancer, there might be thousands of biotech laboratories working on various cures. But with Sanfilippo, there are fewer than a handful. They find one scientist who is developing an experimental gene therapy for Sanfilippo that just might work within the O'Neills' time frame. Cara calls the scientist and gets through. They talk for an hour, and the scientist explains her research. Early testing shows positive signs, but they need funding to bring the treatment to a clinical trial. Cara sits on the floor of the kitchen, taking notes like mad. Glenn leans in behind her, peeking over her shoulder. Every now and again he asks, "What? What!?" It's an intense call, but when Cara hangs up she says, "This is it, Glenn. This is our way out."

It's a long shot. Sure. But at least it's a chance. The parents are normally private and self-sufficient, but they make a deliberate decision to go outside their comfort zones, outside their personality types, a decision to go public and ask for help. They quickly establish a foundation to help raise money for the cure. They create social media pages and start posting regularly about Eliza, about what she has, and about what—maybe—can be done about it. Each day feels frantic, impossible, and when the parents collapse into bed at the end of another day, they review what's in hand and what's needed.

Their fund-raising experience: zero.

Their mission: to raise two and a half million dollars.

Their time frame to raise the money: nine months. An impossibility for a disease no one's heard of.

Their specific hope: to get Eliza into the clinical trial. But even when the medicine is ready, there are no guarantees it will work.

This is a brand-new gene therapy. There's also the chance that even if the O'Neills can raise all the money needed, Eliza might not be picked for the trial. Hospitals and doctors ultimately choose the participants in clinical trials. At the very least, the money raised by the O'Neills will go toward funding research, helping all children with the disease.

The parents know a long shot is all they have, and they also know one important fact, perhaps the first time they've realized it in their lives: they need help.

2

When There's Only One Option

When a need is communicated, people rise to help alleviate it. Over the next few months, Glenn and Cara see this pattern again and again. The more they work to tell people about their daughter, the more people are willing to join their team and help.

The parents read books about fund-raising, create a list of fifty different items they want to do to raise money, rank the items from most likely to least likely, then start to take action, crossing items off the list as the events occur. Some of the items work better than others. They try parties, silent auctions, bake sales, 5K runs, letter-writing campaigns, a golf tournament, bracelet sales, a dance-a-thon. People come out of the woodwork to help. The wife of a colleague of

Cara has fund-raising experience and quickly takes over managing most of the events.

The fund-raising journey becomes a roller-coaster ride of hope and despair. The team mails out a thousand letters. Time passes, and nothing happens. At last one solitary check arrives: one hundred dollars. The parents sit outside the post office in tears, wondering *Great, we'll take it, but time's ticking, and where are the other 999 responses?* The next day they return to the post office and there's one more letter. Only one. But it's a check for $24,000. A father of two daughters with a different rare disease has donated the large amount. The O'Neills and their team are on a high. Those are the only two checks that come in from the letter-writing campaign, and Cara and Glenn say to their team, "We don't have time to knock down closed doors. We have to find the open doors. If only we knew where they were."

Other donations are also hard to predict—but incredible in scope. One person walks up to the family's front door and hands them a check for $10,000. A different person volunteers to do all the design and graphics for the O'Neills. Another person simply comes up to the parents and says, "I'm yours. I want to help. What can I do?" The O'Neills begin to call their support team "the angels"—the people who come into their life to support and encourage them, hope for them, and take action on their behalf.

After six months, the team has raised $250,000. The O'Neills are thrilled about the number, but it's still only a tenth of what's needed for the trial. When they compare the amount of money they've raised with the amount of time they have left, they realize they're not going to make it. They need to enlist the help of a bigger team. This time they're going to ask *the world*.

Glenn types "how to make a viral video" into a search engine and finds Karen Cheng, who runs an agency that makes TV commercials. Glenn emails her: "I'm a dad with a dying daughter, trying to raise money for a clinical trial. Do you have any advice for me?" Cheng responds, and sends the request to a colleague at a photography magazine, who emails the request to a thousand of his colleagues. A young photographer/videographer named Benjamin Von Wong responds, saying, "Hey, I got your story. Do you want to skype?"

Glenn and Benjamin skype. Benjamin says, "I've got a break in my schedule coming up. If I can come to your house and bring a few people with me, I think I can help. We can sleep on your couches. I've never done a fund-raiser like this before, but I've done a few videos and love a challenge. I'm willing to give it a shot."

Glenn asks, "How much do you charge?"

Benjamin replies, "Nah. Forget about it."

Glenn gets off the call and says to Cara, "There are strangers coming to stay at our house." Cara just shrugs. It's so different from their former life, but they have nothing to lose.

Benjamin and his team come to the O'Neills' house and shoot video of Eliza and the family for eight days straight. Three days after Benjamin leaves, a video called "Saving Eliza" is uploaded onto the O'Neills' GoFundMe page. Glenn emails a press release to some news stations, and the story takes on a life of its own.

The video proves to be a game changer. In fifteen days, $500,000 is raised. Benjamin releases two follow-up videos several months later. The $1 million mark is reached, and then the campaign soars past that to $1.8 million, thanks in part to one special donor. On the night of Eliza's fifth birthday, a stranger calls Glenn late at night. He tells Glenn he has been following the story, and has two daughters of his own, one Eliza's age. He shocks the family with a donation of $30,000 and inspirational words to remember during the challenging days: "Keep the faith, and the faith will keep you." The words continue to resonate with the O'Neills, and the dad ends up becoming good friends with the family. From there, the campaign keeps going.

A whirlwind of press coverage occurs. The video helps land the O'Neills on the *Today* show and *The Doctors* TV show, in *People* magazine, and more. More than forty families with children with Sanfilippo syndrome find the O'Neills and join the foundation's network. By the end of the year, the $2 million mark is reached—enough for the trial to go forward. But the trial isn't yet ready. There are lots of steps in the process of getting into a clinical trial. Timelines get pushed back. There can be drug production challenges. Government regulations need to be cleared.

In fact, although the funds have almost all been raised, it isn't smooth sailing by any stretch of the imagination. Shortly after the first viral video is released, the O'Neills decide to take action on one huge sticky wicket that has been thrown into the mix. It's a tiny thing that doesn't sound like much, but it turns out to be a giant obstacle. They learn that there's a common virus—one found on the handles of grocery store shopping carts, monkey bars at playgrounds, and doorknobs at day care centers—and if Eliza contracts this virus, she's out of the trial. Period. Some 30 to 50 percent of all people carry antibodies to the virus, although they don't show symptoms, and contracting the virus would wreck any possibility that the gene therapy might help Eliza. So she absolutely *must not* contract this virus. If she stays healthy, she has a chance. But if she contracts the virus, she's 100 percent excluded from her only chance at life.

Well, then, there's only one option. Quarantine the entire family.

3

The Clock Ticks

A year after the initial diagnosis, Eliza is going downhill. She cries a lot. Extreme hyperactivity is one symptom of the disease, and she can't sit still and be quiet for more than five seconds. She runs. She races. She throws books. She pushes things off countertops and chairs. She's sleepless. She can't follow directions. Imagine your grandfather with Alzheimer's disease. He's slowly losing his mind. This is what's happening with Eliza, except she's got the energy of a four-year-old. The O'Neills love their daughter more than words can describe. But some days are Just. So. Hard.

Add to that the decision to take Beckham, now seven, out of school.

Add to that the choice to limit the family's contact with everybody in the outside world, a self-imposed quarantine. This is how it works: everything that comes into the house is wiped down with disinfectant. Cara's mom goes to the grocery store for the family and leaves the groceries at the front door of the house. Friends go to the post office and bank for the O'Neills. Cara quits her job. Glenn's company lets him work from home. The O'Neills run most of the foundation's day-to-day activities by phone and email, with help from board members. A number of therapists come to the house to help Eliza, and each has his own individual mask, gloves, footies, hair gear, and white suit. All protective gear is kept in the garage. Meetings are held by video conferencing. Beckham chats with his buddies at school the same way.

At first, the O'Neills think the family will be quarantined for a few months, tops. They hang a huge piece of paper in their kitchen with a series of numbers on it. Each day they are in quarantine, they cross off another number. One, two, three.

Ten, twenty, thirty.

One hundred days go by.

The family leaves the house every once in a while, and the kids are allowed to go outside and play in the backyard. Some days the family just get into their car and go for a drive. If they stop to fill the car with gas, only one parent gets out, and he or she wears a mask and gloves. There's one lonely, deserted beach nearby, and sometimes they go there to play. A few desolate hiking trails offer adventure. Sometimes in the evenings, when nobody is around, they walk around the block just to get outside. Eliza doesn't get sick—not even once. She doesn't even get her earaches anymore.

Two hundred days go by.

It's Valentine's Day, and every little girl deserves to go to a special dance. But what's Eliza to do? Glenn decides to bring the dance to her. Eliza puts on her best red dress, and her mom fixes the little girl's hair. Glenn dresses up in a suit and tie. They hold the dance in their family room. First up are some fast songs, where everybody just wiggles around. Then comes a slow dance, and Glenn picks up Eliza and twirls her in his arms. Mom comes in, too, and she and Glenn dance while Eliza traipses around the room with a book. Beckham's nearby, tapping his toe.

A full year goes by.

Thursday-night date nights for the parents are only a memory. There's no having friends over. No cousins. No grandparents. No going to the library or the movies or to see a favorite sports team or to the zoo, which Eliza used to love. No trick-or-treating. No trips to sit on Santa's lap at Christmas. No restaurants. The family read and play games and watch TV and study and work. After a while, the parents let their children draw on the walls. Eliza just scribbles. Beckham is homeschooled now, and he draws pictures of his geography lessons. He and Glenn create trails in the backyard where Beckham rides his bike. Just for fun, and because he wants to, the parents let Beckham cut everybody's hair—and it looks pretty good! Beckham understands that his sister is sick. He loves her dearly and wants to do everything he can to help. Most evenings he's the only one Eliza allows to put her to bed. Beckham crawls under the covers with Eliza, holds her hand, and talks to her until she falls asleep. But Beckham hasn't been told the disease is fatal. He keeps asking his parents when they will get the medicine for her. That Christmas Beckham asks his mom if Santa will bring the medicine for Eliza.

Four hundred days pass.

Five hundred days.

The parents hang on by sheer willpower. To Cara, it feels like one long, rainy weekend. As a parent, she's desperate to keep the kids from going crazy. She's isolated. She's exhausted. She can't talk to people and find relief in that bit of normalcy. And there's no respite. No end in sight, even. In this rainy weekend, Monday never comes. At times she literally goes to bed and pulls the covers over her head.

Six hundred days pass.

Six hundred twenty-five.

Eliza can't say the alphabet anymore.

She can't sing her favorite song.

She can't tell her parents "I love you." That loss devastates Glenn and Cara.

Six hundred and fifty.

The family nears the breaking point. Beckham hears his parents talking about yet another delay in trials and starts to cry. Seeing Beckham so weary prompts Cara to cry, too. She wonders if they should even have started the quarantine. At this point, they still have no idea if a trial is a month away or another year away or even if Eliza stands a chance of being a candidate.

Glenn and Cara make the heart-wrenching decision to send Beckham to his grandparents' house. Beckham turns nine, and the isolation is getting to be too much for him. He doesn't want to be away from his parents and sister, but Glenn and Cara explain the options to him, and ultimately he makes the choice to leave. The handoff to the grandparents occurs in a deserted parking lot. Everyone's in tears. Glenn and Cara don't know when they'll see Beckham again.

Seven hundred days.

Seven hundred twenty-five.

Let's hold that story right there for now. Let it ache in our hearts as we wait for the conclusion.

4

"We" Is Greater than "I":

THE PANDO PHENOMENON

ampson explains: If you hike about a mile southwest of Fish Lake, Utah, you'll encounter a remarkable grove of aspen trees, about one hundred acres total. Picture an area about the size of seventy-five American football fields (including the end zones) all clumped together.[1] At first glance, the aspens in this high alpine grove look similar to other aspens—slim trunks, white bark, high leafy canopy of foliage in season. But what you will soon notice is how uncannily identical the particular trees look in diameter, height, and even shape. Here's what will surprise you. You aren't looking at a *grove* of trees. You're actually looking at *one* tree.

A botanist named Burton Barnes from the University of Michigan first suspected this, and his hypothesis was later confirmed by Professor Michael Grant from the University of Colorado, who named the single organism "Pando," Latin for "I spread."[2]

Pando is one plant. It's an entire forest made up of one single tree. If you could peek under the surface of the ground, you'd find that all its trees share the same gigantic underground root system. Pando is thought to be the largest living thing in the world.[3]

Far too many of us believe we can overcome our obstacles and do it solely by ourselves. We're rugged individualists, lone wolves, single trees. If we want something done properly, we have to do it ourselves, right? But Pando serves as a strong reminder that we're all connected

somehow, some way. We're all in this together. We're a forest of trees with connected roots—and those connected roots make us strong.

Funny: the individual tree trunks in the Pando forest are all relatively skinny. At first glance they appear vulnerable, as though they wouldn't be able to withstand strong winds without blowing over. Yet Pando has been alive for more than ten thousand years and has survived strong winds, forest fires, and various ecological predators throughout the years. Likewise, research shows that no matter what obstacle stands in our way, the process of overcoming it goes better if we don't try to go it alone. I can relate to this principle greatly. A team made up of myself and two friends helped me enormously in my own life, and I'll tell you about the specifics of the pact we made in chapter 6. For now, just know that if each of us had tried to walk the road alone, we wouldn't have made it. But banded together, our roots supported and sustained us. Together, we could accomplish anything.

Just like the O'Neills, what we all need is a team, a powerful group of supporters who help us overcome difficulties and achieve success. A team can help us carry out necessary tasks. A team can provide guidance for the journey. A team can support us physically, spiritually, mentally, and emotionally. A team can share our visions, help us maintain perspective (even have fun together), and become a larger part of our bigger dream.[4]

Maybe the idea of letting people into your life sounds difficult. You're used to taking responsibility for yourself. Maybe others have hurt you, let you down, or disappeared from your life when you needed them most. If so, we understand that. People are flawed— ourselves included. Yet we encourage you to reboot your thinking. One of the most helpful realizations is that a team doesn't need to be flawless or uniform. In fact, team members don't even need to get along—at least not all the time and not toward the front of a team-work experience.[5]

Indeed, these days many people use teams in the form of "support groups," "small groups," and "think tanks." They've become commonplace in businesses, universities, therapy centers, sports groups, and other organizations, and research shows they're effective.[6]

How can you go about building an effective team? The entrepreneur Brad Sugars says, "Supporters generally come in two forms: advisors and specialists. Some you hire, some you pay for, and some you obtain through networking and outreach. Smart people at your side can save you years of hard work—and missteps."

Sugars compares the support team to the safety net below a trapeze artist. A strong support team, he says, can mean the difference between success and failure, between sanity or spinning out of control. Beyond trusting your gut instincts, the invitation is to "talk out your ideas, your trouble points, and your opportunities with skilled individuals. Often, just the process of explaining a situation to someone else will spark alternatives that can give you a new perspective. Discuss, listen carefully, and then go with your gut."[7]

The O'Neills learned this—and they hold a special place in my heart today. In the middle of their quarantine season, a reporter called me for a medically related comment on their situation for a story she was writing about them.[8] As I grappled with the realities of their life in quarantine, my heart broke for them—yet I was so inspired by their incredible perseverance, solidarity, and tenacity. I was so happy to hear that hope was still at hand—thanks in part to their team.

Their team started with family and friends. It spread to include videographers and the power of the world connected by the Internet. During the quarantine period, it shrank to just their family, supported by a larger outside network. It included doctors, geneticists, and a myriad of medical workers. The common denominator throughout was simply that people wanted to help. Each person had something different to offer, yet the team was united in "heart." This is an indication to us that teamwork perhaps isn't as technical as we make it. If you have two hands and energy, then you have something to offer to others who need your help.

5

Family, Friends, Team:
SHARLEE'S CANCER SUPPORT SQUAD

2001

Sharlee explains: My mom and dad are in the waiting room of the doctor's office, and I'm down the hallway from them, getting worked over by my oncologist and his medical staff.

They call it a bone marrow biopsy. The needle is strong and thick, and I can see the needle's sharp glint before it goes into me. I'm lying on my stomach, and they push the needle through the skin all the way to the bone and keep going. They need to drill that needle into my bone so they can take out the marrow to test it. The bone must be punctured. They push hard, and it's not easy going, and it feels like they're grinding away at my insides. In my mind I imagine a Tom and Jerry cartoon where the mouse puts a big nail on top of the cat's head and keeps hammering. Except that nothing about this procedure is funny—that picture is a pretty accurate representation of how it feels. The storm is here. The hurricane has arrived. Of all the pain I've ever felt in my life, this is the absolute worst. The needle is still in my back, and I'm screaming. Crying. Yelling at the top of my lungs, "Please stop! Oh, God, please stop!"

Through my screams I can hear my dad from down the hallway. I'd know his baritone voice anywhere. He's alarmed, saying, "That's her! What are they doing? They're hurting her." He's asking more questions I can't hear. Muffled voices reply. He says, "They need to stop!"

I'm sobbing through my screams. Trying to breathe. I don't know how long this procedure will last, and although it's probably only a few minutes, it feels like forever.

The needle is out. The procedure is over. I feel defeated. I've been keeping it together so well up to now. The surprise of finding the lump on my neck. The doctor's visits. The suspicion of cancer. The decision to go back to school. No problem. But I can't keep it together while getting this biopsy, and I like to think I'm a person who's not easily defeated.

Mom and Dad come into the room while I'm still lying on the gurney. Mom's eyes are puffy and red, and she's still crying, and I'm still crying, too, and my dad's eyes don't look that good, either, and the minute I see them, I cry harder.

I'm bawling now. Sobbing. Saying, "Please don't make me do this again."

They come over to me and hug me. They don't say anything. They just hold tight, and I can see in their eyes a look that says, "We're here for you always. No matter what you go through."

On this day I learn about teamwork as never before, and then, over the weeks and months to come, I learn to rely on my team even more. I've always prided myself on not accepting help from people, but my family and friends become my biggest supporters during this difficult season, and I learn that teamwork is a two-way street. You contribute to your team, and your team contributes to you. My cancer feels larger than just me. My dad and mom are affected by it. Derek has bad days because of it. My friends give and give and give and keep giving because of it. The cancer is mine, but we're all going through this together.

Like this: It's the last semester of my senior year, and I return to college while flying back and forth from Atlanta to New Jersey every other week for the treatments, and sometimes on the phone, when my mom is asking me how I'm doing, I overhear my dad peppering her with questions in the background. The emotions they're showing me on the phone aren't the depth of what they're truly feeling or communicating to each other. I sense that this is harder for them than they ever let on to me.

My brother, Derek, calls me every day. Sometimes more than once. Whenever we are on the phone together, he's always positive, always encouraging, telling me only good things. I don't want to worry him, so I talk to my friends and parents more about what's actually going on. Derek's in a slump this season, and he deliberately doesn't tell anyone what's happening with me. He doesn't believe in making excuses and doesn't want to blame anyone but himself for his performance, but he's getting annihilated in the press. He's at one of the biggest places in his career, but he doesn't want people to make a connection between his performance on the field and his worrying because his little sister is battling cancer.

I realize then that there's a sense of mutual responsibility I feel to my team, and hopefully they to me. I have obstacles in my life that I need help to overcome, and my team members have obstacles in their lives that I can help with. Sure, there might be times when a friendship feels one-sided, but overall there's a sense of camaraderie where each person says, "We're going to walk through these experiences together." This realization helps me feel not completely dependent.

When I am first diagnosed with cancer, I immediately receive a call from my brother's ex-girlfriend. She continues to remain like a big sister to me, even many years later. She's someone who's always looked out for me, even when she's traveling the world or touring or making an album. She always finds time. When I am diagnosed, it's a particularly busy time for her, but there's still a natural kindness that flows from her toward me. She finds ways to check in with me and to support me throughout my treatment.

I always get the same phone call from her: "Kwali-Kwal, are you taking care of yourself? How are you feeling?" She's always had some sort of nickname for me, and it's evolved throughout the years. I went from Lamb Junior to Kwali-Kwal (short for Koala . . . don't ask!). She often calls my parents to see what the doctors are saying. She gets me a portable DVD player and tons of movies to help make my treatments go more quickly. She buys me a new bed set so I can sleep more comfortably in my apartment in Atlanta. When my hair begins to fall out, she makes an appointment for me with her hairstylists in New York City to cut my hair into a shorter style. With the new cut, it won't be as heavy and may be less prone to falling out as quickly.

Each day I take shots in my legs to help my body produce white blood cells, and my bones ache all over from the medicine that goes in—particularly my shoulders, because I played softball in high school and used those joints a lot. Heating pads help a bit, but the pain is so deep within me, it's excruciating.

My father's background as a drug and alcohol abuse counselor has instilled in me a tendency to not take pain medicine that I've been prescribed unless it's absolutely necessary. It's particularly hard for me to sleep due to the pain, so I'm often wide-awake all night long.

My best friend and roommate, Britney, is a big part of my team. She helps get me, along with some of my other girlfriends, to and from the airport every other week for the chemo treatments, even when I want to bail and miss the plane instead. On nights I can't sleep, she stays up with me. I do my routine: brush my teeth, wash my face. But I know I'm not going to be able to sleep, so I don't even hit the pillow. Britney sits up and watches TV with me or listens to music with me. Mostly we talk, and before we know it, it's two in the morning. Three. Four. Five. Britney is still up with me, and she's got class in a couple of hours, and so do I. There's no end goal this night except the hope of becoming so desperately tired that sleep overtakes me. This goes on for days at a time, and Britney stays by my side.

On the nights Britney is unable to stay, my friend Vince helps. He's from my hometown of Kalamazoo and attends college in Atlanta as well. He makes a point of coming over and sitting with me until I fall asleep. He reminds me that it's important always to feel as though I have a piece of home with me—and during this time, Vince is the closest thing to home that I have in Atlanta. Once I'm asleep, he lets himself out and then will visit again in a few days.

My other best friend, Nneka, studies with me almost every single day. We live in the same apartment complex and go to a nearby bookstore. It's our routine: we meet after school, drive together to the bookstore, order a coffee, and study. When we finish, we sometimes treat ourselves to dinner at Chili's before heading home. Chili's for dinner is a big treat for me in college, something I usually experience only when my parents come to visit, yet Nneka knows just what I need. She's a friend who hangs out with me no matter what. We laugh, we study, and we laugh some more. She can always get me to smile. She's a huge part of my team.

My close friend Melissa meets me in New York City each week when I fly home for treatments, and she often plans something fun for us to do the night before my chemo treatments; at times this is the only thing that gets me onto the plane from Atlanta when I'm struggling to return. Although I'm not much fun at this point. On days when I'm super sick, I don't want to do anything, don't want to go anywhere. But my friends come to me, and we do something quiet. Or sometimes they say no to invitations just so I won't feel I'm the only one who can't go. They are all part of the band of brothers and sisters I need to make it through each day. How desperately I need my team around me.

How desperately we as people need one another.

6

Teamwork:

THE O'NEILLS PUT HOPE INTO ACTION

2016

It's April when the phone call comes.

The millions of dollars have been raised. The virus has been avoided. The endless hoops have been jumped through. At last Eliza is to go in for screening to see if she's eligible for the trial. The doctors at the hospital wear gloves, masks, and gowns to reduce Eliza's chance of exposure to germs, and even now her full participation in the trial is not a sure thing. The O'Neills are told that a minimum of six children and a maximum of nine children will participate. The doctors will pick the safest candidates. Eliza gets the screening, then they go home and have to wait some more to find out if she's in or not. It all comes down to the phone call from the medical team that they'll receive next.

Yes, and she's in. No, and she's out. There are no appeals.

Cara and Glenn are sitting in the front seats of their car when the critical call comes. The car is parked, and they switch on a dash camera to record the moment for posterity. Glenn takes the call. Cara listens in. On the video, we can't hear the words, but we see Cara begin to sob. Then Glenn. This is what hope looks like. Sitting in a parked car, eyes closed, bawling. Because you've just heard one word that changes everything: *Yes*.

They travel to the children's hospital in Columbus, Ohio, for the treatment day. Just to get this chance feels like a miracle in itself. Doctors sedate Eliza, put an IV into her arm, and administer the therapy, and then it's over. Gene therapy, at this point, is a onetime thing. You get it, and you hope it works. There's no ongoing treatment other than to monitor Eliza's progress. Eliza is the first person in the world to receive this therapy. Will it work?

With the treatment administered, the isolation can officially end. The quarantine has lasted 726 days. That's four days short of two full years. When Eliza is released from the hospital a day later, one of the first things Cara wants to do is go to a grocery store. It's a surreal experience, so normal it's euphoric. They eat pizza out at a restaurant, and it's the best pizza they've ever tasted. Then they go and get Beckham. He's been with his grandparents for three months. It's an emotional reunion for everyone.

When Eliza comes home, her team is all there for her. They feel that at least she stands a fighting chance. There are no guarantees, and the battle isn't over. The parents are advised not to share anything publicly until the trial is completely over. They don't receive any data from the hospital. The only thing they know for sure is what they can see happening in front of their own eyes with their daughter. They are charting new ground.

Today, eight months after the clinical trial, Eliza just turned seven years old. She's still not speaking, but after the new medicine went in, her parents feel they have more of a connection with her. Her hyperactivity diminishes. Every day she goes to a special school for autistic children. She puts shapes together. She works on puzzles. Therapists work with her to try to get her to speak again.

She's not in a wheelchair.

She doesn't need a feeding tube.

She doesn't have any seizures, which children with the disease often have by this age.

She doesn't cry as much as she once did, which her parents see as a very hopeful sign.

Her parents choose to believe that the gene therapy is helping. Only time will tell for sure.

What have the O'Neills learned during the last few years?

"So many people have skills that can help you," Glenn says. "When you're going through an obstacle, just gather the people closest to you, start there, and then go to the open doors where you can share your story. We use the phrase 'provided for.' In those moments when we didn't feel we could go on, people came into our lives to help at just the right times, and we felt so provided for. Each person who helps you isn't there by chance."

Cara adds, "Your team can help you dig deep. When you feel like you can't go on, your team can help. Sometimes you go on day by day, and sometimes it's minute by minute. Sometimes what you're going through feels like it will never end, but it will. New seasons will come."

The fight isn't over for the O'Neill family. They're still on their journey, still raising funds for their foundation. For them, success means finding a complete cure for Sanfilippo syndrome, one that's available to all children. It's been a long, hard road, and they're still fighting for their daughter and still fighting for other children with the disease.

Ours is a similar call to action. In turning on the engine of the Stuff within us, we need to develop our team and then walk the road together. Our invitation is to go ahead—ask for help, even when it feels counterintuitive. To look for people with proven experience, to find people with skills that match our needs, to value the people with strengths that can make up for our own weaknesses, and to not be afraid of diversity or disagreement within our team.

No, it's not a mandate to go blindly. It's still fine to question everything. To knock on every door. To pester the people who may be able to unearth the answers you need. In the next chapter, we'll look more closely at how to challenge conventional wisdom and stereo-types, and how doing so can often turn an obstacle on its head.

CHAPTER SIX

Push Your Limits

Our children cannot aspire to be what they cannot see.
—The Three Doctors

1
_____

When You Love to Live

S ean Swarner's life feels full of possibilities. He's always been an adventurous boy with a keen imagination who loves the outdoors. At an early age he discovers organized sports and soon throws himself into baseball, soccer, football, basketball, swimming, track, and the pole vault. All his friends know him as the kid you want on your team. The kid who finishes first. But standing in his way today is something no child should ever have to experience.

Eighth grade, thirteen years old, lunchtime at school. Sean scarfs down his food and makes a beeline for the gym, where usually every day he shinnies up the pegboard, arms only. For some reason this day all the pegs are missing, so he turns his attention to a nearby basket-ball game. Sean grabs the ball and goes in for a layup. He sinks the basket, but when he comes down he hears a crunch and feels a sharp pain in his knee. Instantly he knows something's gone badly wrong.

He's a tough kid and hobbles around to his classes for the rest of the day. But by the time he gets home, his knee has swollen to the size of a grapefruit. His mom takes him to their regular doctor, who examines the knee, orders an X-ray, and, since he heard wheezing throughout Sean's lung fields, suspects that he might have pneumonia. The doctor gives him a nebulizer and sends him to a specialist. By now Sean's mangled knee has triggered some sort of biological chain reaction, and his whole body is swollen. Tests are performed, and the specialist cuts right to the chase. "Do you already have any oncologists that you know and like? If not, I can refer you to one."

Sean's mom gasps, but no, she doesn't. She asks for time to consider it and later that day calls a friend who's a hospital CEO and asks for recommendations. At the oncologist's, Sean quickly undergoes a number of tests—a CAT scan, more X-rays, even one of those extremely painful bone marrow tests. It takes a few weeks before a clear diagnosis comes in.

Sean has Hodgkin's lymphoma—cancer of the lymphatic system. Highly advanced. Stage 4. Sean's parents are told matter-of-factly he has three months to live. They don't tell Sean the severity of his diagnosis. He's had a grandmother previously die of cancer, so the parents tell him only that he's sick with Hodgkin's lymphoma, and that the road ahead will be hard.

Sean starts chemotherapy immediately. When he has a good day, he wants to go to school. When he has a bad day, he's stuck in the hospital. The family lives in Willard, Ohio, a small town in the Midwest, and a handful of teachers come to his house to tutor him and help him keep up with his studies. Sean loses his hair. He gains sixty pounds from the steroids he is taking. Once he throws up repeatedly for thirty-six hours straight. He's put on an antinausea medication that makes his eyeballs literally roll back in his head.

But Sean carries on, continually challenging conventional wisdom. One of his favorite comic strips is *Calvin and Hobbes*, about an adventuresome boy and his talking jokester pet tiger. Just like Calvin, Sean imagines that a cosmic ray shrinks himself into the alter ego of Spaceman Spiff. He's holed up in the IV bag in a microscopic spaceship, and a rocket blast propels him forward. Spaceman Sean is on a mission to destroy cancer tumors. The heart valve opens, and Spaceman Sean blasts his chemo missiles at enemy invaders. It's amazing what a kid with a strong imagination can think of.

Officials from the Make-A-Wish Foundation call Sean and grant the terminally ill boy one wish—whatever he wants. Children have traveled to Disneyland, met movie stars and professional athletes, ridden in helicopters. But Sean knows deep inside himself he's going to beat the disease. It's hard for him to fully articulate his confidence, but he's still hopeful, still fighting, still filled with youthful panache. He's Spaceman Sean, and he sees how he's beating the disease; everything keeps looking better and better. He hasn't allowed the magnitude of the situation to fill his mind, and he nonchalantly figures that some other kid is worse off than he is.

So Sean gives his wish away.

Years later he's giving a presentation for the Make-A-Wish Foundation, and the representative says, "You know, we've only ever had one person in the history of the organization give their wish away."

Sean—still nonchalant—says with a chuckle, "Yeah, that was me."

The three-month mark passes, and Sean keeps living. He keeps fighting hard, and, after a year of chemotherapy, doctors use the magical word *remission*. It's time to remove his chest catheter. Sean wants this done quickly because he has a swim meet coming up. The catheter is out and Sean competes, although he feels winded and bloated in the pool. A year later he comes back to the very same meet, this time feeling like his normal self. This time, Sean wins every event he competes in.

Sean has pushed the limits. He's redefined what's possible. He's beaten stage 4 cancer, and his big goal now is just to forget being sick and to return to being a normal teenager again. So he throws himself back into life. He swims and runs cross-country and track. He celebrates his fifteenth birthday and goes steady with a girlfriend, and life is good.

But a few months before his sixteenth birthday, something doesn't feel right. He goes back to the doctor for a thorough checkup. When the diagnosis comes, Sean's parents ask him to wait outside while the doctor talks to them. Sean listens through the keyhole.

"Is it cancer again?" Sean's mom asks.

"Yes, but a different kind," the doctor says.

Then Sean hears the worst news imaginable—it's Askin's sarcoma, a rare and highly aggressive part of the Ewing's sarcoma family of tumors. Cancer of the bone.

This time, he is given only two weeks to live.

2

I'm Not Dead Yet

S ean can't hold back the tears. He's the only known person ever diagnosed with both of these different and deadly types of cancers:
Hodgkin's and Askin's. He knows it might be realistic to accept the
verdict, give up, and die. Or he can push the limits again and fight for
his life a second time. He decides he's not ready to give up. He still
has too much living to do. What he doesn't know yet is how incredibly
dark the road ahead will be.

Doctors discover a golf ball–sized tumor on his right lung. The
same day as the initial diagnosis, they crack open his ribs and surgically remove the tumor. Afterward, he's in and out of consciousness
and sees a priest coming into his room. The priest, thinking the boy
will die, gives him the last rites. Sean imagines the old Monty Py-
thon comedy sequence where a body collector in medieval Europe
walks up and down a plague-ridden street calling out "Bring out
your dead! Bring out your dead!" One elderly man is ordered to get
onto the cart, even though he's still alive. "I'm not dead yet!" the
man protests. "Oh, get on the cart," the body collector says. "You
will be soon."

The two-week mark comes and goes, and Sean's not dead yet. He
keeps hoping, keeps pushing, keeps fighting. For the next year he's in
and out of treatments. Three months of chemo. One month of radiation without chemo. Then ten more months of chemo. About half the
time he's in a coma. Once his temperature soars to 108 degrees

Fahrenheit. He floats out of his body, glances around the room, and isn't sure if he'll return to his body or not. He loses 60 pounds and looks like a skeleton. Radiation destroys the upper portion of his right lung. Both lungs are left intact, but only one remains functional. He misses a whole year of school and doesn't remember much of being sixteen. His family—his team—stays by his side every step of the way. They fight right along with him.

And again—slowly, surely—he beats cancer a second time.

Sean is officially a medical marvel. When the word *remission* is used this time, the medical community is astounded, but Sean just grins. He's always intrinsically lived as though the prognoses the doctors and science had for him simply weren't acceptable. His expectations of himself were to live and push through. And he did just that!

One of the first things he does when he feels well enough is get his driver's license. He's still bald from the treatments and asks if he can wear his hat for the picture. Everybody knows who he is in his hometown, and the DMV official just chuckles and lets him wear his hat.

That's the last cancer Sean encounters. He graduates from high school and heads off to Westminster College in Pennsylvania, partying as hard as John Belushi in *Animal House* for all four years. He parties as though he's making up for lost time, squeaks through graduation, then heads to the University of North Florida, working toward his master's and doctorate. His goal is to become a psychologist for cancer patients.

One day, while he is sitting at a stoplight, the light turns green and the car ahead accelerates, but Sean just sits there, lost in a daze. Horns honk behind him, but all he can think about is that he's not on the right path. He should care that the car behind him is honking, but he doesn't care—and that's the point. It hits him that his caring muscle got turned off somewhere—caring about the car behind him, about other people, about himself, about where he's going. He realizes that though he's gone through trauma, he's never taken time to sort out how that has changed him. Maybe that's why he suddenly feels he's on the wrong path. He knows he hasn't dealt psychologically with his own trauma. He's still carrying the baggage of his ordeals, and the baggage keeps getting heavier and heavier. He feels he's at a crossroads in life, yet with no map to guide him. His brain clicks into gear and he eases into the flow of traffic, but he knows he needs to face this issue.

Sean works part-time as a bartender at a nightclub. One evening a beautiful young woman orders a drink and asks for Sean's phone number. They flirt with each other, and when he's done with work, he offers to take her home. By then she's had too much to drink. She throws up in Sean's car and passes out. He arrives at her apartment complex, carries her up three flights of stairs, and kicks on the door until someone opens it. A party is raging inside, complete with white lines of powder on the coffee table and used needles lying next to blackened cooking spoons. The woman's friends indicate that using drugs and passing out drunk are common behavior for her. Sean sets her down in a safe place, then makes a beeline for the door. He tells himself, *This isn't you. This never was you. You've fought too hard for your life to go down this path.* On the way home he draws his line in the sand. He knows the party scene isn't the right path for him—yet neither is becoming a psychologist.

Over the next few weeks he does a lot of self-reflecting. He's still not sure what career path to follow, but he knows he wants to do something that feels bigger, something amazing. He asks himself a string of hard questions: *Who am I? What do I truly want? What motivates me forward?*

He knows he wants to live life to the fullest, and he has always liked being outdoors. That thought becomes a direction. He has tasted firsthand the fragility of life, the preciousness of each day, and knows how it feels to deal with the possibility of having life taken from him at any moment. He knows how it feels to live each day as though it were his last. That feeling sparks a dream.

Sean drops out of graduate school and moves in with his younger brother, Seth, who's always been part of his team. Oddly, this dropping out becomes Sean's launch point. Seth helps Sean figure out the nuts and bolts of his dream. Together, they establish an official nonprofit organization called the Cancer Climber Association. In a nutshell, they plan to climb the world's highest mountains, raise money for cancer research, and inspire people to live to the fullest. They discover that no one with cancer has ever climbed Mount Everest. So they move to Colorado to train (Sean repeatedly hikes up the 14,000-foot Mount Elbert with a hundred pounds of rocks in his backpack); then they head to Nepal, intent upon climbing the world's highest peak. Sean's mom comes up with the idea of Sean carrying a tribute flag to the top bearing names of people who have had cancer.

Sean creates a motivation statement, *"This* is the best day ever," then repeats the statement day after day after day. It's a reminder to him that today is all he'll ever have. *This moment* matters. Happiness is a choice, and it is a choice he can make right here, right now. This moment is the only thing he's guaranteed.

He knows that the odds of climbing Everest are stacked against him. He's not supposed to be climbing tall mountains. Doctors tell him it can't be done—no one's ever climbed Everest with only one functioning lung. But he wants to test the conventional wisdom. He wants to challenge limits.

He wants to redefine what's possible.

3

How Sampson's Team of Three Pushed the Limits

S*ampson explains:* Sean's story is about challenging conventional wisdom. My story is about "raising the bar." Both of these concepts are different ways people can push their limits.

In many ways, the neighborhood I grew up in is its own battlefield. Mothers act as generals and admirals, sending their sons and daughters out every day with the hope of their returning home in one piece, not destroyed by their surroundings. My mother knows her children will all need to fly solo one day, so she's forced to trust the process.

At first the war is more of a skirmish. The challenge grows more ominous as the battlefield starts to change. It's as if we all wake up one day and the battlefield isn't the same anymore. There are now land mines and booby traps where they have never been before, ambushes where safety once reigned, and clouds of despair that block the skies where rays of hope once pierced the clouds. Some of the generals and admirals, the leaders of the troops, have gone AWOL and changed allegiance, all during the heated battle.

The weapon of mass destruction that ramps up the war is drugs. When widespread drug use invades the community, all of us, children and parents alike, witness an immediate bombardment. My mother holds me tighter, not allowing me to stray very far. But like most teenagers I want my freedom to run with the pack and push the envelope. Still, I am lucky. I have a mother who cares for me and loves me and will give her last breath in exchange for my survival.

My bottom line is that I always want to make my mother proud. I always want to be the kid who shows up one day as a grown-up to say, "Ma, here are keys to a brand-new house" or "Ma, here are keys to a brand-new car. This is a token of my appreciation for all you've done and all you've sacrificed to make sure I was provided for."

The battlefield where I grew up eventually morphs into unrecognizable terrain. Mothers, fathers, and children are forced to adjust. Over time, the unrecognizable terrain becomes the norm and the community acclimates. Lives are lost, tears flow, hopelessness floods the old spaces of hope. I can only imagine what it's like for my mother and other parents to be a part of this change. This is not the life they intended. This isn't the way they grew up, and this certainly isn't the backdrop they want for their children. Certainly, my mother wants to change the conditions we live under, but given her reality, she can't. Yet she decides to be a constant in all her children's lives, watching over us more closely, remaining our general. And that decision saves my life.

A few years before I came into the world, and not long before my parents go through their divorce, Pop bought our family's house on the

GI Bill—not that it's anything to look at. Our house has two bedrooms and one bathroom, and is situated on Ludlow Street in Newark. Our house isn't actually in the projects, but it's directly across the street from the projects—the Reverend Otto E. Kretchmer Homes, to be exact. After Pop moves out, Ma struggles all she can to stretch a dollar and keep us in that house, but things are always tight.

Across the street from our house also sits a graveyard, and the bodies of far too many young men from our neighborhood end up there. Stabbings, muggings, and shootings are regular occurrences in my neighborhood, and when I'm a teen, the harsh reality is that it's rare for youths such as me to survive unscathed to age twenty-five.

I begin to feel the limitations of my surroundings. No one in my family has ever gone to college. No one in any of my friends' homes has ever gone to college. Most people in my neighborhood have never made it through high school. After her own mother passed away, my mother stopped attending school at eight or nine years of age and stayed home to work on the farm, which was common where she grew up in a small town in South Carolina. So I play many roles in my household and take pride in doing so. My mother doesn't read very well, so I help her write money orders when she pays the bills, I help her maintain her bank account, and I help her read the letters that come in the mail.

It's hard for me to see expensive sneakers and not want a pair. It's hard for me to see a luxury car driving down the street and not imagine myself behind the wheel. As a teen, I ask myself, "How am I ever going to get money like that?" I see how people in my neighborhood come up with their own solutions to get by. My family's little two-bedroom home is burglarized four times during my childhood, which is par for the course. I've come to realize that we're a community of imperfections. And like every other kid at that age, I can always find something to make fun of.

I have school clothes, play clothes, and church clothes. We never wear our school clothes outside to play because we know we'll be in *big* trouble if anything ever happens to them. We don't have money to just throw them away. Mom patches them, and they become our play clothes. But I never want to wear clothes with a patch. If I do, the joke's on me that day.

I have a pair of burnt-orange corduroys, and one summer I wear them every single day. I own one other pair of pants, but they get a hole that Mom patches, and the patch shows too much and I'm ashamed to wear them, so I wear my corduroys—day after day after day. We're playing football one afternoon on the big concrete lot, dodging broken bottles on the ground as usual, and the sun is out and we are all sweaty. A kid starts laughing and pointing at me and says, "Hey, aren't you hot with those corduroys on?" and I say, "No, I'm not hot. These are my football pants. I like these pants." Just trying to think of anything to sidestep the teasing. I'm not completely innocent, because the truth is if I'm not taking it, then I'm dishing it out. The teasing is a small thing, but it's constant among us.

I have this friend, Noody, and he lives in the projects, Building No. 6. His real name is Lawrence, but, if your name is Lawrence and you live in the projects, you'd want to go by a nickname, too. Noody and I play two-man baseball with a bat and a rubber ball, and we go to the side of his building and spray-paint a box with a big X in the middle on the concrete wall for our strike zone. One of us pitches and fields and the other bats and runs, and we can play nine innings that way. Ma always makes sure she keeps an eye on me at all times, even if I'm only across the street playing ball with Noody. This is her rule: I'm to stay where she can see me. There's so much happening in my neighborhood, from the growing number of drug dealers to an increase in violence and crime. Against this backdrop, I constantly think about how I'm going to make something different of my life. And when I don't think about it, my mom makes sure to remind me of it—every chance she has.

After my brush with the law that summer before my senior year of high school, I start working at McDonald's because I decide that I don't want to squander my freedom by misbehaving again. School starts in the fall, and I focus on school and work, getting As and becoming an assistant manager, but I still have no idea what I'm going to do with the rest of my life. I am very good at baseball and often think of what it would be like to play professionally, but my being drafted out of Newark seems like a long shot.

I have two good friends, Rameck Hunt and George Jenkins, and one day during our senior year in high school, we have a substitute teacher for second-period class. All three of us focus on school, but, being typical teenage boys, we also have a mischievous side. So we all decide to cut class, aware that the substitute teacher will never know we're gone. Our plan is to go to the gym to shoot some hoops. But on our way, the security guard spots us in the hallway and we dart through the nearest open door, which happens to be the library.

Funny how the course of your life can change with one small move.

In the library that day is a representative from Seton Hall University. She's holding a seminar about careers in health and science, and that's nothing I've ever thought about before, but George and Rameck and I scurry to find seats, still glancing over our shoulders to see if the security guard has found us. We sit down and settle in, pretending that we had intended to come here, and for the first time in our lives we hear an idea that blows our minds.

We can become doctors. And we can do it together.

Us?

That would mean eight long years of post–high school education, followed by residency. That would mean big money for tuition, room and board, and books—money that none of us has. That would mean getting accepted into a premed program to start with—something we have no idea how to do. That would mean not allowing our upbringing to hold us back but instead finding a way to make it propel us forward.

Rameck, George, and I make a pact that day. This is an opportunity we can't let pass us by. We have been hungry to find a path to escape our surroundings, and, even at an early age, we recognize that this is our way out—and we're not going to squander it. We are going to do this. We're going to apply to Seton Hall and go to college together, somehow go to medical school together, and stick with one another to the end.

This is only the beginning of how we redefine what's possible for our lives. Our start of pushing limits. Of raising the bar. Along the way, I can't tell you how many people tell us there is no way three boys from Newark are ever going to become doctors. Friends from the neighborhood. Family members. Even educators. But it takes only one person to believe in us. The right person: Carla Dickson, the administrator from Seton Hall, believes in us from the start.

Most people argue that we don't have the right ingredients to make it as doctors. Given where we come from, it'll be impossible. Many people in my neighborhood laugh at me and tell me it can't be done. They all call me by my middle name (as they did back then) and say, "Marshall, who are you fooling? You will *never* be a doctor. That just doesn't happen for people in our neighborhood." I quickly learn how to tune those people out and focus on the network of people who believe we can do it, no matter how small that network seems at the time.

I know becoming a doctor seems like a long shot, but I need to take the chance, because I know what awaits me if I go with the flow. I don't want to be another statistic. So I have to get up and go. I have to launch. I think, *Just give me a chance, world, and I will work harder than anyone else to make this dream a reality.*

The short version of this story is that George, Rameck, and I all succeed. We harness the power of our team, as discussed in the last chapter, and we beat the odds. We push our limits. We never lower the bar for ourselves or for one another. We redefine our possibilities. Today Rameck is an internist and the medical director of a weight management program at Princeton Medicine. He is an assistant professor of medicine at Robert Wood Johnson Medical School. In 2015, he was named New Jersey Hospital Association's Healthcare Professional of the Year. I'm an emergency-room physician and cover several hospitals in New Jersey, and George is an assistant professor of dentistry at Columbia University and works directly with dental students and residents. Together, the three of us run our own nonprofit organization, the Three Doctors Foundation. We've appeared on major TV shows, been featured in major newspapers, and given speeches all over the country. At times we can't quite believe the amazing opportunities coming our way, and it all started when we challenged the limits society had placed on us, raised the bar for ourselves, and never let anyone lower it for us.

4
———

That Crucial Twofold Decision

Sharlee explains: There are two ways of pushing limits: challenging conventional wisdom, as Sean Swarner does, and raising the bar, as Sampson and the Three Doctors do. In Sean's case, he is pushing the limits that are bounded by facts, research, and what is supposed to take place in his medical battles with cancer. In Sampson's case, he is pushing the limits put on him by what others *believe* he can or can't accomplish due to his circumstances growing up. Society buys into various stereotypes, and when it does so, the bar is lowered for certain individuals. The expectations are not the same, which can be very detrimental to people who do not challenge those stereotypes.

In both instances, there are realistic cause-and-effect things to consider. Neither Sean nor Sampson threw logic to the wind. Sean still had to undergo chemo and radiation. Just because he believed he had more to live for didn't mean he could skip that step of treatment and magically get better. Sampson and his friends couldn't say that because they *believed* they could become doctors, they didn't need to attend medical school. But both Sean and Sampson visualized themselves in a place of success. They both believed they could accomplish their goals.

Sean Swarner's story mentions him visualizing himself battling cancer through a comic strip he loved as a kid. Also, he visualized success while climbing the mountain. Sampson and his friends visualized themselves as fully qualified doctors.

Raising the bar is a type of self-challenge. One expert explains that the concept comes from the athletic world: "In the high jump competition, the bar is raised after each jumper completes the jump, thereby making each jump more challenging. [Similarly] a leader in the business environment will continually set higher goals. As goals are reached by the business module, higher goals are set in order to reach new highs, raising the bar, so to speak."[1]

Here's how it might work in the academic world: If you tell yourself you can score only 80 percent on a test because that is what people expect you to do, then most likely you will push yourself only enough to score 80 percent. But what if you tell yourself, "I can do better than what is expected of me. Not only can I meet the expectations of others, but I can exceed those expectations. I will not allow others to lower the bar for me because of my circumstances."

When you continue to set your goals higher and higher, it is a known fact that you can usually meet those goals with hard work and determination. It is very easy to allow society or your friends and family to make excuses for you, to allow others to set the level of your achievements based on what they assume you can accomplish. But why allow others to dictate your ability? That's your own privilege.

Whatever your situation is in life, do its specifics need to dictate your limitations? Could it be true that people who come from specific neighborhoods, people of certain genders, people with particular medical ailments, people with learning disabilities, people with certain body types, or people from specific family structures must necessarily be limited by those circumstances? Or are those boxes just begging to be broken open?

Conventional wisdom is the accepted way of looking at things; it provides shortcuts to solutions and prevents us from spending our lives reinventing the wheel. We don't want to denigrate conventional wisdom. We can learn from the experience of others and from past generations by receiving conventional wisdom.

But there's a downside to conventional wisdom, and negatives can emerge if we never question the tried and true. Conventional wisdom has a way of saying to new challenges, *It can't be done. It's not realistic. It's impossible. We do things only one way around here.* If we accept those statements as fact, it might be the same as accepting limitations, never thinking outside the box, and settling for a diminished life. What we found in our interviews is that people with the Stuff consistently challenge expectations and limitations. They are continuously pushing the limits.

Auren Hoffman, the CEO of SafeGraph, a company that seeks to understand human movement and how people interact with the world, doesn't dismiss conventional thinking but warns against accepting it with an uncritical mind-set: "Protect yourself from experts through contrarian thinking. Conventional wisdom is often very conventional thinking. Before accepting opinions as truth, think through the issues yourself. Don't just look for agendas but look for biases. . . . Seek out other opinions. Seek out outcasts. Seek out non-expert experts who often challenge the status quo. . . . Of course, experts can be right. They often are. You don't have time to question everything. . . . For instance, even if you cannot prove the earth is round, it is not a good idea to think the world is flat. It is likely that the government did not fake the moon landing. And when you were born, you probably were not delivered by a stork."[2]

Understand, too, that obstacles are real and the process of overcoming an obstacle is seldom easy. Yes, an obstacle can be overcome, but no, it probably won't be overcome overnight. And the positive changes accomplished by pushing limits don't occur instantly. The process involved in challenging limits is real, and that process needs to be respected. Knowing this helps take the pressure off us. It lets us breathe as we wrestle with our obstacles. It allows us to be patient with ourselves. We can grieve our losses and feel our pain as we move on in our growth and toward opportunity. But at the same time, we choose never, ever to allow anyone to determine our limits based on our circumstances. We will determine what our limits are. And all of us—Sean, Sampson, and I—know how good it feels when we show everyone, including ourselves, that we can meet a challenge head-on and exceed expectations!

5

_____

Standing on Top of the World

The climb up Mount Everest begins, and Sean Swarner is able to apply many of the lessons he learned during his two cancer ordeals. When the oxygen grows thin, he uses visualization techniques similar to his childhood Spaceman Spiff practices, imagining his body manufacturing more red blood cells, imagining the oxygen going to all the needed places in his body.[3]

When most people climb Everest, they arrive at the mountain with a team of thirty to forty people: porters, cooks, Sherpas, and other climbers. But Sean and his brother don't have enough funds for a team that size. Their team consists of one cook, who stays at base camp, and two Sherpas, who climb with Sean. Seth helps organize the base camp but doesn't plan to climb to the top.

Climbing Mount Everest is no simple matter. You have to establish at least four camps on the way up, stopping at each camp so your body acclimatizes. Time is spent shuttling gear back and forth from one camp to another. Sean and Seth establish their base camp on April 8. Their plan is for Sean to reach the summit in about a month, mid-May, depending on the weather conditions.

Each climbing stage is a huge feat. Freezing temperatures chill the bones. High winds buffet the body, threatening to shove a climber off the mountain. Deep chasms form in the ice and snow and must be crossed on aluminum ladders. The air toward the top is so thin that climbers have been known to die from lack of oxygen.

It takes about two weeks even to arrive at base camp, and on the way, Sean meets another climber named Peter. They quickly become friends and stay in several of the same villages and hostels. Peter speaks with an English accent and looks like a mountaineer, with a strong build and dark hair. He has a quick sense of humor, and there's a genuineness to his personality that Sean appreciates right away. They laugh at their accents and idioms. Peter orders a "pint," drives on a "motorway," and "overtakes" people. Sean orders a "beer," drives on a "highway," and "passes" people. They part ways when they reach base camp, and Peter and his team of Sherpas climb on ahead.

One day when Sean is shuttling gear up to Camp 2, he sees Peter just as Peter is ready to leave for Camp 3. They give each other a quick hug for good luck and promise to connect later at base camp, after both men have summited and descended the mountain. But a few days later, news arrives via the Sherpa grapevine that a sudden storm came up at Camp 3. Hurricane-force winds. A climber was caught outside his tent when the storm came up. He stumbled around in the blinding snow and finally found his way to a different tent, but nobody was inside. There he spent the next two days riding out the storm with no food or water. When the storm passed, he was in a weakened state but wanted to keep climbing. He and his Sherpas encountered a mile-long sheet of ice that angled upward at 45 degrees, but he misclipped himself onto a fixed guide rope, slipped, and fell. He tumbled two thousand feet into a crevasse.

A report goes out on the international wire: "Anonymous hiker dies on Everest." Sean calls his parents and lets them know it's not him. They're in tears together, because Sean knows who it is: Peter. It's another reminder that life is so fragile.

Sean is grieving, but he decides to proceed with the remainder of his climb. He's carrying the tribute flag with names of people whose lives have been affected by cancer, and he doesn't want to let them down.

When he approaches Camp 3, there's no sudden storm, but he begins to feel sick—*really* sick. He has a horrible headache and feels nauseous, suffers from vertigo, and can barely walk. His ability to digest food shuts down. Slowly he plods onward, straining to put one foot in front of the other. He reaches Camp 3 and collapses in a tent. He's so close to his destination—only a day and a half from the summit—but it might as well be forever. Sean's come down with altitude-induced swelling of the brain. He can barely move. He's put on oxygen and sleeps in his tent for two days solid.

When he finally wakes up, he lies on the floor of his tent, contemplating his next move. He feels a bit better, but reports of bad weather have come in. Other groups have staggered into and out of

Camp 3 but have been forced to return before reaching the summit. The weather is just too dangerous. Sean does not want to give up on his dream. He pictures himself reaching the summit.[4] He smells the ozone, hears the crunching of crampons beneath his feet. He feels the wind, sees the sunrise. He visualizes himself taking the last three steps to the top. He wills himself forward, up and out of his warm sleeping bag, and onward, one foot in front of the other.

Sean and his two Sherpas climb straight to Camp 4, then keep going. The weather is perfectly clear and calm, but it's so dry that the moisture from Sean's eyeballs frosts over much of the insides of his goggles. He doesn't want to remove the goggles to clean them because he is so close to the sun that even a few minutes without protection can induce blindness. The top is within reach, and he wills himself to keep going. Only a hundred more feet to go. Fifty. Twenty-five. Ten. Five. Three-two-one.

On May 16, 2002, Sean Swarner stands on top of the world—29,035 feet above sea level. He is the first cancer survivor to summit Everest and finds out later that thanks to the lousy weather he's one of only three people to reach the top that entire season. The day is beautiful and clear—and he can see the curvature of the earth and the dark blueness of the sky as it nears the outer limits of the atmosphere. He plants his tribute flag. He radios Seth at base camp and asks him to call their parents and share the news: "Your son made it to the top of the world." Sean takes a picture and feels an overwhelming sense of pride and accomplishment. He's come a long way from that day as a thirteen-year-old when he was told he had only three months to live, from the day as a fifteen-year-old he was given only two weeks to live. He's living proof that no challenge is too great, no peak is too high.

The first hospital Sean visits is in Nepal, as soon as he comes down the mountain. He meets a Nepalese teenager fighting cancer and gives him a T-shirt he wore as a boy, which he'd brought along for good luck. Cancer truly knows no international boundaries. But neither does hope. Sean tells the boy to give the T-shirt to someone else after he gets better.

Sean knows he's only begun his life mission. Over the next few years, he summits the highest peaks on all seven continents—Kilimanjaro in Africa, Elbrus in Europe, Aconcagua in South America, Kosciuszko in Australia, Vinson in Antarctica, and Denali in North America—completing the famed "Seven Summits" mountain-climbing tour. He plants a tribute flag with names of cancer victims at the top of each peak, and he develops a second motto along the way: "Keep climbing. Never give up."

He returns to the United States and continues to visit hospitals to encourage other cancer patients. He speaks about his trip at universities and business campuses. His message is that the conventions of human limitations can be challenged. Odds can be defied, endurance can be tested, and people can overcome, heal, and triumph no matter what the obstacle. He tells people that they, too, can climb their own Everest—no matter what their particular Everest may be.

Yes, it can sometimes be scary to push the limits. But fear can actually become an ally, as we'll see next.

CHAPTER SEVEN

Refuse to Give In to Fear

You gain strength, courage and confidence by every experience in which you really stop to look fear in the face. You are able to say to yourself, "I have lived through this horror. I can take the next thing that comes along." You must do the thing you think you cannot do.
—Eleanor Roosevelt

1

There's Always a Way Forward

Today is a happy day for Traci Micheline, a day she's looked forward to for a long time. Today she's giving birth to her first children, twin boys—soon to be named Nicholas and Vincent—and everything has been set into motion perfectly. She's already in the birthing room. She's already on the gurney. Her mom and her husband, Jay, are by her side for support. The babies are positioned correctly. She is just about ready to push. So why, just now, does she feel Baby B do a sudden flip? Because if that's the case, then that will change everything.

This is supposed to be an incredible moment, in part because Traci wants more than anything to deliver the boys naturally. She's had lots of doctor visits over the past nine months; she's made her wish known, and the doctors have assured her that nothing is wrong and delivering naturally, even twins, will be okay. She developed gestational diabetes during the pregnancy, so lots of tests have been done. Yet she has repeatedly been told there's nothing to worry about. Everything will be fine. But a flip—if what she felt was indeed a flip—means a cesarean section will be required. Traci tells her nurse about the flipped feeling.

"Nah, you don't understand what you're talking about," the nurse says. "That can't happen now."

"I'm not crazy," Traci says. "I'm telling you, I just felt him flip."

"Don't worry." The nurse's tone is calm and even. "There's no possibility of that happening now."

Just then the delivery doctor walks into the room. Traci blurts out—"Baby B just flipped." The doctor stares straight into Traci's eyes, and Traci stares straight back.

"Nurse, get the sonogram machine," the doctor says. The nurse darts out and wheels the machine back into the room. She's shaking her head. But the sonogram machine doesn't lie.

"Okay, that baby has definitely flipped," the doctor says. "We need to do a C-section right now!"

The twins are born at 5:00 p.m. and 5:01 p.m. Nurses hold the babies up to Traci's face for a quick picture, then they're scooted to the neonatal intensive care unit, standard procedure for emergency C-sections. By the time Traci gets out of surgery and is wheeled to the recovery area, it's after 7:00 p.m. A room for longer care is set to become available at midnight. Traci sees the weariness on the faces of her husband and family and knows that if they stay, they'll just have to sit around for the next five-plus hours. So she tells them to go home, get some sleep, and come back early next morning. They hug her good-bye and leave.

Traci waits in the recovery bed and watches an old episode of *Friends*. Everything is calm.

Suddenly a tall doctor bustles into the room, all business, and says, "Mrs. Micheline, there've been some complications, and I need to explain some things about your son Vincent. While I talk, I need you to sign these papers right now." Fear shoots into Traci's heart. As the doctor talks, Traci scribbles furiously. The doctor leaves. Traci locates a phone and calls her husband.

"You have to get back to the hospital," she says.

"I just arrived home," Jay says. "What do you mean?"

"You just have to get back."

Alarmed, Jay rushes to the hospital. By then Traci has fallen apart. It's difficult for her even to speak.

Jay asks, "What's going on?"

"I don't know," Traci says.

"What do you mean you don't know?"

"I mean I don't know. Go find out. I don't know if Vincent is even here or if they're transporting him to another hospital."

Jay rushes to find out. It turns out that Vincent, the baby who flipped, was born with a hole in his diaphragm. When the baby took his first breath, everything in the stomach area was sucked through the hole. The doctors say he doesn't have a high chance of surviving, although if he does survive, the problem can be corrected surgically.

He is now on a ventilator, and the next few days will be touch-and-go. For surgery to take place, the baby needs to be breathing 70 percent on his own, and if Vincent can live for a week, the doctors think he can be saved. The one silver lining is that the emergency C-section proved a blessing in disguise. If he had been born naturally, he most likely would have died immediately, because the process of natural childbirth puts too much pressure on a baby's stomach, and organs can get crushed.

It's small comfort for Traci. She's walking down the corridor leaning on her IV pole, and she's completely forgotten her expectation that this would be her happy day. That's been eclipsed by a huge dark cloud of unknown, and her focus is totally on her needy son. She goes to see him and finds his tiny body completely surrounded by beeping machines and tubes.

Traci snaps into action. A decision needs to be made quickly: Do the parents want Vincent to stay in this hospital or be transferred to a different one where the personnel will be better able to pump his heart? A snowstorm is raging outside, so a helicopter, the quicker option, can't be used. An ambulance *can* be used for transport, but it'll take longer for Vincent to get to the other hospital, and there's a chance a battery might die on one of the machines used to keep him alive. How do parents ever make these decisions?! Traci and Jay opt to keep Vincent where he is. They reason: if something happens to him, at least the family will all be together. The newborns are scheduled to have photographs taken, and Traci says yes for both of her sons. Even if the parents have Vincent for only a few days, Traci still wants pictures of him. A nurse asks if Traci wants Vincent to be baptized. *Now. In the hospital. Just in case.* Traci frowns and says, "No. He'll get baptized with his brother. We're going to have a big party later on." Already her strength is showing; she is choosing to hope for the best.

A few days later Traci is instructed to go home with one son, Nicholas, but she can't stand the thought of being away from Vincent. She dutifully heads back to the house, takes one look around, and says, "I can't stay here in the house, I have to be back with my baby," but the doctors insist she must stay home. She takes a deep breath.

One week after the birth, the home phone rings at five in the morning, and doctors say Vincent is breathing at 70 percent. A surgery to repair the diaphragm is scheduled for that day. Traci learns that Vincent and two other babies are set to have the same procedure on the same day—one other boy and a girl. Traci sees later just how life-threatening this problem is. Vincent and the other boy survive, but the baby girl doesn't make it. For the next month Traci and Jay shuttle back and forth from home to the hospital, caring for Vincent. They're told that even though he survived, the news is still grim. "He's likely to be very weak his whole life," a doctor says. "He will never be able to play sports."

But Vincent pulls through. The short version of the rest of this story is that he survives and thrives, and years pass and he becomes a teenager, and he's perfectly healthy, strong, and able to play sports. You'd never know he started life in such a precarious condition.

Somewhere along the way, Traci learns her first lesson in surviving fear. She describes it this way: "A troubling situation can happen to any person at any moment, even on a day that's supposed to be happy. When trouble happens, you often won't know what to do. It'll be a dark season, and you'll be turned into pudding. Yet fear must not get the upper hand. You have to go forward anyway. Because there is always a way forward. And the outcome might not be as bad as you first think."

When Baby Vincent is back safe from the hospital after his surgery, Traci watches her son breathe. He's beautiful and progressing well, and for now the initial crisis has passed.

Little does Traci know, her life lessons in fear have only begun.

2

___

Don't Let Fear Have the Final Say

A year and a half after giving birth to the twins, Traci gives birth to her third child, a son, Jason, named after his dad. Jason is perfect: healthy, vigorous. But when Jason is five months old, Jay, the dad, experiences a bout of diverticulitis. He needs a few heavy surgeries and is fitted with a colostomy bag, no simple procedure. When the sickness is over, he needs another surgery to have the bag removed. The procedure does not go as planned, resulting in his needing three additional surgeries. All in all, the situation turns into a medical nightmare that takes about two years to traverse. Even then, that's not the biggest challenge the family will face.

Jay isn't able to lift their newborn during most of this time, so he doesn't bond as closely with baby Jason as he did with the twins. He isn't able to detect small changes in the baby. But Traci can. When Jason's about eighteen months old, Traci begins to suspect that something's "off": the new baby doesn't interact with anyone besides his mother.

Friends say, "Oh, he's just attached to you," but Traci knows this situation feels different. She grows afraid for her son. When Jason is two years old, he goes through a round of tests and is diagnosed with apraxia, in which a child's mouth has problems correctly forming words, and—worse still—autism. It's a difficult diagnosis even for professionals to make, as there are a number of levels of autism. Some autistic people are fully functioning. But a neurologist delivers the bad news to Traci: "Your son will probably *never* speak."

"When you have a baby, you have all these dreams for his life," Traci says of the experience today. "You dream he's going to get older and he's going to do all these wonderful things. But autism can shatter so many of those dreams. And autism can be so complex; there's no pamphlet to read to figure things out. They gave me a list of therapies to try, and you sort of need to try them all. A lot of your child's development will be up to your own research and initiative. Honestly, I felt thrown as a parent. Very afraid. There was a tremendous question of 'Okay, well, our two-year-old is autistic. What now?'"

As Jason grows older, he goes through his therapies and shows a little progress here and there, but one day turns into the next, and a lot of days Traci simply functions. When Jason turns five, he begins to bond with his father more and becomes more independent and playful, but he still doesn't speak, and the parents are told that if he is not speaking at age five, there's little hope he ever will.

Jason has a great speech teacher, and he learns to communicate using a program on an iPod touch that allows him to pick a picture and then the program says the word. But when he starts school, district officials want him to use a different system to communicate, one that isn't computerized. Traci tries the other system with Jason, but the noncomputerized program simply doesn't work with him. The district digs in its heels. Traci presses as hard as she can for the district to make an allowance for her son, even enlisting the help of a lawyer. Gradually the district relents.

When Jason is seven, he begins to say a few words on his own. He doesn't hold actual conversations, but he'll speak a few words here and there, then pick up his computer and use it to communicate. Even better things are ahead. One day his teacher calls Traci from school, elated. Jason has spoken a full sentence: "Time to go again." He even repeats it. Another day, a speech teacher sends Traci a video of Jason sitting on a swing. The teacher asks, "Jason, what do you want me to do?" And Jason says, "Push me." Traci is as happy as can be. The words linked together indicate that he is interacting with his world.

Traci is told that Jason will never read, but she doesn't believe it. He proves to be a whiz at anything computerized, and if Traci asks him to tape a TV show at home, he can use the remote to scroll down to the correct show and tape it for her. She sticks labels on every item in her house: *Toaster. Fridge. Door. Microwave.* She believes that if he sees the words, he'll gradually learn to read them. The twins come home from school and ask for help with their spelling words. Traci makes flash cards and mixes them up on the kitchen table. All three boys sit looking at the pile of cards. Traci tells them a word, and the game is to find the correct card. Jason grabs the correct cards right along with the other boys. Traci is convinced that he can read.

Somewhere during this season of life, Traci learns her second lesson in fear. It goes hand in glove with what we discussed in the last chapter. She explains, "Limits are meant to be pushed. Life can throw you situations that evoke fear, but fear doesn't need to hold you back or have the final say. Just because you are told your child will never speak or read, that doesn't mean it'll turn out that way in the end. You have to push through the fears and hold yourself open to possibilities."

Little does Traci know that she'll encounter one more experience with fear, and this lesson will prove to be the hardest of all.

3

_____

When Life Is a Blur

The twins have just turned nine. Jason is seven. Everyone's doing fine. Husband Jay, who builds elevators for a living, is hurt on the job one day and needs back surgery. He goes in for the surgery and comes home to rest. It's a Thursday—Valentine's Day—and the family has a nice meal together. The kids eat chocolates. There's lots of friendly banter around the dinner table. That evening, after the children are put to bed, Jay goes to sleep early because he's still recovering and he's used to getting up early. Normally he gets up at 4:00 a.m. to take the train in to work, although he won't be going tomorrow. Traci's up late watching *Grey's Anatomy* in the living room, and Jay gets up to use the bathroom. He stands in the hallway, looks at Traci, and asks with a chuckle, "You're still watching that?"

Traci laughs back and says, "Ah, go back to sleep."

It's a simple interaction that shows their love. They have been married for eleven years, and they've been through hard times and come out the other side, still smiling.

After the show, Traci's usual routine is to let the dog outside, wait for him to come back in, and then go to sleep herself. She goes into the bedroom and falls asleep, then hears the dog bark. It's 2:30 a.m., and Traci realizes that she didn't let the dog out. She gets up, tends to the dog, and returns to the bedroom. Normally Jay snores, but early this morning, February 15, Traci doesn't hear him. She thinks he's gone to the bathroom again, so she turns on a light. She sees her husband lying there, and it takes her a moment to realize what she's looking at.

Then it clicks.

Traci does not remember screaming. The kids are sleeping, after all. Traci's mom lives in a little suite downstairs, and Traci runs to her mother and wakes her up. She remembers speaking to the 911 operator. She remembers running back upstairs and doing CPR on her husband.

When the police and paramedics arrive, they instruct Traci to go into the other room. The twins are up by then, rubbing their eyes, wondering what's wrong. Jason isn't up yet, but the twins are crying because it's all confusing, and Traci keeps thinking, *They're going to bring him back. He's fine. Everything is okay. Everything is going to be just fine.*

Traci's mother instructs the paramedics to take Jay to the hospital. To revive him *at the hospital*. Traci hears one of the policemen say to her husband, "Oh, hey, Jay, we're going to take you to the hospital now." But those little mercies are only for the children's sake.

Traci's sister is at the house by now, and Traci's mom watches the children. The paramedics put Jay's body into the ambulance, and Traci's sister drives Traci to the hospital.

There's no way anybody could have known—all these years, Jay has had a ticking time bomb inside his chest, an enlarged heart. He's died in his sleep. At age forty-two.

Traci feels incredibly blank inside. She doesn't want to believe her new reality. She "freaks out" at the hospital, as she puts it—*How could they not have revived him?*—and then shuts down. That's the only way she can explain it today. She comes home and tells the boys that they've just lost their father. It's the hardest conversation she's ever had.

When the day of the funeral arrives, Traci drives her boys to the church in her minivan. She doesn't want them in the limo. Limos are for graduation. For getting married. For happy times. After the service, she is walking outside with her boys and overhears someone say, "Oh my God. Do you believe she's actually driving her children?" She stops and asks her mother to please put the children into her minivan. Then she turns to the person and says, "Yes, I'm driving my children. My children's first ride in a limo is not going to be to bury their f—— father."

She's ripped raw inside. It's hard for her to breathe, but she has to keep functioning for the sake of her children.

Life becomes a blur. The morning after the funeral, she wakes up, looks into the faces of her boys, and doesn't know what to do. Jason pounds on a picture of his father, and she tries to explain to him: "Sorry, Daddy's not here. Daddy's in heaven." She goes to another room so she can fall apart. Then she comes back and asks her mom to watch the boys. She grabs her passport, wallet, and insulin—nothing else—and says simply, "I'll be back."

She knows she's not leaving her children for good. But she has to get away so she can take a breath somewhere, or else she feels she won't survive. She drives forty-five minutes to the airport, parks her car, walks inside, and studies the departures board full of flights. She has no idea where to go. She just needs to pick a destination and leave. Anxiety washes over her. Panic. Fear. She begins to cry. She knows she can't leave her boys. Not yet. Not even for a few days. A sense of duty fills her, a sense of love.

She turns around, heads out of the airport, and mentally walks herself through the next steps. *Find car. Start engine. Shift transmission into reverse. Back out. Shift into drive. Go home.* Before she reaches her house, she stops at the grocery store to buy something so she can explain her absence. She reaches home at last.

The boys stay home from school for a week, but Traci sees fear in their faces and knows they have to get back to school. What are they afraid of? Of being abandoned. Of losing their other parent.

Traci gathers them together one afternoon and says, "Listen, fear will always be part of your life. But if you give in to fear, then fear will become who you are. It's okay if you don't want to do something—you don't have to do it. But if it's simply fear holding you back, then never let the fear stop you."

4

Embrace Fear, Don't Avoid It

Sharlee explains: I met Traci Micheline several years ago at my son's christening. Traci and Jay were good friends of my son's father— and over the years Traci has become a good friend of mine, too. After Jay passed away, Traci and her sons came to my son's third birthday party, and that's when I first realized what an incredible person she is. It's not easy to manage three active young boys as a single mother. Yet the way she interacted with her sons at the party was so seamless, it was truly awe-inspiring.

If you meet Traci in person, you'll find that she's upbeat, pleasant, even optimistic. Everybody likes her. She's funny and warm and kind, very easy for people to interact with. She has raised boys who are polite, kind, and caring to others. So much has happened to her. It would be understandable if she were angry and resentful, as life has given her some tough obstacles to face. Yet her life is a perfect picture of someone who's stared fear in the face and hasn't given in to its pressure. Her life shows that although fear itself can be a scary thing, it can be a managed thing, even a useful thing.

We like how Traci acknowledges the universal reality of fear. If you're afraid, you're afraid. You have permission to feel whatever you're feeling. In life, you can be happy. You can be sad. And yes, you can feel afraid. But Traci makes it clear that you can't let your fear call the shots. You can push against fear and learn to control it—and that's how you keep going in life, how you overcome obstacles.

What do we mean when we say fear can be even a "useful" thing? Sampson and I learned in our research that we can harness fear and use it instead of letting it lock us into immobility. If a fierce grizzly bear is threatening you, fear will kick in and you'll do whatever it takes to put distance between yourself and the animal. If your child is swimming and struggling to keep his head above water, you'll jump in and rescue him, impelled by fear. This kind of fear of real and present danger has been useful for the survival of the human race throughout history. Fear that moves us to take action is a hallmark of a successful life.

The confidence we gain in facing tangible fears is actually transferable. We can use this confidence to face intangible and even imaginary fears. Because of that, educational programs have sprung up that incorporate fear training into the curriculum, especially recreation and outdoor survival programs. Activities such as rock climbing, rappelling, winter camping, white-water rafting, and other types of stressful activities are used to study fear, to experience personal testing, and to build our skills in dealing with fear.

We don't need anyone to tell us what fear feels like. Physically, our palms may sweat, our throats go dry, our muscles tense, "butterflies" go crazy in our stomachs; we can feel our blood pressure and heart rate rise and our breathing quicken. In some situations, that's just for starters. We may also experience a physical "freezing" phenomenon, where we simply can't move or speak, regardless of the danger. An extremely fearful situation may spark incontinence or even a heart attack or stroke. Those are all physical reactions to fear.

Dr. Alan Ewert, a professor at Ohio State University, studied fear in environmental-education programs and found that we also express fear in a variety of other ways—ways that aren't as instantly recognizable as symptoms of fear. They include talkativeness, irritability, a lack of focus, hostility, becoming overly precise, and forgetfulness. When a person suddenly acts outside his normal patterns (such as a very talkative person going silent), that may well be a sign he's afraid.[1]

Ewert developed a questionnaire and used it with students in an Outward Bound summer program. Participants rated their level of fear. Surprisingly, he found that the situations that caused the most fear were the following:

- Not getting enough to eat

- Keeping others from reaching their goals

- Not fitting in with the group

- Not getting their money's worth from the training

Do you see a pattern? Most of these fears are socially oriented rather than situationally oriented. We're most afraid of people—or what they think of us—rather than actual physically dangerous situations. What is truly surprising is that fears of medical emergencies, dangerous animals, and injuries from falls or deep water were much farther down the list.

Two researchers at Purdue University studied the effect of fear on competitive gymnasts who train at Olympic levels. Their hypothesis was that the gymnasts' environment would prove a perfect platform for examining fear and seeing how it can be overcome.

Competitive gymnasts must fly through the air and leap, spin, and twist in nearly superhuman activities, any of which pose a threat of real and serious injury. Their question was this: How do gymnasts learn to cope with fear? Researchers found that to overcome the fear of injury, gymnasts need to learn how to use psychological skills as well as physical skills. A variety of techniques emerged, which the researchers gave catchy names:

- *"Just Go for It"* describes a thought-stopping technique in which a gymnast consciously chooses to stop any chatter in her head that worries her about being injured. She blocks thoughts such as *I can't do this* and replaces them with *Just go for it*. When this exchange happens often enough, her body goes into a kind of autopilot to attempt the gymnastic acts she needs to accomplish.

- **Superstitions** describes a process in which a gymnast relies on a certain object or routing to bring positive results, such as a lucky leotard, a blue hair ribbon, or eating pancakes for breakfast. This method proved less reliable in combating fear, but its value is that it puts the athlete into a positive mind-set.

- **Trusting the Coach** is another popular strategy gymnasts use, in which they choose to believe in the coach's decision that they are capable of doing a particular move. One gymnast said, "Coaches always say, 'I wouldn't have you do it if you couldn't do it.' They believe in you."[2]

The gymnasts also used relaxation techniques, visualization techniques, and positive self-talk, although they weren't as popular as the first three techniques.

Do these methods actually work for ordinary people?

Dr. Noam Shpancer wrote an article called "Overcoming Fear: The Only Way Out Is Through." Read the title again if you need to, because his advice, in a nutshell, is exactly that: to get rid of fear, we must first embrace it. That sounded counterintuitive to us at first, but here's how Shpancer explains it: The technique many people use to deal with fear is to avoid it, but that doesn't work. If we avoid what we fear, then our nervous systems never get toughened up. In fact, avoiding the things we fear only keeps our anxiety level high and ultimately magnifies our anxiety. By avoiding the things we fear, we actually grow more afraid, not less.

When we deliberately expose ourselves to our fears, we familiarize our nervous systems with the fears, lower our emotional responses, and ultimately feel a sense of empowerment, because we haven't let fear have the final say. Shpancer wrote, "Exposure is by far the most potent medicine known to psychology. If you're anxious about spiders, you will have to handle spiders. If you're scared of the elevator, you will have to ride the elevator repeatedly. If you dread talking in class, you will need to start talking in class. You will have to stay in the feared situation and stay with the heightened fear response until it begins to subside, which it will. Staying in the terrain helps to learn how to navigate, manage and work it."[3]

The therapist Mark Tyrrell recommends deep-breathing techniques to overcome fear. Whenever we feel fear coming on, we simply stop, focus on our breath, inhale for a count of seven, then exhale for a count of eleven. The idea is to make the out-breath longer than the in-breath. We can repeat it until we calm down. It's also a good idea to employ a different part of our brain. In the grip of fear, it's hard to think clearly. Emotions tend to take over.

Tyrrell also advises that when we're feeling anxious, we should describe our fear with a number on a scale. Is our fear a seven or a five? That simple act will reduce our fear, because we've kick-started the thinking part of the brain and diluted the emotional part.[4]

The big point we want to make in this chapter is that there will always be frightening things in life. We'll always encounter unforeseen and unknown situations, just as Traci Micheline did, and the unforeseen and unknown parts can fill our hearts with fear. Yet when we discover and develop the power of leaning into our fears, pushing against them, and not letting fears gain the upper hand, it's all a part of discovering and developing the Stuff. As we learn to use the Stuff, we aren't fearless, but we develop the courage to push through our fears. What follows is a great example of how Traci did exactly that.

5
———

Just Think of What You'll Miss

Four months after the death of Jay Micheline, a cousin of Traci decides to renew her vows after twenty years of marriage. The cousin lives in South Carolina, and Traci lives in Long Island, New York, which means it will be a three-day trip for her to attend. In many ways, she doesn't really want to go, but she knows she *must* go. She can't let fear hold her back.

Traci has her ticket. Her bags are packed. Yet during the week leading up to the trip, her boys are a wreck. "Why are you going?" they ask. "You can't go."

Traci feels caught in a tumble of emotions. Guilt. Worry. She's scared to be away. She runs through every possible scenario. What will happen to her boys if something happens to her? She tells herself that questions like that are exactly why she must go on this trip. She knows if she coddles the fear, then the fear will become who they are as a family.

She tells her children, "Look, you can't be scared of Mommy taking this trip. Mommy can walk out the door and be hit by a bus anytime. So you can't live your life scared. You can't think that just because Mommy is taking a trip on an airplane that she's not coming back."

Traci goes on the trip. She "hates every minute of it," she says, because she battles fear the whole time she's away. She leaves on Friday afternoon and is back on Sunday morning—and her mind and heart churn the entire time she's gone. She comes home exhausted. But she also comes home with a huge sense of relief and accomplishment. She took the trip, and her boys are okay.

———————

A few weeks after Traci's trip, Traci is home with Jason, working on some flash cards with him. Jason is working on his vowels, sounding out words. From out of the blue, Traci looks at her son and says, "Jason, Mommy loves you."

"Mommy," Jason says. Just the one word.

"Yes, *Mommy*," Traci repeats. "One day you gotta say, 'I love you, Mommy.'"

Jason looks at his mother but doesn't say anything.

Traci continues working with the flash cards. Then she stops and asks, "What does Jason say?"

There's a little pause. A glimmer of recognition. And Jason says, very slowly, the full sentence that Traci has been longing to hear: "I . . . love you . . . Mommy."

Her fears are abated. Many years ago she was told her son would never talk, but now here he is, telling her he loves her.

She cries for hours.

Traci remembers that when Jay was still alive, he promised her a trip to Tahiti for their fifteenth anniversary. When she told her boys about it, Nicholas said, "I don't want to be on a plane for that long," and Traci answered, "I don't, either. Nobody likes to be on a plane that long. But if you give in to fear, then just think of what you'll miss."

Today Jay has been gone for more than four years. Traci describes her life this way: "Are we sad? Yes, always. The sadness is something we'll always have. But we are resilient, too. We have coping skills—all of us—and we can all go on. Sometimes people will say to me, 'Oh, you're so strong.' But I don't think I am. Nobody wants to be forty-two and a widow with three children, one with special needs. There's no 'handling this.' But I'm doing it, even though it's not easy. I lived with fear for so long: it was there from the beginning, a fear of what you don't know. But you can't let fear win. Two weeks ago, the boys were playing basketball and Vincent was holding himself back in a game. I said, 'You're not being assertive. You can play well. You can get the ball and you can shoot, but you still have to go for the point. You can't fear getting hit. When you get scared like that, just think of what you'll miss if you hold back.'"

6

_____

My Friend Mindi, Who Lived Across the Street

Sharlee explains: I want to close this chapter with a story of someone very special to my personal journey with cancer. You'll notice that several stories in this book revolve around cancer, and we did that for a reason. Maybe it's not easy for us to immediately identify with the experiences of a burn victim or an orphan from Liberia, but every one of us knows someone whose life has been affected by cancer. That's why we chose to tackle this subject from several angles. I've experienced cancer firsthand, and I've lost loved ones to the disease, too. One friend who battled cancer was a neighbor named Mindi Maikoski.

The Maikoski family moved across the street from us when I was in fourth grade. This Mormon family had ten children, and I became best friends with Abbie, who was exactly my age. I watched as her oldest sister, Mindi, a diminutive dynamo with beautiful black hair and thick glasses, graduated from high school, went to college, and went on her mission overseas, only to return early because she had been diagnosed with glioblastoma multiforme, a form of brain cancer. For the most part Mindi was a superhappy person, always smiling, and her laugh was infectious. But I know, deep down, that she had to have been battling the fear that cancer can bring into a person's life.

Mindi was never my "buddy." She was older than I, more like a big sister. Yet sometimes she'd have discussions with me and even get upset and yell at me like I was any other family member in the house.

By the time I was in high school, Derek had signed with the Yankees, and he'd bought a Mitsubishi 3000GT VR-4. Man, that car was beautiful. I persuaded one of the other Maikoski girls, Shaeli, to take a joyride with me. The Mitsubishi had a stick transmission, and I didn't drive a stick, but Shaeli did, so we looked both ways, carefully backed out of the driveway, and drove around town with the music blasting. We later found out that Mindi saw us as we pulled out of the driveway. Sure enough, that night Shaeli phoned my mom, and I could hear my mom say, "Stop crying. It's fine. Nothing happened to the car." And I thought, *Wow, why would Shaeli call my mother to tell her what we had done?* But I soon discovered that Mindi told Mother Maikoski, and then Shaeli had to call my mother as a result. The incident didn't make us enemies; it was just one of our numerous adventures over the years. Eventually it became a family joke, that anytime I had a bright idea to do something, I would always call one of the Maikoskis to join me.

Mindi was full of surprises. When I went off to college, she wrote me a long letter and told me how proud of me she was. She heard I'd been a bit homesick, so she encouraged me to stay the course. Her kindness really showed through, and I so appreciated her for that.

Three years later, when I was a senior at Spelman and going through cancer treatments of my own, I heard the sad news that Mindi had passed away after a long and very rough battle. I knew I had to go to the funeral. It was the middle of winter and freezing, and I was in the middle of my classes and treatments. I was very sick, and I wasn't supposed to be flying any more than needed.

But I had to go. For the first time since I had been diagnosed with cancer, I realized the magnitude of the disease: People die from this. What I had was real. Fear came over me.

The funeral was held in Kalamazoo, Michigan, where the Maikoskis still lived, and I just felt I had to be there. So much of my young life had been spent around that family, and a bond had developed that was more than neighborly. It was a bond of friendship, laughter and suffering, and growing up and going through hard times together. I got onto a plane and went.

I don't remember much about the service or who I talked to or what was said. But a memory of Mindi came to me, and it's something I hold close to this day. Many years before I was diagnosed with cancer, when Abbie and I were fourteen years old, Mindi was in her family's living room. She was twenty-two and had lost most of her hair by then, and we know now that her battle with cancer was beyond anything I could ever imagine. She wore a hat if she went outside, but if she was inside around family members, then she didn't wear her hat, so she didn't have it on that day. I prided myself on the fact that I was part of the family and could share these intimate moments with Mindi and the rest of the Maikoskis. Mindi was standing in front of the TV watching the music video for the song "The Emperor's New Clothes," with the volume cranked. There were plenty of other people in the house, along with the ever-present dogs and cats, but Mindi wasn't distracted by anything. Her eyes were closed. She swayed back and forth and danced to that loud song in the middle of the room, and on her face she wore a triumphant smile. I didn't interrupt her, and I didn't join in. Abbie and I just watched her and grinned. I know now that unconventional weapons can be used in our battles against fear. Think of these weapons as ways of coping that aren't about direct confrontation but are, like Mindi's dancing, unusual yet effective methods of fighting. Troubles press against us from every side, and some of our obstacles won't be overcome in the traditional sense of the word. Sometimes cancer does get the upper hand. But Mindi had the Stuff. When I returned to school in Atlanta after Mindi's funeral, I often thought about her and how strong she was through everything she experienced with cancer. From that point on, if ever I had to face something that filled me with fear—which was often, as I continued on my road to recovery—I would try to think back to what Mindi would do. She showed me and so many others how sometimes, whatever the outcome is going to be, you battle fear by doing what you have to do.

You turn up the music. You close your eyes.

And you dance.

That's the Stuff in action.

CHAPTER EIGHT

Focus Your Rage

Look—we outlasted it. The walls crumbled. We didn't.
—Classmate of Wess Stafford

1

When You're Furious

W ess Stafford slithers on his belly through the tall elephant grass. He's seven years old and is out bird hunting with a group of five other boys his age or younger. Each boy carries a slingshot. Each boy is already a skilled hunter. Overhead, Wess sees horizon-to-horizon blue sky, a beautiful day in Africa. Yet one of the littlest boys in the group gives a sudden start and cries out. He's maybe five years old, and the rest of the boys stand and run to their friend. The littlest boy's eyes are wide with fright, and he's holding his arm, wincing in pain.

The children are hunting in Ivory Coast, near the edge of the

Sahara Desert. They're about a thirty-minute hike away from a cluster of mud huts and thatched roofs called Niellé, a little village where Wess's dad and mom, Americans, work as linguists and translators. Aside from the elephant grass, the landscape is dry and arid. Thorny acacia and baobab trees dot the land. The temperature hovers at 120 degrees Fahrenheit, just another average day outside for the boys. Each year, Wess and his older sister, Carol, spend three months in Niellé with their parents and the other nine months at a boarding school in the neighboring country of Guinea.

Wess hates his time away at school. He loves the time he spends in Niellé, except for days like today.

With his smattering of four languages, Wess is able to ask the little boy what happened. The boy points to the dirt, where a short, slim snake with a sharp-tipped head still lurks. The sight is nothing unfamiliar. The boys have all killed uncountable numbers of venomous snakes in their young lives. They call these particular snakes "pencil vipers," and the boys all immediately attack the snake with rocks and kill it. It's small consolation to the littlest boy, however, who's crying now. His arm is swelling.

The snake has bitten him.

Today's outing, as always when the boys are hunting, is not about sport. Anything the boys kill, except for vipers, will be used for food. It's the mid-1950s, and in that time and place, even young children are seen as important to the Senufo tribe's survival. Already, Wess and his friends have learned how to hunt and fish and cultivate the fields. They're given free rein to roam the land, and they've learned how to battle the ever-present baboons, who aren't anything like the cute monkey-type animals you might see in a modern zoo. Baboons, to Wess and his friends, are huge attack animals, bigger than the boys themselves, with fangs the size of German shepherds' teeth. Baboons run wild through the tribe's cornfields, destroying a main food source of the families of Niellé, and one of the boys' jobs is to guard the fields with their slingshots. Elephants are also known to stampede through the cornfields, and the boys bang pots and pans together to scare away the huge nuisances. None of the boys sees his activities as hard work. On the contrary, they feel useful to the community. Vital. Valued.

The skin on the boy's arm is splitting now; the bite location is swelling so much that Wess knows they're in big trouble. They try to lift their little friend and carry him back to the village. But the boy is unwieldy, heavy; the village too far away. They yell for one of the boys to sprint back to the village so adults can come and carry him home, but they all know enough about snakebites to know that the round trip will take too much time. Besides, the nearest hospital is a hundred miles from the village over unpaved roads—a full day's drive away. The hopelessness of the moment hits the boys. There's absolutely nothing they can do.

Wess sits and holds the little guy in his arms, cradles him close. The other boys begin to sing, and Wess joins in. Their voices are ragged, brokenhearted. They are not new to seeing death close up, and this year has been particularly difficult due to drought and measles. Life expectancy rates are so low that parents don't name their children until they're several years old.

Wess stops singing, looks up, and begs God out loud not to take the boy. Then he realizes the boy is afraid and needs comfort in his last few moments, not heavy theological questions. So Wess meets the boy's eyes and addresses him directly as a mighty warrior, in imagery the boy will understand and appreciate.

"Where you are going there is no pain, death, or even tears," Wess says. "Don't be afraid. You are deputized to be our scout. Go and find out what kind of animals are in heaven and where they all are. Keep looking over your shoulder, because the rest of us are coming right behind you."

It's meant as a badge of honor. The boys all promise to their friend that they will try not to live very long, so they can all join him soon. Then they start up their singing again. The littlest boy's body shakes. His head rolls to one side, and he dies in Wess's arms.

Blame it on poverty. Blame it on not having helicopters or modern medical facilities nearby. Blame it on the horrific potency of snake venom inside a small boy's body. A fury begins to take root in Wess's heart. He's felt it before, although he doesn't yet know how to give it a name. But he can sense it's there. It's an intense and increasing emotion, and it shows no sign of diminishing.

During another summer, disease sweeps through the village. It's compounded because locusts plagued the villagers during the previous harvest season and food has become scarcer than usual. Normally the villagers can fight off the sickness, but this time many people are weakened. For two weeks straight, at least one funeral is held every night. Wess's parents try to help out wherever they can, but they're not specifically trained in medicine. Wess's dad transports villagers to the hospital in his rickety truck. He works to secure funding for medicine and supplies. A nurse is sent to the village from the hospital. But there's only so much anybody can do.

One of Wess's good friends is named Kolo. He's a few years older, maybe fifteen, and all the boys look up to him because he is the best hunter with his slingshot. He is also known to be the kindest and most generous young man around, traits highly valued in this caring and communal village. To withhold something from a neighbor in a time of need is considered a grave offense.

Wess learns much about leadership from Kolo and other villagers. He sees how traits such as joy and hope and courage and love are not dictated by what a person owns, or even by what a person suffers. These traits are decisions that people make. All around him, he sees people choosing to be joyful. Choosing to be hopeful. Choosing to be courageous. Choosing to love. Wess learns that if you become strong, the strength is not meant to push you ahead personally; it's to champion and protect those who are not brave. If you become a fighter, it's not to win battles for yourself; it's to win battles on behalf of the weak.

Twenty boys come down with the sickness. They are taken to a covered area used as a sick bay and told to lie down in a row on mats to recuperate. Each day the nurse gives each boy a pill. But Kolo sees that the little boy next to him is sicker than he is. The little boy is so young. He cannot fight like Kolo can fight. So each day Kolo hides his pill in his cheek, then spits out his pill after the nurse has passed and gives the medicine to the other boy instead.

The other boy lives. A week later he tells the story at Kolo's funeral. Kolo chose to die so the other boy could live.

Wess is deeply conflicted to see the deaths of so many of the boys he's growing up with. He does not contract the sickness himself and asks his father why. His father sighs heavily and says, "Because years ago, back in America, you were vaccinated."

Wess feels for the first time what it's like to be privileged. He feels thankful but also burdened, ashamed, and something else: *furious.*

Later, as a teenager, he will travel to the United States and see grocery stores lined with aisles of food. He'll see pharmacies full of medicine. By then, almost half the village boys he's grown up with will have died of one thing or another. It hits him: those little ones back in Niellé didn't need to die.

But there's more to his boyhood story.

As a child, Wess learns to feel fury on behalf of children for another reason, a different reason. A reason that affects him personally.

A reason that drives him to the breaking point.

2

A Badly Broken Boarding School

For the three months each year that Wess lives in Niellé, he is nurtured, protected, and cared for by all the adults in the village. As a young boy, if he falls down and scrapes his knee, one of the village mothers picks him up, dusts him off, dries his tears, and sends him on his way. Each night Wess and his sister are invited to the tribal campfires, where the village elders know Wess and Carol by name. Sometimes the elders chide Wess good-naturedly for chasing the communal goats to see them run, a bit of mischief no boy is supposed to get into in the village. But any chiding by an adult is always done with a smile and a wink. Overall, Wess feels highly valued by adults in Niellé, always welcomed, always cherished.

The nine months each year when he lives at boarding school,

however, are another matter entirely. "My childhood was split between the best of times and the worst of times," he says today. "It was almost incomprehensible, the things that happened there. I felt violated, vulnerable, and overwhelmed by a grief I still cannot fully explain."

Wess is sent to boarding school in the days long before home-schooling is heard of, accepted, or widely available. When, if your parents work in a remote, impoverished village, there are simply no other options: you are sent away for your education. When corporal punishment is still practiced in some schools. Practiced and *unregulated*.

About fifty children live at the boarding school in Guinea. Wess is first sent there when he is six and his sister, Carol, is eight. Today he describes the school as "a cacophony of frightened children. All being hit. All pleading for help. All pleading for mercy."

One day when classes are over for the afternoon, Wess heads back to the dormitories. There's a stone wall next to a little cement staircase, maybe ten steps in all, near a tree with a limb sticking out horizontally. An active boy sees instantly that you can either go down the stairs the regular way or leap to grab the limb and swing down. But it has rained that day, and the branch is slippery. Wess leaps and grabs the branch, but slips off. He comes up for air and tries to wipe the dirt from his school clothes, but his arm hurts like the dickens.

At first he tries to hide his injury. Carol is nearby, her eyes filled with concern. She looks at the arm, sees a big dent in it, and announces, "You broke your arm. I'm taking you to the nurse."

Wess doesn't want to go to the school nurse, a woman in her mid-thirties who grew up in the school and never knew any other way of life. She examines the arm with a stern look and declares, "This is what comes from being disobedient. You know you're not supposed to play in your school clothes. You'll never amount to much in life. You got what you deserved."

The nurse reports the injury to the school's houseparents, who take Wess to the hospital in town. The arm is put into a cast (wrongly— years later it needs to be broken again and reset), and Wess is sent back to school.

That evening, because he got his school clothes dirty, Wess receives a spanking—broken arm and all. And not just any old light slap on the wrist.

The three favorite instruments of beating at the boarding school are the buckle end of a leather belt, the narrow edge of a ruler, and a sandal made from an old rubber truck tire. The rubber sandal actually leaves tire-print impressions on the children's skin. Wess is ordered to bend over at the waist and grasp his ankles so the skin of his buttocks is stretched tight. He'll receive a minimum of three swats, although the normal practice is to beat a child until he wails. Younger students learn to cry right away to end the session. Older students grow more defiant; as a show of honor among themselves, they see how long they can take it.

"You'd get beaten for as long as it took to break you," Wess says today.

This is certainly not the first beating Wess has received at the school. Anytime any rule is broken, a beating results. Dust on your dresser? A beating. A forgotten sock left on the floor? A beating. A wrinkle on your quilt? A beating. Didn't eat every bite of disgusting eggplant on your dinner plate? A beating. Crying yourself to sleep at night? Homesickness is not allowed; a beating.

When Wess is nine years old, he learns how to calculate averages in math class. For several weeks he keeps a tally in a notebook under his pillow. *Beat again. Beat again. Beat again.* After five weeks he does the math. He's received, on average, seventeen beatings each week. Not seventeen whacks in total. But . . . Seventeen. Beatings. Each. Week.

That's only half the horror. Each night, all the children are "kissed" good night. None of the children wants to be kissed by these adults. None of the children feels safe. An hour after the electricity goes off, everything in the building is as dark as can be. Adults prowl the halls of the dormitory and enter the rooms. Fondling. Rubbing. One male houseparent is notorious for walking into the girls' sections with a flashlight, seeing a little girl awake, and saying "Oh, you're not asleep? What's wrong? Here, let me rub your back." After five minutes he says, "Good. Now turn over."

This happens to many of the little girls. For years and years and years.

Some of the older children, both boys and girls, who were abused when they were small became predators as they grew older. Those older children make the younger children do things.

"We felt like little hunted animals," Wess says today. "We were in an abusive environment with nobody to protect us, nobody to run to. The very people who should have been protecting us were doing us grave harm."

Why don't Wess or Carol—or any of the other children—tell their parents?

During the school year, the children are not allowed to talk to their parents on the phone. Parents are not allowed to visit the school. The faulty belief perpetuated by school administrators is that children in boarding-school situations focus on their studies better if parental contact is severed. Children are not even allowed to keep pictures of their parents. As the year progresses, they forget what their parents look like. Each week, on Sunday afternoons, the children are ordered to write their parents a letter. But each letter is checked and censored, and the children quickly learn to write only bright and bubbly phrases that make it past the administrators: "It was sunny today. We rode our bikes. I miss you."

If a child ever writes, "Please help me," he'll only be beaten again.

Wess describes the experience today: "The school administrators warned us, 'Don't ever tell your parents.' Our parents were doing important work, and the threat was that if we told, then it would only trouble our parents, and we would destroy our parents' work. You're six years old, carrying that burden? You learn to keep your mouth shut. It's amazing how much abuse a child will absorb to protect the people he loves. We were a society of silent lambs, each protecting our parents from horribleness. All of us buying into the lie."

Toward the end of each school year, the beatings always let up, enough so any cuts or bruises will heal. On the final day of the school year, the administrators warn each child one final time. Then the children return to their parents and feel so relieved to be home that nothing is ever said. When the three months of reprieve are over and the children are sent back to school, many children become anxious, but parents dismiss their feelings as normal homesickness or general anxiety.

This goes on year after year after year.

3

The Breaking Point

A t age ten, Wess and his family return to the United States for an entire year. The parents are taking a furlough to go on a speaking tour and raise funds. When the year is finished and it is time to return to Ivory Coast, Wess grows anxious. Several families who work for the same organization are heading back at the same time, so the plan is to send all the children across the Atlantic first together on an airplane, and then the parents will follow by ship, which is less expensive.

At the airport, the children are saying their good-byes to their parents. The children are being as stoic as they can be. Wess's mother kneels down to give Wess a hug, but Wess holds her at arm's length and stares into her face for as long as he can.

"What are you doing, Wess?" his mother asks.

"Mama, I don't want to forget what you look like," Wess says.

His mother bursts into tears, and so does Wess.

Suddenly, it all floods out. Wess says, "Please, please, please don't send us back to that place. They hate us. They beat us. I can't even tell you all the horrible things they do to us."

The plane is boarding immediately. Wess's mom is confused by the sudden outburst. Agitated. Distraught. She tries to make sense of his statements, but there's no time to sort out any of it. She wonders if his words indicate normal separation anxiety or if something is truly, horribly wrong. The plane ticket is already purchased and can't be refunded. Wess and the other children board the plane and head back to school.

But Wess's mom is left full of questions, angst, and alarm. It takes a month for the parents' ship to cross the Atlantic, and by the time she and Wess's father reach the docks on the other side, she has suffered a nervous breakdown. Wess's father soon sends her back to the United States so she can receive help, while he continues on to investigate what's truly happening at the school.

Before Wess's father gets to the school, however, word reaches school officials that Wess's mom has gone "crazy." The head houseparent, one of the worst abusers at the school, decides to turn the occasion into a "teachable" moment.

He grabs Wess one day at lunch and stands him up on a metal chair. About fifty children are watching, stone-faced in fright. "Boys and girls," the houseparent sneers, "I want you all to look at this little boy. I want you to see what Satan's tool looks like. We told you not to worry your parents. But now his mother is not in Africa anymore doing important work. She's having what they call a nervous breakdown— and it's all this little boy's fault!"

The children sit mortified. Wess stares at the floor, crushed. The houseparent continues, "You can't serve both God and Satan, but this little boy tried. And all this trouble is the result! It's just like you can't burn a candle at both ends." The houseparent walks to the cupboard and takes out a pink birthday candle. He reaches into his pocket for a knife, trims off the blunt end so the candle has two wicks, and asks, "You want to see what it's like to burn a candle at both ends?! Do you?!" The houseparent strikes a match, ignites the candle at both ends, and calls out to the class, "Just watch what happens when you try!"

With that, the houseparent places the candle in Wess's hand. Wess is ordered to pinch the middle of the candle with his thumb and forefinger. Flames from both ends of the candle creep toward his skin.

The houseparent turns his back on Wess and continues to lecture the class, but suddenly it hits Wess: *This has to stop! Sometime. Somewhere. This man is lying—and we all know he's lying. Everybody in this room is a victim of this abuse, just like me.*

Wess is still holding the candle. The two flames lick closer to his fingers.

And something turns in Wess. He thinks, *This houseparent has just leveled the playing field. It's always been him—strong, and me—weak. He wants me to drop the candle to prove his point, but if I can just hold on long enough, then I can win this one. This is where it stops! This is my moment to win for us all—and I will not retreat!*

The class is paralyzed, petrified by fright, as the scene of terror unfolds in front of them. This is Wess's showdown with his abuser. The flames reach both sides of Wess's fingers, but Wess continues to hold on. His fingers grow red from the heat. He's determined to fight. He will not lose. The flames touch his skin. Blisters bubble up. A strange smoky smell wafts through the class. Wess's whole body is clenched tight.

The houseparent is staring at Wess now. Staring—and letting the child's fingers burn.

Wess has difficulty today explaining this next part; even to him it sounds weird, but at this pinnacle moment of intense anger, Wess floats outside his body.[1] He no longer feels pain. His vision drifts somewhere to the ceiling of the classroom, and he can actually look back at himself, at the little boy, and see himself standing there with the candle burning his hand.

Just then one of the boys sitting in the front row can stand it no longer. He bursts up from his seat and slaps the candle away from Wess's hand.

Wess instantly finds his consciousness back inside his body. His fingers are burnt and blistered, but he thinks, *Wow. I didn't give in. I just won.* Today he describes this as the moment he became a warrior.

The moment he became *the one who speaks up.*

Today he says, "It all came to me in that one intense moment. At age eleven, I found my life's calling. From that day forward, I knew I would fight for abused children for the rest of my life."

This is the day Wess Stafford launches.

Wess's father soon reaches the school and intervenes. Word gets around to the parents, and children are pulled out of the school in droves. People are fired, new houseparents and staff members are sought. Eventually a new school is built, and in 1971 the old school is formally shut down. But it all takes time, and Wess's father doesn't leave his children in the situation for the transition. He takes his family back to the United States and is reassigned to work in Arizona for the remainder of Wess's school years.

Years pass, and in 1995, when Wess is in his mid-forties, a group of thirty of his classmates arrange for a formal, independent investigative panel to be convened. The classmates want to bring to light what actually transpired at the school. Wess agrees to participate, along with eighty other alumni who eventually provide interviews showing that widespread abuse occurred in the school. A report is prepared and published[2] that identifies nine offenders—most of whom are retired or deceased by now. A formal apology is eventually issued by the school's umbrella organization. The organization's policies and safety mandates are formally changed, and an account is set up to pay the bills of any alumnus who seeks psychological counseling to help heal the effects of abuse.

On the day after Wess gives his interview to the investigative panel, he flies to Dallas on an unrelated trip to give the keynote presentation at an association of psychologists. More than 2,400 trained counselors fill the event hall. Wess stands at the podium and begins his talk, then slows, stops, and ultimately breaks down in tears, still overcome by grief from the previous day's events. He composes himself, lays aside his speech notes, and simply shares what's just happened, stopping only when he explains how those who'd abused him repeatedly accused him of lying. He is overcome by emotion again, unable to go on.

Silence fills the hall for a few moments. Then, from the back of the room, a woman's voice breaks the silence. "I believe you!"

Immediately a man's voice from the other side of the room calls out, "I believe you, too!"

One by one, all over the darkened auditorium, people rise to their feet and shout, "We believe you!"

And the place breaks out in wild applause.

4

The Making of an Advocate

(SHARLEE AND SAMPSON)

f you walk into Wess Stafford's office in Colorado today, you'll notice a few curious items. Many of them have to do with who Wess has become and the tremendous work he's done on behalf of children over the past forty years. But other items are harder to figure out. Those, you need to ask Wess to describe. But first let's get a picture of who Wess is today.

Wess's career rose directly out of the heart of the little boy who'd witnessed the effects of poverty upon children in Niellé and the effects of abuse upon children during his boarding school years. He grew up to become the president (now president emeritus) of Compassion International, one of the largest and most effective humanitarian organizations in the world. The organization helps feed, clothe, and educate impoverished children in twenty-six countries. It helps develop their sense of self-worth and social skills and ultimately helps prepare them to become their countries' next generation of leaders. Programs have also been established to empower new mothers and help at-risk infants through prenatal care, nutrition education and provision, and infant survival training.

During his tenure as president, Wess hired quality staff members (only 1.7 percent of all qualified applicants are hired at Compassion) and attracted an extremely loyal donor base, and he gives much of the credit for the charity's effectiveness to them. But the facts also point toward his effective leadership. When he took over as president, the organization helped about 180,000 children annually. That number grew to 1.9 million. At the time he started, about 20 percent of sponsors canceled their support each year; today that number is half. Today Compassion operates with an $850 million annual budget—and more than 83 cents of each dollar donated goes directly to helping children, *not* to administrative costs or fund-raising. This is one of the highest percentages of all charities worldwide.

So what are the curious items in Wess's office?

As you might guess, on the walls are university degrees. Pretty good for a kid who was told he'd never amount to much in life. Despite his troubled early school years, Wess is deeply committed to education, and he has four earned degrees, including a doctorate in education from Michigan State University, as well as four honorary doctoral degrees.

You'll see on his shelves books he's written, thank-you cards from gatherings he's spoken at, and other testaments of his clear communication ability. This is significant because he experienced some speech problems when he was a boy. A teacher at the boarding school once grabbed him by the front of his shirt, picked him up, yelled, "Enunciate! You little idiot!" and threw him on the floor. Wess returned to his seat, shaking from nervousness, and promptly wet his pants—and in the process learned a new big word: *enunciate*. Years later, after he became the host of two radio programs, he was driving in his car one day listening to the radio, hearing his own bold, clear voice, and he thought, "Well, there you go, teacher, your little idiot is now enunciating."

So you'll see awards and photographs. Wess's work has been honored by many people, groups, and organizations, and Wess has shared the world's stages at global leadership summits with some of the world's most influential thinkers and activists, including Bono and former British prime minister Tony Blair.

None of those office items is terribly surprising. Here's what is: in a small bookcase with glass doors there are several strange items, including:

- A crumbling piece of plaster

- A piece of hardened cement in the shape of a heart

- An old sandal

"There are no good memories in that bookcase," Wess says. "It holds memories of where I came from—and it's a deliberate choice I make to keep them. Those memories keep me tapped into rage. The items remind me to stay true to my mission."

See, the crumbling piece of plaster was taken from the boarding school. The school is now demolished, and a friend of Wess who visited the site brought some plaster home and sent it to Wess. A note said, "Look—we outlasted it. The walls crumbled. We didn't."

The hardened cement is a reminder that children are pliable. "You can make a lasting impression in their lives either for good or harm," Wess says. "You can easily imprint children's lives with dignity, joy, leadership, and beauty. Or you can harden a child's heart—and I never want that to happen on my watch."

The sandal is made from an old rubber truck tire. It's one of the sandals that were used to beat children at the boarding school. "I want to remember the huge terror of that place," Wess says. "I remember for a reason: to remind me to fight. Rage is what drives me, the positive side of rage. That's what has driven me to fight for children all these years."

Those statements stunned us when we visited Wess in his office, because Wess doesn't appear to be an angry man. His faith in God is strong, his demeanor intense and wise. In fact, we approached the interview knowing a bit of his story already, thinking perhaps he'd talk about fear or hope or turning negatives into positives or succeeding in giving back. But time and time again, Wess mentioned the topic of rage. He kept circling back to it, discussing how he wasn't defeated by it. The rage didn't frazzle his nerves or destroy his family or career. Instead, he deliberately used rage as his motivation. He used rage to find and fuel his fighting spirit.

For him, rage became a necessary part of the Stuff.

5

The Benefits of Rage

(SAMPSON AND SHARLEE)

As we sat in the airport one day waiting for a flight, on our way home from one of our many trips for this book, we saw a dainty four-year-old. We learned that her name was Chelsea. Chelsea was playing with some other children—happily, or so everyone thought. But suddenly she stopped her play, stomped over to her parents, threw back her shoulders, and exclaimed in her loudest voice, "I'm the Incredible Hulk! Everybody out of my way!"

Of course it brought a smile to the face of every adult sitting nearby, astonished by the contrast between Chelsea's delicacy and the mental image of the television hero who turns green with rage and, yes, does incredible feats.

But a few of the adults smiled because they saw through the incident to something more. They were proud of the little girl, and why? Because she was just beginning to understand the power of rage.

Chelsea is not the only one.

Arun Gandhi, a grandson of Mahatma Gandhi, explains in his book *The Gift of Anger* how he learned from his grandfather that anger can be powerful and useful. When his grandfather was first married as a young man, he observed his wife's responses during disagreements between them. Whenever the two argued, Mahatma shouted, but his wife responded calmly, graciously, and rationally. The more Mahatma thought about her responses, the more he saw that shouting matches are only unproductive. He became convinced that he—and all people—must learn how to use anger intelligently.

Mahatma Gandhi passed this lesson on to his grandson. Arun was a citizen of South Africa during the height of apartheid, the vicious political and cultural system that mandated the separation of races within the country. At age twenty-two, Arun traveled to India to visit relatives. There he met a kind and beautiful nurse named Sunanda who eventually became his wife. But when Arun tried to return to South Africa with her, the country's government, thanks to apartheid, refused to grant her a visa.

For more than a year, Arun tried and failed to get the necessary paperwork. The system remained rigid. He was forced to make the heart-rending choice between staying in India with his new bride and returning home to South Africa to care for his sisters and widowed mother. He chose to remain in India, but a burning anger toward the government of South Africa was born in him.

Ten years later, a South African member of Parliament named Jackie Basson visited India and asked Arun for help in navigating the country. Arun immediately thought, *No.* He was still furious at South Africa's government for denying his wife a visa. Yet Arun remembered his grandfather's teaching about the necessity of channeling anger into good.

Arun writes,

> . . . *I swallowed hard and decided not to act rashly. I shook hands with him . . . got [him] settled; then, for the next several days, my wife and I took Mr. and Mrs. Basson around Mumbai, treating them warmly and showing them the sights. We talked about apartheid and how it had pulled our family apart. On the last day, we said good-bye—and both of them began weeping.*
>
> *"You have opened our eyes to the evils of prejudice," Basson said, embracing me. "The government I have supported is wrong. We will go back and fight apartheid."*
>
> . . . *I was dubious . . . [yet] the moment Basson got back home, he . . . was so ardent in his opposition that the ruling party threw him out and he lost the next election. But he remained steadfast, and his strength no doubt helped persuade others.*
>
> *Observing his incredible change confirmed for me the*

power of Bapuji's philosophy of using anger intelligently. If I had snapped at Basson . . . as I wanted to when we first met, I would have had some momentary satisfaction. . . . [But he] would have gone back home more convinced than ever that racism was the correct position and that he should stay away from blacks and Indians.[3]

We all get angry—no question there. It's a natural emotion, a normal part of the human experience. What counts is whether we master anger or it masters us, and then what we do with our anger, because our anger can be used for either destruction or construction. In the best of times, anger can be caught and tamed, harnessed and redirected. In the worst of times, anger can create barriers and destroy relationships and property; it can put those things and those we love into harm's way. Our encouragement is always to choose the positive.

Consider the strong physiological responses that anger can create in us. It's helpful for us to know that strong emotions are a natural response to the emotion of anger.

"These emotions . . . are primal in nature and help guarantee our survival," writes the medical professional Marcelle Pick. "When you become angry, there are neurotransmitters (catecholamines) in your brain that release and cause a bolt of energy. Your heart beats faster; your blood pressure rises, and your arms and legs get extra blood flow. You get a rush of adrenaline, norepinephrine, and cortisol, and enter an altered state of consciousness, ready to 'fight.'"[4] That's not all; the surge of adrenaline causes your pupils to dilate and your breathing to accelerate, and "If you're really angry, even the hairs on the back of your neck stand up! Your liver responds by releasing sugar, and blood shifts from your internal organs to your skeletal muscles, causing a generalized state of tension. You're energized and ready for action."[5]

No matter which particular physical reaction we experience when we're angry, we can't deny that anger evokes power. This can be a good thing if used positively. Anger can be the tool we use to dig ourselves out of ruts, to counteract feelings of inadequacy or hesitation, to simply "launch." Anger is a can-do emotion that can allow us to tap into our fighting spirit and become a force of effective change in the world.

For instance, if we feel anger about a situation of social injustice, hopefully we'll have the courage to stand on stage and give a speech about it, or join a cause, or write an article, or phone our representative in Congress, or unite with others battling the injustice. The anger helps fuel us forward.

All the while, we'll watch our responses to ensure they're positive. How many times have we wanted to send an angry email to a colleague or friend or family member? Usually, immediate reactions are not the best course of action to take, because the response to the email in that angry moment only intensifies the situation. Far better, experts say, to go ahead and draft the email—get all our emotions and thoughts written down—and then wait twenty-four hours before we even think of sending it. Before we do, it's good to read through the email again after we've had a chance to decompress. Get someone else to check it, and weigh the pros and cons of what might happen if you do send it. If we're still okay with everything we wrote before, then—and only then—should we send it.[6] This is also an effective course of action when it comes to relationships.

DR. SAMPSON DAVIS and SHARLEE JETER

Anger can be used for all sorts of positive functions, including:

- Achieving breakthroughs over problems and barriers.[7]

- Producing optimism and reducing fear.[8]

- Creating or interpreting art.[9]

- Helping relationships, particularly when anger helps people communicate a sense of injustice rather than venting or clamming up and hiding the anger.[10]

- Providing self-insight. When we're in touch with our angry feelings, we can learn where we need to change and improve.[11]

- Reducing violence. We usually think of anger as *producing* violence (and indeed it can). But it can also reduce violence, because controlled anger is "a very strong social signal that a situation needs to be resolved."[12]

- Negotiating a fair deal.[13]

Researchers at the Mayo Clinic suggest ways to get anger under control so we can be in charge of it, not the other way around: in the heat of the moment, it's good to take time to pause, breathe, collect our thoughts, then state our concerns and needs clearly and directly. Spend time in physical activity to help reduce the stress that sparked the anger. Take a time-out if needed. Then, instead of focusing on the anger and the impulses it sends that make you want to break something, work on resolving the issue at hand. Do so without laying blame. Be respectful and specific. Keep in mind the power of forgiveness, which can actually work together with the power of directed anger to change things. Don't leave out humor as a tool to defuse tension. Now you are prepared to work on the positive changes that your redirected anger demands.[14]

6

Unclench Your Fist, Move Forward, Get On with Your Life

That's what Wess Stafford did. And our big question was, how did he get from there to here? How did he transform himself from an abused, frightened, grieving little boy into the grown-up leader of an organization that does so much good?

For Wess, the secret was forgiveness—not forgiving and forgetting; not forgiving and pretending the harm never occurred; but practicing a forgiveness that deliberately remembers yet goes forward anyway.

For several years in his teens, Wess lived as a self-described "lost and broken soul who spent much of his time trying to be invisible." One weekend while working at a camp as a young man, Wess listened to a speaker during a campfire session. Wess can remember the talk, almost word for word.

The speaker began, "Some of you have been really hurt in your lifetime, and you're really angry about it, and it's dominating your life."

Wess thought, *Whoa, that's me.*

The speaker continued, "It's very possible that you're the only one paying the price for all that hurt. The people who hurt you may not even remember you. They may not be sorry at all for what they did. The pain and sorrow and confusion are dominating your life. If that's the case, then you're letting these people live in your life rent-free. You're the only one paying. And there's only one way out. It's called forgiveness. If you don't forgive the people who hurt you, then you keep on carrying the burden, and you carry it alone. When you forgive, you lay down the burden. You can be set free."

That way of looking at things was new to Wess. The talk finished and the campers left the fire pit area, but Wess stayed, mulling over the speaker's words. When the campfire had died down and Wess was all alone in the darkness, he spoke these words out loud to his abusers, even though they weren't there to hear: "You people! You stole my childhood. You can't have my adulthood. You took my past. You cannot have my future. I choose to forgive you. Now get out of my life!"

Today, Wess describes his action as "an effective, albeit crude sort of forgiveness." His choice centered on not letting anyone dominate his life anymore. And the action proved to be healing, although not instantaneous.

"As time has gone on, I've learned more about forgiveness," Wess says. "I've learned how difficult yet necessary it is. You must forgive, and forgive all over again. Forgiveness doesn't mean that what they did to you doesn't matter. It doesn't mean you need to reengage those people and bring them back into your life and maybe get hurt again.

But it does mean you unclench your hatred. Not your rage but your hatred. You drop your candle. You move forward. And you get on with your life. That's what has propelled me to overcome insurmountable sadness and hurt. That rage is what I use to fight for children in poverty today, for children who are abused. Rage is my motivation against injustice."

Wow, we like that.

To tap into the Stuff, we need to discover and develop hope, forge our vision, push through fear, set a launch date, push our limits, and channel the anger we feel toward positive good. But none of this will be easy. In fact, it'll probably be really difficult. Yet that needn't discourage or dissuade us from overcoming whatever obstacle may be in our way.

CHAPTER NINE

Lean Into Hard Work

Nothing will work unless you do.
—Maya Angelou

No Easy Answers, No Simple Fixes:

THE JOURNEY OF DEBRA PEPPERS

Debra is sixteen. Tonight is the night of her high school junior prom, and all her friends are going, but she isn't. She's five feet, four inches tall and weighs 260 pounds, and she's sitting in her parents' kitchen eating a bowl of ice cream with Oreos crumbled on top, crying as she eats.

Debra has plenty of girlfriends and they all have dates, but they don't want her along as a third wheel. She tried asking several boys to the prom, but none of them agreed. She considered going by herself, but that didn't seem right. She called her old standby, Don, an overweight boy who is usually up for anything, but Don said sorry, he can't go. In desperation, she even called a guy named Benny, who kinda likes her. But Benny is already out of high school, already married and divorced, and her dad heard of the plan and said, "No, not with Benny." Debra bought a pattern for a prom dress for tonight—a frilly pink creation that her grandmother needed to work over because she could never find an off-the-rack dress that fit. But the dress stays in the closet tonight, and as she eats, she looks out the picture window to the street in front of her house. She sees convertibles go by with the tops down. Friends of hers are inside the cars, all dressed up for the prom, laughing, smiling. Debra feels absolutely miserable.

"When I say I was eating a 'bowl' of ice cream," she recalls as an adult today, "I mean I was eating a *mixing bowl* full, just mindlessly stuffing my mouth, stuffing my feelings down with every bite. Nothing filled my emptiness. I thought of myself as despicable. A failure. Unlovable. And it wasn't like I was trying to go to the dance with the captain of the football team. I was willing to go with anybody, but even 'Fat Don' turned me down. I felt like something was seriously wrong with me. I was a mess."

When the last car has passed, Debra scoops up her last mouthful of ice cream, blows her nose, and switches to her hidden stash of whiskey. Southern Comfort is her favorite. Even as a teen, she can drink an entire pint straight down without stopping. "That night I turned from one addiction to another," she says today, "from overeating to overdrinking. I needed help, but I didn't know where to turn. I didn't have a plan. I felt like I didn't have the means to cope. I was aimless in my hurt."

It's not as though Debra has a life filled with difficulties. When she looks back today on her teen years, she says they should have been "picture perfect." She has two loving parents who do whatever they can to support her. She lives in a small town in Missouri and has the support of her community and the educational system. Her older sister, Donna, is a friend and role model. Donna always gets good grades. She's a cheerleader and prom queen and a perfect size six who ends up the valedictorian of her high school graduating class. But when Debra walks into class on the first day of high school, a teacher takes one look at her, asks, "You're Donna's little sister?" and shakes her head.

Oooof. She might as well have punched Debra in the stomach.

Yet the incident points to part of the problem.

"Absolutely, I couldn't compete with Donna," Debra says today. "Donna was perfect. She liked me and talked with me and was my friend, but I just couldn't compete with her. At least, that's how I saw myself. I was at least a hundred pounds overweight and a size twenty-two. As a child, my nicknames had been 'Cutie' and 'Sweetie.' But my nicknames in high school were 'Fatty' and 'Lard Bucket.'"

After the prom incident, Debra decides to run away. She tries once but doesn't make it far. Then she tries again. This time she drops out of school, intent on never coming back. Her plan is to travel all the way to California, sit on a beach, and be just like the singer Mama Cass from the Mamas and the Papas and sing "All the leaves are brown . . ." But after six weeks on her own she runs out of money, so she crawls back home and begs her parents to take her in. Her parents, highly relieved, welcome her in but insist she finish high school. Debra appeals to the superintendent to be readmitted. She remembers the conversation word for word. He says, "Debbie, I like your family. I like your parents. I like Donna. But I'm not sure what I think about you. Your grandfather was in the state legislature under Harry Truman—doesn't that make you want to succeed?"

"Actually, it makes me want to fail," she tells him.

"Well, if you don't stay in school this time and graduate, there are no more chances for you. If you drop out again, you're out for good."

Debra nods. She's readmitted to the high school, tries to make amends with her teachers, tries to pull her grades up a bit. But it's slow going. She's still drinking in secret. Still struggling with overeating.

Along the way, there are one or two bright lights. The first shines from a teacher named Miss Alma. Miss Alma is elderly, with gray hair. The students joke that she's so old she has varicose veins in her forehead. She teaches English, speech, drama, and journalism, all classes Debra likes. One day when Debra is walking down the hall, Miss Alma appears by her classroom doorway and asks her to come inside and talk. Debra's missed a lot of assignments, so she figures the conversation will be about school and goes into the classroom, troubled. Miss Alma shuts the door behind her. Debra stands by the teacher's desk, trembling, wondering if Miss Alma is going to lay down the law and chew her out. But the teacher walks over to the pupil, looks Debra in the eye, and puts her arm around Debra's shoulders.

"Debbie," Miss Alma whispers, "God's going to do something great with your life if you let him. And I'm here for you, too. You are *not* your sister. You have your own gifts and talents. Someday you're going to soar."

"I didn't know what any of that meant," Debra says today. "I thought Miss Alma was just feeding me lines. But I remembered what she said long afterward, and it made me think. No, Miss Alma didn't turn around my life right then. I still had problems. But I liked that she told me that she was there for me. And that someday I was going to soar." Debra turns this over and over in her mind, trying to grasp the meaning and the possibilities.

Debra buckles down and is able to graduate and slide into college at the University of Alabama on academic probation. Her parents drop her off on opening day. Her room is on the twelfth floor of the dorm, and her dad waits down in the lobby for Debra and her mother while they arrange her room. Dad's wearing a Cardinals shirt, and he strikes up a conversation in the lobby with a sophomore from the baseball team. Dad, ever the matchmaker, tells him he's got a daughter who's an incoming freshman. The boy gives him his phone number with a request to pass it along to Debra.

Debra has always been a Cardinals fan. She waits a few weeks, then calls the boy. They hit it off on the phone. He has a little Volkswagen Karmann Ghia convertible and says he's going to put the top down, would she like to come for a drive this afternoon?

It sounds like fun to Debra, who says, "Well, sure. I have this other thing I'm going to do first. If you don't want to meet right now, I could go do that, and then we could meet another time."

He says, "Nah, just come on down to the lobby and let's meet."

So Debra puts on makeup, a pretty white blouse, and her new skirt. She does her hair—and she's always been told she has pretty hair and a pretty face. She takes the elevator down from the twelfth floor and meets him in the lobby.

The boy takes one look at Debra and says, "Uh, maybe you ought to go on back to your other engagement." He turns his back on her and keeps talking with his friends.

Debra's been rejected before, but never this quickly. This starkly. She flushes red from embarrassment and says, "Okay, see you around campus." But the cheeriness in her voice is a mask. She starts crying in the elevator on the way back upstairs. Back in her room, she grabs the phone and orders a huge Dagwood sandwich from a nearby deli, along with two big bags of cheese curls. The deli delivers, and she's already working through a stash of candy bars by the time the sandwich arrives. She sits in her room and eats for hours. In the process, she downs an entire bottle of vodka, hating herself and her life more with every swallow.

It's only one blow of many. She ups her grades enough to stay at the university, but she describes how she basically "runs wild" during her first year of college—binge drinking, partying, smoking marijuana, and endlessly overeating. She experiments with voodoo, Eastern philosophy, Transcendental Meditation—constantly trying to find peace and soothe her inner pain. But nothing helps.

Then she meets a student named Ralph Peppers, who goes by the nickname Bud. He's a year older than she is, a chemistry major, strong and well organized. They go to a Jimi Hendrix concert on a date and hit it off.

Soon after, Debra heads home on a break, and a doctor prescribes a diet pill called Eskatrol. It's basically speed, an amphetamine weight-loss agent that's eventually banned by the US Food and Drug Administration, but she feels desperate and eventually loses some weight on the pills, although they "just made a mess of me," she now says. The pills are only one of countless weight-loss methods she tries over the years. She even tries a big long pair of jogging pants that hook up to a vacuum cleaner. The idea is that the pants are sucked close to your skin while you jog in place and make you sweat.

With Bud in the picture, Debra develops a bit of hope. Maybe, she thinks, she has some value after all. She gets a gym membership.

She starts eating a bit more healthfully. Her weight drops below 200. Then to 180, 170, 160. In sixteen months she loses 100 pounds. She feels "normal again," she remembers. Her grades rise, and she begins to succeed in her classes. She and Bud get engaged and then marry right before Debra graduates with her teaching degree.

After she graduates, however, she can't find a job. She starts eating again, and her weight begins to climb. She applies to every school in the district, then to every school in the state; then she crosses state lines and applies everywhere she can. Nothing. Again she feels as though nobody wants her.

Debra spirals into depression. The marriage grows strained. Her weight soon reaches 260 again, then goes even higher—so high that she doesn't even weigh herself anymore. She's drinking again, too, and one night she's home alone, feeling as low as she can possibly go. She thinks there's only one solution left. She gets a razor blade and walks into the bathroom, intent on slitting her wrists. But she glances in the mirror and is startled by the expression staring back at her.

"It's hard to explain fully," she says today. "But it was like I looked straight into the eyes of evil. Like the face of a madman or a serial killer. Yet the face was mine. I felt absolutely terrified. So I threw that razor blade away as far as I could, ran into the bedroom, gritted my teeth, and said, 'Okay, God, let's just see a miracle.' Nothing happened, no lightning bolt, no shaking of the room. Instead, I cried myself to sleep. But when I woke up, for the first time in a long while, I actually felt some peace. I don't know where it came from or why I felt it. I remembered that when I'd been just a kid I'd gone to Sunday school once and learned a portion of the Twenty-third Psalm. I think the only reason I went was so I could get a gold star. But the line from the psalm came back to me all those years later: 'Yea, though I walk through the valley of the shadow of death, I will fear no evil, for thou art with me.' That's what it felt like, that night I tried to kill myself. I was in the valley of the shadow of death, but God still cared. He was still with me."

At last Debra finds a position teaching freshman grammar and drama at Lindbergh High School, a large school in the suburbs of St. Louis. She hears students whisper, "Ugh, there goes that fat teacher," as she passes down the hallway, and she knows that her life has reached a new turning point. She knows she needs to get to the root of her issues once and for all.

2

A New Way Forward

Debra joins Weight Watchers and begins to learn how to find balance in her life, physically, spiritually, mentally, and emotionally. Through counseling, she begins to confront her lack of confidence, her depression, her perfectionism, her fears. The marriage improves, and Bud is ever supportive. Her parents are supportive, too. It takes a lot of sheer grit, yet within eighteen months, she's lost the hundred pounds again. She loses even more, eventually landing at 140 pounds. This time she keeps the weight off—and she keeps it off for good.

"A lot of the positive change was because change was happening on the inside," she says today. "I was seeing myself as valuable and needed. A second component of the positive change was spiritual. I was doing some good sorting out of matters of faith, and I experienced a new sense of fulfillment. I wasn't feeding my emptiness anymore. Another big factor was something I call 'daily diligence.' I needed to learn healthy habits and then live by them—and those habits took sheer hard work to implement. There's no quick fix."

Her job at the school is difficult, but she loves it and wants to be the best teacher she can be. She develops an appetite to know more, read more, and be around people who influence her positively. She begins working on a master's degree in education, and this time she reaches and keeps a 4.0 grade point average. Students begin to see her as a trusted teacher, someone who's been where they've been, someone they can confide in when they've got issues of their own. Debra continues with her education and completes a PhD in communication. She officially becomes "Dr. Peppers" and gets a lot of good-natured mileage with her students because of her new title.

At Lindbergh, Debra finds she has a special heart for students who have problems, either academic or social. She feels she can identify with them. She can understand their struggles and easily put herself into their shoes. Each morning she opens her classes with "moments of inspiration," during which she tells her students motivational stories and gives them inspiring quotes to help them throughout the day.

The way forward isn't always easy, but over time she trains student leaders and helps start a "care team" at her school that offers peer-to-peer counseling and support. She starts a communication skills program to help students with their friendships and home life.

She's instrumental in helping to start an alternative high school to help students who don't fit in with "mainstream" learning. She and her students write a play to help teens combat a variety of issues: eating disorders, drug and alcohol abuse, teen pregnancy. The play takes off, and she and her students perform it at other schools in the area. The *St. Louis Post-Dispatch* picks up the story about the play and does a huge spread about what Lindbergh High School is doing to help teens. A corporate partner sponsors the production of an educational video based on the play, and the play and project are taken nationwide.

"I absolutely fell in love with helping others," Debra says. "This is what I had been made to do. And once I started doing that, it was amazing how doors opened."

In time, Lindbergh High School votes her "Teacher of the Year."

Thirty years of teaching pass so quickly. Shortly before she retires from teaching, Dr. Debra Peppers—the onetime high school dropout, addict, and teen runaway—is inducted into the National Teachers Hall of Fame. The award recognizes the best teachers in the country—only five a year. As of 2017, only 130 teachers have ever been awarded the honor.

"How did my life turn around so dramatically?" she asks today and insightfully answers her own question: "It involved making plans, holding myself accountable, turning stumbling blocks into stepping-stones, and forgiving myself for my imperfections. So much of my life was symptomatic of the hurts in my heart. My addictions, my alcohol use, the weight—they were part and parcel of the same thing. And little by little my life became balanced. It took work and discipline, sure. The hard work comes in finding the balance. And then I focused on helping others. Here, hard work was paired with compassion. I needed to be kind to myself, and then I needed to be kind to others, too, helping them find balance in life. Every person is struggling with something. Each person has battles they're fighting and obstacles they need to overcome. There's no easy road. But it can be a good road, even a joyful road, in the midst of trials."

Even then she doesn't slow down. After she retires from teaching in the public schools, she teaches at Webster University and becomes a speaker and trainer for an educational company, taking her story internationally and appearing in more than sixty-five countries and in all fifty states.

One day she's speaking at a women's conference in El Salvador. Some four thousand attendees are at the event, and Debra shares the story of Miss Alma, the inspirational high school teacher who was one of the initial bright lights in her journey. After the conference, a woman takes her by the arm and says, "You talk about Miss Alma. You know what *Alma* means in Spanish?"

Debra shakes her head. She's never thought about it.

"It means 'soul,'" says the woman. "The teacher who spoke to you was named 'Miss Soul.'"

Debra can only smile.

3

The Facts of Hard Work

S*harlee explains:* When it comes to overcoming obstacles, the power of hard work cannot be underestimated. Difficult tasks can be achieved by determination, by sweat equity, by not giving up even when the way grows hard. The evidence is clear: a onetime high school dropout, addict, and teen runaway is inducted into the National Teachers Hall of Fame—and Dr. Debra Peppers credits much of her success to finding balance, then doing the hard work necessary to keep it. In the story to come, we'll see how a plane crash survivor with a brain injury learned how to walk and talk again and went on to do amazing things. How much hard work did it take for Austin Hatch to achieve the seemingly impossible?

Though most of us don't have those kinds of tasks in front of us, we do have dreams and challenges that require hard work. How hard? Harder than we may expect. Yet the more practiced we become in doing hard work, the more we realize that it is simply part of the Stuff. The more committed we are to a strong work ethic, the more likely we are to succeed.

When we asked the participants in this book the secrets of their success, we always heard the answer "hard work" somewhere in the mix, if not at the very top of the answers. It wasn't easy for John O'Leary to heal after being burned so badly. Once Rich Ruffalo went blind, he needed to relearn how to function as an educator and an athlete—and that wasn't easy. Spending two years in quarantine was hard work for the O'Neill family. Succeeding in business—again—took tremendous grit for Mindee Hardin. It certainly wasn't easy for Sean Swarner to climb Mount Everest with only one functioning lung.

And when we went outside this book to look at examples of hard work in other areas of life, we found this factor cropping up again and again—and in tremendously different fields of operation.

For example, Colin Powell, former chairman of the Joint Chiefs of Staff, said, "A dream doesn't become reality through magic; it takes sweat, determination, and hard work."[1]

The cosmetics diva Estée Lauder said, "I didn't get there by wishing for it or hoping for it, but by working for it."[2]

When I battled with cancer, I was on a personal mission to prove to my doctors, and most important my parents, that I'd made the right decision by going back to school and commuting to New Jersey every other week for treatments. I worked hard to get through the treatments and take care of myself. So I spent a lot of extra time getting help from my professors. I studied harder than ever before. I wanted to prove I could do it.

All my free time went to working hard to pass my classes, because I spent so many hours and even days feeling sick from the cancer treatments. This all came during my senior year of college. I was a math major, and that meant handling some very difficult courses then. So I needed to do everything for those courses in half the normal time.

Absolutely, hard work was a huge factor in my success.

4

From Tragedy to Accomplishment:

THE AUSTIN HATCH STORY

For as long as he can remember, Austin Hatch has dreamed about playing basketball for the University of Michigan. His mom, Julie, went to Michigan. Both grandfathers went there. His dad, Stephen, did research at the University of Michigan before going to medical school. Austin attends his first football game when he's only a year old, and as he grows up, he sees how Michigan is deeply ingrained in his family's fiber. Austin can hardly wait until the day he sets foot on the Michigan court himself.

During Austin's early childhood years, he plays basketball anytime he has the chance, constantly working to hone his skills. He thrives in the love of his parents. His father's a doctor, incredibly smart and compassionate. His mother's a homemaker, so lively and loving that she "lights up the room everywhere she goes," Austin says today. Austin's older sister, Lindsay, is really into ballet and loves to dance. Austin's little brother, Ian (the family affectionately calls him "Mr. Big"), is already a star on the soccer field. Ian plays forward, and he's really fast.

But all that changes on September 1, 2003.

Austin is eight years old. Today, looking back, he doesn't remember many details of the weekend. His grandfather built a lake house years ago in northern Michigan, and the family flies up there in their tiny single-engine plane to enjoy the last of the summer's good weather. Austin's father pilots the plane. The family spends the weekend inner-tubing and splashing around on the lake. Then it's time to go home.

The family boards the plane together.

The plane crashes.

Austin can't remember the accident today. Only flashes of memory come to him about that horrific time. Snippets of a wonderful life he once knew. Lindsay, the ballerina, is twelve and loves to dance. She does cartwheels across the yard at the lake. *Flash.* Ian, the little brother, five, dribbles a soccer ball in the backyard. So much talent. So much potential. *Flash.* Austin's mother, playing tennis with the three children and laughing so brightly, so warmly. *Flash.* "She had a spirit about her that made everybody happier when she was around," Austin says today. "She was an incredible mother."

Austin and his father are the only survivors of the plane crash.

Their grief is crushing, but somehow, through struggle, determination, and faith, father and son continue forward. Some days are almost intolerable. They have lost so much. There is hard work in grieving. Some days all they can do is put one foot in front of the other. Some days it hurts even to breathe.

Years pass, and slowly but surely life takes on new rhythms. Austin's father remarries, to a woman named Kim. As a teenager, Austin grows to six feet, six inches tall and becomes a standout player on his high school basketball team. He averages twenty-three points and nine rebounds each game. Recruiters come from all over to watch him play. Austin has worked so hard to get to this level. His longtime dream of playing for the Wolverines is nearly in sight. Every day he works to be the absolutely best basketball player he can be. On June 15, 2011, as a sixteen-year-old, he verbally commits to the University of Michigan on a full-ride scholarship.

But nine short days after Austin makes the commitment to the University of Michigan, he, along with his father and his stepmother, are flying in his father's plane near Charlevoix, Michigan. Again his father is piloting the plane.

No, Austin can't tell you much about what happened.

It's all simply unspeakable tragedy—*again*.

A second plane crash.

This time Austin's left in a coma. His injuries are nearly fatal. He can't walk. Can't talk. He's survived two plane crashes within eight years. And perhaps hardest of all—the second plane crash kills both his father and his stepmother.

"I don't remember anything from the accident itself," Austin says today. "I told people I committed to the University of Michigan, and I've seen footage of the interview, but I don't remember anything about that interview. In fact, I don't remember anything for about a month before the accident. I played in an AAU tournament in Kansas City in May—that's the last thing in my memory. Everything else surrounding the accident has been wiped clean. I don't want to remember either of those accidents. I don't want to have those images in my head."

Due to a traumatic brain injury sustained in the second crash, Austin must battle back to regain his health and functionality. Rehabilitation is extremely difficult. His skull and ribs are fractured. He has two punctured lungs. He's on a respirator. He must fight his way out of the coma. He must relearn how to do everything. Walk. Talk. Shower. Get dressed. Tie his shoes. None of this comes easily.

"I don't remember many of the specifics of my recovery," he says today. "Every day was hard—I know that. Yet I remember that as soon as I realized I still had a life to live, I decided to give everything I had."

Austin has a few memories of learning how to walk again. Since he was only sixteen, he was in the pediatrics ward, and he describes himself as a six-foot, six-inch baby. "They'd never had a patient so tall," he says today. "My therapist, Michael, put a belt around me, and he'd hold me so I wouldn't fall. Just to get my legs to move was a big accomplishment. To have my brain send the signal to put one foot in front of the other was so complicated. Michael worked as hard as I did. After we'd work for an hour, we'd both be dripping with sweat."

Austin is discharged from the hospital on October 8, 2011, less than four months after the second crash. He's still relearning how to do many things, still talking slowly, sometimes frustrated because his brain knows what he wants to say but his mouth struggles to make the right words. But that January he feels well enough to return to high school for half days. He moves to Sherman Oaks, California, to live with relatives and finish high school there, graduating a year behind his class in 2014.

Life catches a hint of normalcy again, but the hard work is by no means behind him.

5

The Hard Work of Being "Uncommon"

S omewhere in the midst of all that grief and change and recovery work, Austin picks up a basketball again. Begins to dribble the ball. Starts to take shots. Starts to work out with his high school team. The coach brings him along slowly. Austin doesn't play in an actual basketball game for three and a half years. Then one day toward the end of his senior year's season, his team is up by twenty points. Coach comes down the bench, crouches in front of Austin, and says, "Okay, Austin, today's the day."

Austin grins and heads out onto the court. Coach calls a play. Austin has the ball and shoots. It's a perfect three-pointer. Nothing but net.

"It felt like old times," Austin says today. "I hadn't done that for a while. Making that shot didn't mean I was totally recovered, but I was heading in the right direction again. There were a lot of tears in the locker room afterward. It felt really cool to finally get into a game after everything and then to hit a three-pointer."

But the hard work is not yet over. Part of the work continues to be dealing with grief, but Austin's personality is resilient. He deliberately chooses to focus on the future rather than the past. "I can't help what happened to me," he says today. "No one can control that. But I can control my responses. And I chose to focus on what I had, rather than what I'd lost. Did I miss my family members? Yes, absolutely. I miss them so much. All the time. But I decided that I would use my life to honor them. I had to keep going."

Is Austin somehow angry at his father as the pilot of the planes? "No, I'm not angry at my father," Austin says. "Never. He was the most incredible man who ever lived. He played basketball with me in the driveway all the time. Even though he was a doctor and very busy, he was home every night to have dinner with us as a family. He was incredible. My best friend. My mentor. Everything. I miss all my family members so dearly. My desire is to honor them, including my father, by how I live my life today."

University of Michigan head coach John Beilein says he will still honor Austin's scholarship. A deal is a deal, and Austin respects him greatly for it. Austin joins Michigan's Wolverines for the 2014–15 season. He's still mourning his family members, still working to recover fully, yet stepping onto the court for the first time feels like a dream. In an exhibition game in the preseason, he is allowed to play with just 1:41 remaining on the clock in the second half. He gets onto the court and is fouled. He's sent to the free throw line. Only twelve seconds remain in the game. He misses his first toss but sinks the second. The clock ticks down. Game over. He's scored a point for his university's team. His dream of playing for the University of Michigan has officially been reached.

At his peak, Austin would have been one of the best players on the floor, but he's still coming back, still recovering. He continues to work incredibly hard, often putting in extra time after a regular practice ends, but over the next season he and his coach and supporters all see that due to his injuries he won't be able to become the elite player he once was. Austin plays in five games his second year, mostly toward the end of the fourth quarter, and after his sophomore season is over, Austin makes the difficult decision to take a permanent medical red shirt status. In his case, that means he'll become a student assistant to the team and keep his scholarship. The team won't have Austin's scholarship count against the player limit. But it also means he won't play anymore.

Austin remains undaunted. He continues with his studies. He develops strategies to help him remember things. He writes down everything. If someone tells him something, he instantly puts it into his phone or calendar so he won't forget it.

"When it comes to cognitive stuff, I'm still rehabbing today," he says. "It'll be a lifelong journey, and even if I didn't get hurt, that's the approach I take to life now: I'm constantly trying to get better every single day of my life. My accidents have made me appreciate life more. Obviously, both of the accidents were awful, but I'm proud to have made a pretty solid comeback. People sometimes say I have a 'cool story,' but I want to be more than a cool story. I don't want to be defined by what happened to me. I want to be defined by how I chose to respond. By what I do today. By the positive impact I can have on other people. That's what really matters. I see now that my parents chose to raise me to become an uncommon man, and I strive to be that every day. Uncommon people are gritty, and everybody can be uncommon in this sense, by doing things differently than other people. Uncommon people take the high road in every circumstance. We form habits and get the job done. Marriage, family, work, whatever it is, I want to be someone who honors my commitments and follows through on everything I say I'll do, even if I don't feel like doing it. I know I owe it to myself to keep going."

Today, Austin's heading for a career in business leadership, and he recently got engaged to his longtime girlfriend, Abby. They're looking forward to their future together.

"If we truly make the decision to overcome something," Austin says, "there's no limit to how great a recovery we can make. For me, every day I need to choose to honor my family, God, and the people who have invested in me. That's the reason I do things. That's my big purpose in life. My encouragement to anybody is to work as hard as you possibly can to overcome the obstacles you face—and then work harder. How you respond to adversity will have an impact on far more people than you realize. Life isn't only about ourselves. It's about the people whose lives we touch. We can be a source of encouragement for them. We can honor them every single day by how we live our lives. And we can make them proud."

6

You've Got What It Takes

(SAMPSON AND SHARLEE)

Whether experts are born or made is a debate that psychologists love to chew on. "It is clear from decades of research that, to a very large degree, success in music, games, sports, science, and other complex domains reflects knowledge and skills acquired through experience," write psychologists David Hambrick and Elizabeth Meinz, although they acknowledge that "basic abilities, which are known to be substantially heritable, also contribute to performance differences."[3]

That means it's a combination of both. Yet even if a person is born with genius-level smarts, that doesn't discount the value of hard work. As early as 1970, the psychology pioneer John Watson said, "Practicing more intensively than others is probably the most reasonable explanation we have today not only for success in any line, but even for genius."[4]

Hambrick and Meinz studied people playing chess, doing crossword puzzles, and exercising other skills and concluded that both basic talent and hard work are important predictors of success, yet the data they looked at repeated over and over that *deliberate practice* improved performance, regardless of a subject's basic abilities. In fact, "It seems clear that deliberate practice is necessary to acquire a very high level of skill."[5] In other words, inborn talent alone won't cut it. Hard work is a mandate for success.

But here's another question: We can all see that hard work is important, but what will help us actually buckle down and do it? Several factors play into making hard workers—and this is how the Stuff can be summoned and developed.

- *By studying the example of positive influencers.*
  If you're lucky enough to have parents, mentors, or positive role models who are hard workers, studies show that you are likely to be a hard worker. You grew up watching people work hard (and probably being required to work hard at age-related jobs yourself). Thus you acquired the understanding that hard work is part of life. It's just something people do. You accepted that. This foundation makes it normal for you to tackle hard tasks for the rest of your life.[6]

- **By seeing the value of a task.** This simply means that if you value it, you'll work hard at it. This is true whether or not you enjoy the task. A recent study shows that "To effectively self-regulate, people must persevere on tasks that they deem important, regardless of whether those tasks are enjoyable."[7]

  Let's say you are on a road trip and determined to get to a destination by a certain time. If you place a high value on that goal, you'll be more likely to push through traffic challenges, fatigue, temptation to take side trips, and the desire to quit and even to ignore others in the car who are asking "Are we there yet?"

  The study found that when a task was fairly taxing, people benefited most from relating their hard work to the importance of the task. In other words, if you really care about a task, you'll do it.

- **By committing to determination.** Determination is sometimes used as a synonym for hard work, but it's actually a decision that you make ahead of time. Determination is a mind-set that produces the hard work.

  In a recent study, children's IQ levels were tested with puzzles. One group of children was told their scores and praised for their intelligence. Another group was told their scores and praised for their effort. Then the students were offered a choice for the next test: they could either take a test that was harder than the first, or take a test at the same level.

  Most of the children who had been praised for

their intelligence picked the easier second test. But a whopping 90 percent of the children who had been praised for their effort chose to tackle a harder test.

As the testing progressed, the researchers found that the "intelligence kids" no longer enjoyed what they were doing and lost interest. But the kids praised for their effort enjoyed the difficult tests even if they couldn't always score high on them. This study found that children respond more favorably to an acknowledgment of their hard work than of their level of intelligence, and are then more willing to seek out more challenging tasks. The researchers called this a "growth mind-set," and concluded that "dedication and persistence [determination] in the face of obstacles are key ingredients in outstanding achievement."[8]

Besides being the precursor of hard work, determination is what keeps you going. "Determination means having the ability to stay on course, to remain focused on your goals, to stand up to the problems and obstacles with conviction, to be fixed and firm about your decisions, solutions and intentions, and to apply the power of your will to your dreams and desires."[9]

There's one more key component of hard work—and this is a fun one, albeit crucial. The old proverb "All work and no play makes Jack a dull boy" reminds us to balance hard work with breaks for play and pleasure, and there's proof that this is true.

Professor Lonnie Aarssen, a biologist at Queen's University in Kingston, Ontario, and his colleague Laura Crimi of McGill University surveyed 1,400 undergraduates, measuring their attitudes and pairing their complementary life factors. The students' answers were distilled into six measurements about how attracted they were to the following life roles: parenting, accomplishment, religion, leisure, understanding of death, and negative moods.

One correlation proved stronger than all others: an attraction to accomplishment and an attraction to leisure, showing a clear link between work and play.[10]

What practical factor helps most when we encounter the need to do hard work? The participants in this book have described how sometimes a job seems overwhelming. It feels as though there's no way we can tackle something so monumental, so the tendency is to give up before we start. We just can't envision getting to the other side of the mountain.

That's when we need to break a huge job down into smaller tasks and tackle them one at a time, in order of priority, order of demand, or order of chronology. We shouldn't even think about the whole mountain. What matters is simply concentrating on the portion in front of us. Just think about the riddle "How do you eat an elephant?" The answer: "One bite at a time."

Whatever your obstacle is, your invitation is to lean into the hard work required to get to the other side. But even though hard work is tremendously important, we want to stress that hard work isn't *every-thing*. Sometimes we need to be open to unforeseen inspiration.

CHAPTER TEN

Stay Open to Unforeseen Inspiration

We all have possibilities we don't know about.
—Dale Carnegie

1
_____

The Unlikely Gift of Vulnerability

At first, Christine Magnus Moore isn't searching for inspiration. She's simply doing her job as a nurse. She's a mid-thirties California resident and world traveler. Condominium owner. Single with a busy social life. Independent. Energetic. Highly capable.

Christine *helps other people*—that statement defines her—and she absolutely loves her work and life.

She remembers clearly why she went into nursing. She was nineteen and studying at junior college, not sure what to do with her life, when her dad was involved in a collision on a two-lane highway. A motorist coming from the other direction passed the car in front and slammed into Christine's dad head-on. Christine will never forget seeing her father afterward in the trauma center. Brain injury. One broken leg. Lung injuries. Connected to a ventilator that breathed for him. Surrounded by monitors and IV tubes. Doctors said he wouldn't live. Clenched by worry, Christine stood at her father's bedside crying. But a nurse put her arm around Christine's shoulders, took time from her busy demands, and explained what the monitors and tubes were for.

"She only spent about fifteen minutes with me," Christine says today, looking back. "But I deeply felt the care she held out to both my dad and me. I was amazed she knew how to care for someone so injured. And after that, I knew I wanted to be a nurse."

Christine's dad astounded everyone by pulling through.

And Christine's dream took flight.

In fact, by the time Christine reaches her mid-thirties, she's working two nursing jobs. Her background is in oncology, and for many years she worked in that field, but she shifted slightly and now works as an emergency-room nurse as her first job, caring for people with broken bones and heart attacks. Her second job is working at an outpatient surgery center. She's very busy, but she loves it.

Whenever she's not working, Christine's athletic self sends her outside into the fresh air for some fun. On her calendar are a trip to Europe and a competition in a fifty-mile bicycle race. She's trained for the race and is looking forward to both trips immensely.

Why, then, is she so incredibly fatigued? Surely her tiredness comes from working two jobs. Or maybe she overtrained for the race.

But there are the night sweats, too, dark hours when she wakes up drenched with perspiration.

That's odd, she thinks. But for weeks she just keeps going.

One morning she's in the shower, getting ready for another twelve-hour shift at work, and she feels a strange, spongy lump in her left groin area. The lump itself is not painful, but her heart skips a beat with anxiety. She pulls herself together, puts on her scrubs, and heads to work.

In the ER, she casually mentions the lump to a colleague, who tells her to see her primary care physician. Within a week Christine sees him, and he sends her to a surgeon. The surgeon examines the lump, doesn't look hugely concerned, and schedules a biopsy.

Christine says, "Okay, but I've got to take my trips first." She's adamant; the trips are already planned. She races the fifty miles on her bike in Mexico, then heads home only to leave shortly thereafter for the next trip to Europe with her boyfriend. She spends much of the European trip lying on the beach in her bikini, lump sticking out and all. She develops a strange sort of sunburn, like nothing she's experienced before, a sunburn that doesn't fade.

"My body was really doing some weird things," Christine says today. "I spent a lot of time on that trip covering up. My body. My *reality*."

Back home in California, Christine's mom takes her to have the biopsy done. In the surgical room, Christine sees familiar faces preparing to operate on her. They remove the lump and a few lymph nodes, biopsy the lump, and then wheel her to a recovery room. Everything feels odd—to have her colleagues look at her this way.

After the procedure, the surgeon, now in a suit and tie, walks up to Christine, who is still in the recovery area, looks deep into her eyes, and says, "I'm so sorry to tell you this. You have non-Hodgkin's lymphoma."

She knows the surgeon personally and in a visceral response asks him to hug her, which he does. Christine bursts into tears. Other nurses bring her mom into the room. She's crying, too, as are some of the nurses.

Later the cancer is deemed stage 3. It's not in the bone marrow yet, but it's very aggressive. Christine doesn't ask the survival rate, and her doctors don't offer the information. The cancer is under her arms, in her abdomen, all through her lymph system, and in her neck.

Christine feels devastated, shocked that her life has taken such an ugly turn. She's always been the one who cares for patients, never the other way around. She's always the confident, capable, calm one, but now she feels just the opposite. She calls her insurance company to fill in the people there about the disease but breaks down when she hears the words come out of her own mouth. She cries and cries.

Christine chooses to go back to work. Independent and determined as always, she handles the work at first, but as she undergoes more testing and then has a procedure to put in a Port-A-Cath (a device that administers medicine directly into the chest), she finds that she feels sicker than she first thought. She can't be on her feet for twelve hours straight anymore. She realizes she's sicker than many of the patients she sees. She quits both jobs and goes on disability.

Her first trip to the chemo room feels as though she's entered another universe. She's in the room with a dozen other chemo patients, all elderly, all sitting in lounge chairs while being administered chemo. Non-Hodgkin's lymphoma affects adults in different age ranges, but as the population ages, there's a risk for all cancer types. Christine takes one look around and thinks, *What am I doing here? My body shouldn't be failing at my age!* Other patients try to make eye contact with her, but she just puts her earphones on and zones out.

"I was angry," she says today. "I didn't want to look at the other patients, and I couldn't believe I had to endure this disease at my age. I was mentally shocked that I had to be on this journey."

Christine's boyfriend drives her home. In the car, she feels nauseated and starts salivating excessively. Whatever's down won't stay down for long. She clutches at the door handle as her boyfriend pulls into her driveway and parks. Christine climbs out, stumbles on the grass, and throws up repeatedly on the front lawn. The vomiting is forceful, dramatic. *This*, she thinks, *only a few months after I raced fifty miles on my bike.*

"On the lawn, I felt so sad, confused, humbled, and angry," she recalls. "I was livid at cancer, my enemy. I had helped people my whole life, but now I felt helpless. The very thing I'd been fighting was now attacking me. I felt like a target. It was trying to destroy my life, and it was doing a good job."

Late one night she's at her boyfriend's house, sleeping, and wakes up with a sudden stabbing pain in her back. It's hard to breathe. She spends the rest of the night sitting in a chair, feeling slightly better but still working to take each breath. In the morning she calls her surgeon, heads into the office, and gets an X-ray. Turns out her lung was accidentally nicked during the last surgery. The nick will heal. But it feels like one more dark panel added to her nightmare.

Christine says today, "Everything just felt like it was crumbling—all at once. I'd always been 'Miss Independent and On the Go.' But now I could hardly climb the stairs. I wasn't working. I didn't feel productive. I lost my hair. I had bags under my eyes. I felt depressed and lonely. I didn't even know who I was anymore. My mom told me to think positive, but that only made me angrier. The cancer infuriated me, and I needed to feel that anger. I needed to go through a season of despair. My mom understood and bought me a Bozo punching bag, and I punched that thing forever. I started to have dreams of being violated, my home being burglarized, of someone hurting me. The cancer was playing with my mind. I felt violated during the day—so I dreamed about it at night."

2
———

The Turning Point

On the way to the fourth chemo treatment, Christine's boyfriend is driving. Christine sees people going to work, shopping, eating at restaurants, just doing normal, everyday activities, and she feels so empty inside. She grows shaky. Her breathing becomes labored. Her mind races, and she starts to cry. She tries to refocus her mind, but soon she is sobbing, then retching. The woman who'd always been in control now can't control her own body—physically, mentally, or emotionally. She's experiencing a new depth of anxiety, a fear she's never felt before. She tries to do breathing exercises, tries to pray, tries to look outside at the beautiful California sunshine, but nothing seems to work.

Her boyfriend pulls the car over and says, "Look, you've got to pull yourself together. You need to go to this treatment. You have no other choice."

But Christine can't help herself. "I'd never felt that vulnerable in my life before," she says today. "I just could not stop crying."

Her boyfriend pulls back into traffic and heads toward the cancer center. They park and go inside. Christine is still crying, still dry heaving. A nurse leads her back to the chemo room, and brings her a Valium and a basin to throw up in. The room looks the same as before. Patients are sitting in recliners, all being pumped full of toxic medicine. But this time something changes inside Christine's heart.

"I was so pathetic, so incredibly sad," she says today. "I felt like a basket case, just so demeaned and embarrassed that I couldn't keep it together. But then the other patients started comforting me, saying things like 'It's okay. We're all here for you. We know how you feel. You're almost done. Your treatments will be finished soon. This is hard, but you can do it.' These were the same people I didn't want to associate with—yet they were comforting me. They were offering me camaraderie, and this time I accepted it."

After this treatment is over, a nurse takes Christine to see the oncologist. Christine has worked with him before. He's a bit of a father figure to her, and she's expecting a lecture. *C'mon. You're an oncology nurse! Get yourself together! Why are you not handling this better?*

Instead the oncologist sits Christine down and says, "So I heard about what happened."

His voice is soothing, calm, and reassuring, and Christine starts crying again at the unexpected kindness. He encourages her to keep going forward, and he validates the sense of confusion and loss she feels. And he recommends an antidepressant.

"Normally I would have said no," Christine says with a chuckle. "But I was taking so much medication by then I thought, *Oh, well, what's one more?*"

From that day forward, Christine's spirit is lighter. She begins to laugh at herself. At the absurdity of life sometimes.

One of the many side effects of chemo is constipation, and Christine doesn't have a bowel movement for three days. She's very uncomfortable, so she takes a stool softener, drinks a lot of liquid, and starts to power walk around the inside of her house, all in the attempt to get things going. Finally the glorious outcome occurs. Christine and her boyfriend give each other high fives.

"How is that not funny?" Christine asks today. "We're high-fiving over a poop! These small victories can be such big victories, and laughter helps a lot. It truly does."

Christine begins to change her outlook, too. She looks at her obstacle of cancer as a new adventure. She has traveled the world, raced her bike in Mexico—and now she's traveling the cancer journey. It's a painful journey in many ways, but she sees it as a learning voyage, a deepening tour, an expedition in fortitude.

Her unlikely inspiration? "It came that day I was so vulnerable," she says today. "The people who helped me saw the state I was in and inspired me forward, absolutely—and that was only the beginning. After that one humbling experience in the chemo room, I just saw how my fears and anxieties were exposed in front of everyone, yet I was still accepted by them. In fact, I'd become one of them. None of us wanted to be in that chemo room, but there we all were. And strangely, it was okay. None of us were going to be in that room forever."

Christine endures seven months of chemo, eight cycles total, before it's all over. But she never breaks down again like she did on the drive to her fourth treatment. Things are calmer now. She feels a strange new beauty within her vulnerability. And once her new door has been opened, inviting her into this adventure, she doesn't want to close it.

"In the midst of the worst time of my life, I learned to accept help from people, even though I had never accepted help before," Christine says. "I told myself that it's okay to allow people to help me. I told myself that I can't make it through this time without having people help me."

And help comes in droves. People drop off food. They call, send cards, and write encouraging messages. Former coworkers at the hospital donate more than two hundred hours of paid time off to help supplement Christine's meager income. Doctors send checks to help with expenses. Paramedics send flowers.

One nurse, whom Christine's always been a bit afraid of because she acts so hard-core, sets the alarm on her watch so she can regularly pray for Christine. Friends send her motivational books and memoirs by other cancer survivors. When Christine loses her hair, her sister gives her a beautiful scarf. Coworkers bring her a ficus tree decorated with yellow ribbons they've all signed with messages of encouragement. A coworker gives her a hand-decorated journal. A friend gives her a warm blanket handmade by a ninety-year-old great-grandma, who, Christine is told, "crochets all day and prays for the people the blankets go to."

"The outpouring of love and help I received from others was incredible," Christine says. "Their support catapulted me into a stronger frame of mind to help battle the beast. I realized that whether or not these people knew what to do, they all gave me love and help. It's not about the gift or the size of the gesture, it's about their heart and how it touched and helped heal mine."

Christine ends up beating the cancer. Cured, she's able to work again and gets a new job, this time as a cancer nurse for children.

That was fifteen years ago. Today she's married to a wonderful husband. She still travels. She's written a book, and she speaks to cancer survivor groups, medical groups, and book clubs.

"When I approach cancer patients now," she says, "I find I'm more empathetic. I've been both in the bed and at the bedside, and from a depth of tears can come great strength. I know how overwhelming cancer can be, and I see how burdened my patients can be, because I've lived it. I don't always tell my patients I'm a cancer survivor—but if they're open to it, then I do. This becomes a point of bonding between us. It takes so much courage to be a cancer patient. I knew that as a nurse, but I had no idea of the amount of courage until I became a patient."

3

The Look on My Mother's Face

Sampson explains: In some senses, Christine Magnus Moore's story is about cancer. But in other ways it's much broader than that. Her story is about receiving help from unexpected places. It's about how, when she was in an intense, low place in her life, Christine discovered the unlikely gift of vulnerability. She allowed herself to be open to inspiration, and when she was in her most vulnerable place, her fellow patients and colleagues became her caregivers. Thanks in part to the new gift of support they gave her, she succeeded and overcame the cancer.

Part of the Stuff involves this choice to keep our minds and hearts open to unseen possibilities. It is all too easy, when we are overwhelmed by a challenge, to shut down mentally. We are determined to succeed, focused on the task at hand. These are good things. But we continually need to expand our thinking, to keep an open mind, even as we focus on our goals. Some of the greatest opportunities presented to us are ones we could not have imagined, and if our eyes are not open, then we don't see these opportunities even when they are right in front of us.

On the long, hard road to becoming a doctor, I kept on the lookout for unlikely inspiration. In college, I used to listen to an old song—"Be Optimistic"—and I saw how maintaining a positive attitude is half the battle. But even before that, during that time when I got into trouble with the law right before my senior year of high school, inspiration came from an unlikely source. I was struck by a specific look on my mother's face the day I was led into the courtroom.

She was in her late fifties then, but she's always looked younger than her age. She's a very attractive woman. Yet that day in the courtroom I saw a look of incredible agony on her face. It wasn't hatred toward me; it was a look of helplessness and disappointment that revealed the intense pain she was feeling because of my actions. As a mother, she felt she was all out of options for me. I remember seeing her face, her eyes, and it was as though all the chatter in the room disappeared. All I could see was my mom, and I wanted to say, "I'm so sorry for putting you through this."

The three other guys I'd been with during the crime were also sentenced to prison. Each case was handled separately. They all had more priors than I did, so one received a sentence of seven years. The second received five years. The third got three years, and he was only fifteen years old.

Word came that the prosecutor intended to try me as an adult. Depending on my behavior inside, I'd do a minimum of three years in jail and a maximum of ten. Then the offer of a plea bargain came. I didn't know whether to accept the plea bargain or gamble with a jury. Who was I kidding? I'd already been arrested. Why would a jury ever show mercy to a kid like me? I prepared myself to accept the plea bargain and steeled myself for the reality of serving jail time.

The day I appeared before the judge for the final time, he called the prosecutor and my attorney over to his bench. They had a discussion. Then came the surprise. My mother had always been a person of great faith, and while I was in juvie, both she and I had prayed every night that God would give me another opportunity. For reasons I can't fully explain, the judge offered me a different sentence from the plea bargain: a two-year suspended sentence. Potentially, that meant two years in jail if I misbehaved again. But if I toed the line, it meant only two years' probation. No jail. I wouldn't even go to juvie. I would be an adjudicated youth, not a felon, so I wouldn't have a record.

I was free to go.

That was the second chance my mother and I had prayed for. I felt elated and overjoyed but also numb. I couldn't believe how close I'd come to doing time. I'd been given an unforeseen gift—from the look on my mother's face to my personal freedom—and this gift became my inspiration, a huge boost into a journey to do something worthwhile with my life.

4

_____

Are You Open to Unforeseen Inspiration?

(SAMPSON AND SHARLEE)

Think about what inspires you. Maybe it's a beautiful sunset or a line of a poem. Maybe it's your country's flag. Maybe it's a particular memory of a stellar day or of someone you love. It can even be a fragrance, a line of a song, or the excitement you feel when the umpire shouts "Play ball!" Maybe it's even something negative—like the disappointed look Sampson saw on his mother's face in the courtroom. Or the anger that inspired and motivated Wess Stafford, as we saw in chapter 8. Whatever moves you deeply is probably a source of inspiration.

People who have the Stuff, who face their obstacles, overcome their challenges, and follow their dreams, are people who stay open to inspiration—even from unlikely sources. Because you never know when you'll get stuck at an impasse. That's when you will desperately need something—anything—to set the wheels turning again. The tricky thing about inspiration is that you never know where it's going to come from. Inspiration resists programming. You just need to be open to it popping up whenever.

Back in 1815, the English Romantic poet William Wordsworth wrote the poem "Surprised by Joy."[1] More than a century later, in 1955, a professor at Oxford University, Clive Staples Lewis, was moved by Wordworth's poem to write a book of the same title that described his own encounter with inspiration, an encounter that began to radically change his worldview and the course of his life. Lewis wrote, "As I stood beside a flowering currant bush on a summer day there suddenly arose in me without warning, and as if from a depth not of years but of centuries, the memory of that earlier morning at the Old House when my brother had brought his toy garden into the nursery."[2]

Note Lewis's words above: "there suddenly arose in me without warning." This is what it can feel like to encounter unforeseen inspiration.

When we are open to inspiration, it might come from an appreciation of art, a receptivity to experience emotions more fully, a willingness to try new activities or go new places, an eagerness to consider new ideas, or a desire to reexamine our social and political values.[3] We can self-evaluate along these same lines and see where we need to be more open.

Maybe the inspiration for you to overcome the obstacle in your business will come from listening to Beethoven's Fifth Symphony. Maybe the inspiration to keep going toward the finish line in your relationship challenge will come from rereading your favorite book. Maybe you'll find the key idea you need to solve an intellectual impasse by leaving your desk and going for a walk or trying out a new sport, anything from tennis to skateboarding.

Certainly, our openness to inspiration promotes optimism. The more we're inclined to hope, to expect good things in the future, the better we do. One study found that optimism has a huge impact on mental health, especially on helping people push through challenges toward specific goals. "Optimists are significantly more successful than pessimists in aversive events and when important life-goals are impaired."[4] Which means a positive outlook may make the difference in finding the key to the challenge in front of you.

Where will your inspiration come from? Our point is that we don't always know. Our best advice is simply to watch for it! The openness itself is part of the Stuff. Sometimes you will find inspiration—and sometimes it will find you.

Even when you're at a very low place.

5
———

One Blow After Another:

THE MARTHA HAWKINS STORY

M artha Hawkins isn't searching for inspiration. Mostly, all she wants is a soft, safe hospital bed to lie down in. It's 1975, and she's just being wheeled into Greil Memorial Psychiatric Hospital, a shattered woman. Her mother checks her in. Martha remembers seeing the tiled floor, a green-and-white pattern. She remembers seeing a receptionist behind a glass partition. For a state mental ward, everything looks fairly friendly—there aren't any bars on the windows or anything like that. Martha is shown to her room. Her mom kisses her cheek good-bye and says she'll come and check on her soon; family members aren't allowed to visit for the first two weeks. Martha lies down on her bed and begins to cry. Her life has seen far too much brokenness, hurt, pain, and despair. How did she get into Greil? More important—how is she ever going to get out?

Martha is born the tenth of eleven children in Montgomery, Alabama, and grows up in the projects. Her father works at a fertilizer factory; her mother manages the home. The children sleep crossways, four to a bed, with some on the floor when it isn't too cold and others on a couch in the living room.

Martha loves to cook as a child and dreams of opening her own restaurant someday. But she also experiences her share of societal hard knocks. Schools in the Deep South are segregated, and the kids in the white schools always get the new textbooks. When the books are raggedy and torn, they are passed along to the black kids. Downtown Montgomery has separate bathrooms and water fountains for African Americans, and a person of color is required to sit at the back of the bus.

Martha is homecoming queen of her class in eighth grade, but she never thinks of herself as pretty. The next year, when she is a high school freshman, a boy in twelfth grade holds her hand at a basketball game and asks to kiss her. Martha doesn't say no. They start going steady, they grow close, and the next year, as a sophomore, she finds out she's pregnant. The boy joins the military and marries her, but the marriage doesn't last long. In those days, teen moms aren't allowed to stay in high school. Martha is a single mother and a high school dropout by the time she's sixteen.

Around then, a "voice" in her head starts showing up, as she describes it today. The voice isn't anything mystical. For the most part it's her own voice sending her negative messages. The voice says, "You're stupid. You're ugly. You're worthless. You're a failure. You can't follow your dreams."

People often hear this kind of thing in their minds and dismiss it. Problem is, Martha starts to believe the voice.

Over the next few years, she has three more sons, four boys in all: Shawn, Quintin, Reginald, and Nyrone. None of the boys' fathers sticks around for long. Martha knows she has brought some of her hardship on herself and feels uneasy about it, yet she works diligently to provide for her children, first in a clothing factory, later doing shift work in a glass factory. She earns enough to buy a car and even enough to buy her very own little house for her family in a new subdivision outside the projects. She goes to hear the Reverend Martin Luther King, Jr., speak at a church. Change is truly coming, the reverend says; hope is at hand—and Martha grows excited at the words. But then Reverend King is shot dead on the balcony of a motel room in Memphis. Martha sits with her family in the living room, watching the news on TV. Everybody is crying. The news seems too painful to bear.

The shift work at the glass factory takes a lot of her energy. Working graveyard, from midnight to 8:00 a.m., is okay, although her days and nights get messed up. Martha's nieces stay over to babysit the boys. The day shift is 8:00 a.m. to 4:00 p.m., and that's Martha's favorite because life feels normal. The shift from 4:00 p.m. to midnight is the hardest because that's when her boys are home from school. When she works that shift, she never sees her boys.

She manages. That is, until her appendix bursts and she needs to be off work for six weeks. She recovers and goes back to work, but one day she starts bleeding really badly and needs to go to the hospital again, this time for a hysterectomy. She's twenty-six years old. Then kidney stones come to plague her. Her temperature spikes to 105 degrees. One kidney shuts down completely, and surgeons have no choice but to remove it. The hospital bills pile up, but Martha keeps going forward, keeps getting by.

Then the sky falls.

One evening she's out shopping for her boys, who are over at her mother's house. Martha is in an area of town that's considered "safe." It's not late, only a few minutes after 6:00 p.m. She is walking to a bus stop with a package under her arm when suddenly a car pulls over to the curb. It's nobody she recognizes, a complete stranger. Music blares from the dashboard radio, and a man jumps out, runs around the front of his car to the curb, and shouts and waves. Martha is momentarily dazed, and he grabs her, quickly opens the side door, and shoves her inside. He jumps back behind the wheel and squeals off into the night.

Martha thinks she's being robbed. She begs for him to take her purse and let her out, but the car is traveling at highway speed now, flying through traffic. The man snarls and swears. He pulls a revolver from inside his coat pocket, points it at her, and tells her to shut up. He drives her to a secluded area outside of town, yanks her out of the car, and throws her down on the ground.

Martha never gives in. With the man on top of her, she punches and kicks, claws at his face. He slams her head against the dirt and starts to choke her. Martha feels herself blacking out, although she never does so completely.

When the man is finished, he leaves in his car, and Martha is left alone. She doesn't see any lights or houses or stores nearby. She tries calling out, but no one hears. She gets up and stumbles forward, walking somewhere, anywhere. She doesn't know how far or for how long she walks.

Two police officers find her. They pull over in their cruiser and take her to the police station. They are kind, but there's only so much anyone can do.

Martha is told to look through a book of mug shots. Two of her sisters come and get her. They bring her a change of clothes, and the police keep the clothes she was wearing as evidence. The sisters take her to the hospital, where she's given a pain reliever and ice and stitched up. They take her home. She climbs into the shower and stays there until the hot water runs cold. Her boys stay over at her mother's house that night. The next day Martha doesn't go to work.

The perp is never caught.

Martha must go back to work and she does, but she stumbles through her days, barely functioning. For many months to come, all Martha feels like doing is lying down, closing her eyes, and crying. The voice in her head is still there, but now the voice is telling her something else: "You're never going to feel normal again. Your life is ruined. Why are you even living?"

Martha hangs on this way, barely surviving, for more than a year. Doctors say she is severely depressed, and she tries a variety of medications but none seem to work. She even tries electroshock treatments at a hospital, but they don't seem to do much good.

One day she's at home. The boys are at school. The voice asks her, "Is this really the way you want to spend the rest of your life?" She tells herself no. She takes one handful of pills, then another. She loses track of how many she takes. It's an overdose and she knows it, but it's not enough to kill her. She stays in bed for three days straight, and she hears the voice say, "Hmm. Better try again."

So she does. For her second suicide attempt, she swallows pills until she can't swallow any more. Her mother calls the house but doesn't get an answer. She sends Martha's father and uncle over to check on her. They find her and rush her to the hospital. Martha's stomach is pumped. That's when Martha is sent to Greil.

6

In a Hospital Nightstand Drawer

Martha looks back today and says, "Greil was known as a person's last stop. I was at my absolute lowest. I didn't see any possibilities. All I saw was doom. Here I was, the mother of four young boys, and I couldn't take care of them. I was physically sick, mentally sick, rejected in relationships, physically and sexually assaulted. I was hurting so bad on the inside, and all I could think was *My sons will be better off without me.* The pain was so deep, so indescribable, and I was holding all that pain deep inside. A few weeks in, one of the doctors said to me, 'You know, Martha, you've got to open up. You're just as worse off as you were when you came in here.' But I couldn't. At least, that's what I told myself."

At first she does not participate in the group therapy sessions. All she can do is attend the sessions and cry. She feels dazed and mentally unclear from the various medications she's been prescribed. She is unnerved by the behavior of some of the other patients in the hospital, although she feels compassion for them, too. One woman in her group therapy sessions speaks in a flow of nonsense words strung together: "So even with triangular noodle you know motorcycle but he river flow amber rod."

After two weeks, Martha's boys come to visit. The visit isn't long, and Martha finds she's still bottled up so tightly she can't say anything to them. The boys just hug her. Nyrone brings her a picture he's colored with crayons at school. Martha returns to her room and cries. But she also feels a twinge of hope. A very small twinge.

Today she describes the twinge this way: "I remember saying to myself, 'I'm gonna do everything I can to get well again, because I want to make my boys proud of me.' My boys became my motivation. That's who I started living for. I wanted to make sure I didn't bring them any shame or harm, because they had made me proud. Even despite everything I went through, they weren't getting into trouble. They were still doing well in school, because they didn't want me to worry about them. My boys made me proud of them, so I wanted to make them proud of me."

The only problem was that she didn't know where to begin. And here's where unforeseen inspiration enters her story.

Late one afternoon at Greil, after she has spent the whole day crying, she opens the drawer of the nightstand next to her hospital bed, looking for more tissues. Inside is one of those free "hotel Bibles," placed there by Gideons International, a group of interdenominational businessmen and -women who believe that people can find inspiration through faith-filled books. Martha went to church as a child but never considered herself terribly religious. She lets the Bible fall open and reads a number of passages, including these words: "God . . . comforts us in all our troubles."[5]

Martha thinks, *Well, I could sure use some comfort right about now. Maybe I'll keep reading.* She reads all the rest of that afternoon, skips supper, and keeps reading that evening until it's time for sleep. Nothing much seems changed in her life—except Martha notices one thing. As she drifts off to sleep, for the first time in a long while she isn't crying.

The next afternoon she attends her group therapy session. One by one, the people around the circle share, and the time comes for her to talk. She feels her throat starting to shut tight, as usual, but she grabs the chair as firmly as she can and says one sentence—and

Martha remembers it exactly to this day: "My name's Martha, and I been feeling real poorly for a long while."

Her voice is quiet and she's trembling, and that's the total of her words this afternoon. But the counselor smiles at her, and so do a few other people, and when Martha goes back to her room, she falls asleep again—and this time, too, she isn't crying.

That's how the next few days and weeks progress. More reading. Little by little, more talking. More rest. Less crying.

Very soon she finds she wants to do something to give back, although she doesn't know what. She doesn't feel completely healthy or whole—not by a long shot—yet she has noticed that other patients' hair is often uncombed, so she volunteers to help them comb it. It's a simple task, yet she feels empowered by the help she can give. She begins talking to the other patients, getting them to talk and listening to their stories. She finds that many of the patients are highly intelligent and highly functional; they're just going through really rough times. She says today, "You never, ever think you're going to need mental health services. But it's amazing to find out that so many people do. Life can be incredibly difficult sometimes. The people who seek mental health services are just like everybody else."

Martha progresses in her therapy sessions and is soon able to go home to be with her boys on weekends. Back at Greil on weekdays, she starts writing in journals, filling pages and pages with everything she's feeling. She keeps reading the nightstand Bible, searching for more comfort and inspiration. She often writes letters as prayers. A snippet from one of those letters reads:

God, the past year and a half have been pure hell for me. My needs are so great. I thank you for letting me hold on to my

mind, my life. It feels now that my soul is being set free from
sickness, from death. Thank you for guiding me to a place
where I can heal.

And the voice inside Martha's head begins to say something very different.

"The voice had always been what I was telling myself," Martha says. "But that old voice had been part of my life for far, far too long. That old voice told me I was stupid and crazy and worthless, and I believed it. I bought into that lie, because I couldn't see the possibilities. The new voice helped me tap into possibility. Once I got connected to the power of God, the new voice told me, 'You're valuable. You're wanted. You're loved. You can do this. You can dream. You can start again.'"

After spending three months at Greil, Martha is pronounced well again, although her road to full recovery will continue for some time to come. She's open and talking in therapy sessions. She doesn't want to commit suicide anymore. She's still on medications, although the doses are decreasing. She packs her suitcase, hugs the doctors and nurses and the patients she's come to know so well, and says goodbye. She is able to go home for good.

But her new life is only beginning. She doesn't want to return to factory work. For the first time in a long while, she believes in herself. In the possibility of what she might accomplish. She decides to "launch."

First on the agenda: more education. As a strategic move, she accepts public assistance for a limited amount of time. She returns to school, gets her GED, and begins to attend college business classes. Next she starts her own catering company—small at first, but enough to get off public assistance. She caters for family functions, then for neighbors and friends, then for the business community. Word of her excellent food gets around, and the bigger part of her dream slowly begins to take shape. With the help of business grants, she's able to rent a tiny old building in downtown Montgomery, fix it up, and— open its doors. It takes a lot of hard work and the support of her family, friends, and community, yet Martha Hawkins—high school dropout and onetime patient at the state mental institution—now owns and runs her own restaurant. Thirteen years have passed since Martha's stay at Greil. Her restaurant's name?

Martha's Place.

On the menu are all the comfort foods she's grown up cooking. Roast turkey and dressing. Fried pork steak. Southern fried chicken. Collards. Fried green tomatoes. Pork chop casserole. Baked ham, smothered cabbage, black-eyed peas. For dessert, there's pound cake and apple cobbler and banana pudding and sweet potato pie. Pure comfort food.

Newspapers write up her story. Friends tell their friends. A line forms outside the door. Martha's Place soon becomes a go-to spot in Montgomery. Tour buses stop by for lunch. Even celebrities stop in to enjoy Martha's cooking: Maya Angelou, Whoopi Goldberg, Sissy Spacek, Walter Matthau, Angela Bassett, Jesse Jackson, Bernice King, Ted Koppel, the governor of Alabama, professional football players, businesspeople, artists, and musicians.

One of the biggest fans of the restaurant, before she passes in 2005, is none other than civil rights legend Rosa Parks.

"Mrs. Parks always took cornbread muffins to go," Martha says today with a grin.

Martha often hires people who've been down on their luck, in- cluding people struggling to make ends meet, people with special needs, recovering drug addicts, and people who've been in jail. Martha believes in giving people second chances—and her employees flourish.

Today, more than forty-two years after her stay in Greil, Martha is in her early seventies; she's thriving and shows no sign of slowing down. She continues to run her restaurant, although it's moved to a bigger location. Martha's Place serves about four hundred people a day on weekdays, up to six hundred on Sundays. Martha employs twenty-three staff, and she's now spoken in forty-one states. She's even been called before the US Senate to talk about low-income housing.

How did her four boys turn out?

Shawn is a retired FBI agent. He has his master's degree in homeland security. Martha has a picture of him shaking hands with the president.

Quintin is a lobbyist and owns his own company, doing fine.

Reginald is a mortgage lender, doing well.

Nyrone became a minister and works as the executive director of the First Tee, an international youth development organization that introduces young people to golf and helps them succeed in life.

Martha's oldest grandchild recently graduated from Vanderbilt with her master's degree and is now doing cancer research. Her second oldest grandchild graduated from the University of Tennessee in biochemistry and is getting ready to go to medical school. Her third oldest is on a full-ride soccer scholarship at the University of Mississippi. And the younger ones are all doing well, too.

"When I came out of Greil, life opened up for me, and it was amazing," Martha says. "I didn't fear anymore, because I was seeing myself and the world through different eyes. I was listening to a different voice—not the old voice that told me what I couldn't do. But the new voice that told me what I *could* do. I was discovering who I truly am, and I was finding out that good possibilities lay ahead."

That's what it can look like to stay open to unforeseen inspiration.

The point is not that we will all find a Gideon Bible in a night-stand drawer of a state mental ward, as Martha Hawkins did. Or that we will all become vulnerable and open ourselves to being helped in a chemo room, as Christine Magnus Moore did. Yet part of discovering and developing the Stuff means that we don't close ourselves off—we stay on the alert because we never know where our best inspiration may come from.

And inspiration often becomes the jump-start that enables us to flip negative situations to positives.

CHAPTER ELEVEN

Flip Negatives to Positives

The essence of optimism is a source of inspiration, of vitality and hope where others have resigned; it enables a man to hold his head high, to claim the future for himself, and not to abandon it to his enemy.
—Dietrich Bonhoeffer

1
—

Take Life On, No Matter the Challenge

A li Stroker is two years old. She and her four-year-old brother, Jake, are in the backseat of the family station wagon. It's October 20, 1989, and Mom is piloting the car down a street in suburban New Jersey. Lots of leaves have fallen this autumn, and residents have blown them into the middle of the street. Visibility is poor. Mom swerves to avoid a big pile. A sickening crunch. Their car crashes head-on into another vehicle.

In 1989, full five-point-restraint car seats for infants and toddlers aren't promoted anywhere close to the level they are today. Ali and Jake are both wearing seat belts around their laps, but the lap belts cause their heads, shoulders, and torsos to fly forward while their hips stay restrained. Shoulder belts for rear seats don't become standard equipment for all cars until the 1990 model year.[1]

Sadly, both children are severely injured and rushed to the hospital. Ali's spinal cord is injured. Jake has a traumatic brain injury. Mom has broken her foot and a tooth. Ten hours after the accident, Ali suffers a spinal stroke that leaves her permanently paralyzed from the chest down. She has no memory of the accident or stroke today, even though the events become the catalyst of great change for her. No medical miracle arrives. She's two years old and unable to move her legs. Doctors say she will be in a wheelchair for the rest of her life.

Ali and Jake are in the same hospital room during rehabilitation, and this togetherness as siblings charts the course for much of their long-term recovery. Ali is fitted with a wheelchair, and it soon becomes her new normal. Jake's brain injury proves unpredictable in healing and development. He walks with a limp, can't move one arm, and will face many learning challenges in the years to come.

Ali's father, Jim Stroker, is a physical education and health teacher at a middle school, and devotes much of his time to helping his children heal and adapt. Ali's mom, Jody Schleicher, is "very smart," Ali says today, looking back, "and handled the medical side of things for us. Caring for us became a full-time job for her. As a family, we were a team through it together. In many ways we had the opposite of a carefree childhood because of all the therapy. It was a childhood of nurses and medicines and wheelchairs. Yet a lot of love and attention came our direction. We became the focus of our family, in a positive way. We were always taught that we could do anything and be anything. Nobody with a bad attitude was ever around us. We dove into all the inspirational stuff—it became our religion, and we believed it."

Ali remembers being five years old and in physical therapy. The therapists are trying to build up her upper-body strength so she can become independent later in life. They want her to be able to lift her entire body weight so she can get into and out of bed, into and out of a shower, onto and off of a commode, into and out of a car. Twice a week she throws herself into her training sessions. Soon she can do three sets of fifty bar dips, three sets of ten pull-ups, and three sets of fifteen chin-ups—all as a five-year-old!

"It's painful to try and get so strong when you're that little," Ali says today. "My physical therapist was amazing. He was so tough on me, yet today I wonder how difficult that must have been for him, needing to interact with a child in that way. Yet I knew even then that I had no other choice than to do the PT exercises. This whole concept of 'never giving up' was instilled in us very early. That's helped me out enormously in my career today."

As the years go by, Ali figures out how to play tennis and ride horses. She learns to play the piano and becomes a proficient singer. The message that's constantly drilled into her is that she *can* learn how to do things—it'll be in a different way, her way, but a good way. Her parents consistently tell her to focus on what she is able to do, not on what she's unable to do. "We were never allowed to feel sorry for ourselves," Ali says today. "We weren't allowed to say 'I can't do that.' Because we were always taught to take life on, no matter our challenges. There was always this attitude, 'We'll make it work, no matter what.'"

Still, each of the children learns to deal with challenges in different ways. When Ali was seven, she says, she was "very shy, not outgoing at all, undoubtedly still traumatized by the accident." Their next-door neighbors have three children, and that summer the oldest daughter comes home from theater camp and decides to direct a neighborhood production of *Annie*, the classic musical about a fiery young orphan. The littlest sister in the neighbors' family has had a brain tumor and still has a number of special needs, so the family is never unnerved or fazed by Ali's chair. The oldest sister casts Ali in the lead role of *Annie*, and Ali thrives in the role.

"With *Annie*, I really came out of my shell," Ali says today. "That's where I found my purpose. I learned the play, memorized it, and loved it. I thought the play was the most sophisticated and passionate thing I'd ever been a part of. I was used to getting attention because of my chair, but with theater I got attention apart from my chair—and that helped boost my confidence. From that moment onward, my dream was to someday appear in a Broadway play. I'd never heard of any actors in wheelchairs being on Broadway, but that wasn't going to stop me."

As Ali grows up, she is always mainstreamed in public schools, and strategically, she never has an aide to help her. Her parents want Ali to learn to navigate on her own. "Elementary school was the hardest," Ali says today. "Every kid loves recess. It's your favorite time of the day—running outside to play. But I dreaded recess. It was socially painful. Recess and gym class were the hardest."

Ali's difficulties continue in middle school. She doesn't have many friends, and she spends most of seventh grade eating lunch with her teacher. The school's cafeteria is downstairs, and every day at noon Ali maneuvers her wheelchair onto a lift that slowly moves her down to the lower floor. Today she describes the lift as "a strange cubical thing next to the stairs, like an elevator but out in the open." She hates that she can't walk down the stairs like everybody else.

"Even though I was hearing a lot of positive encouragement at home, there were many days when I didn't feel positive at school. There were just so many moments when I wanted to be an athlete like everybody else. I wanted to be the cool girl in middle school who plays soccer and has friends and hangs out after school at a friend's house. But that wasn't happening for me. I didn't fit in. I'd have to move through the hallways with my books on my lap, and I felt like I was taking up space and didn't belong. I felt like everybody was staring at me, and I was in my own world, just so uncomfortable. I hadn't yet owned my world, and I didn't want to be different. I just wanted to be like everybody else."

Again, theater helps her out. Ali auditions for a variety show in New York put on by the Kids for Kids Project, and she and the cast raise money for muscular dystrophy. She meets several children with muscular dystrophy and hears that due to the disease they'll probably die in their twenties. She realizes that her life could be much worse.

"It was a reality check for me," she says. "To be a kid with a disability helping another kid with a disability. It felt empowering to help yourself by helping other people. It helped me see all people as needing help—me included. My confidence as a middle school student grew by being in the show."

When Ali goes to high school, she finds that her school has a strong theater program that puts on five shows per year. She throws herself into theater and loves it. She plays Cosette in *Les Misérables* and Maria in *West Side Story*. She develops real and strong friend-ships through the theater. She has her first kiss on stage in a play. And then she has her first real crush, first real boyfriend, and first real breakup, all with a student in the theater department.

Ali explains, "I'd always wanted a boyfriend. Since I was about five years old, I'd had crushes on boys. When I was a little older, my mom and I talked about relationships and boys, and she expressed to me the reality that young guys might be nervous around my chair, and not to take it personally. But then I had my first kiss on stage, and then my first boyfriend, and these were huge moments for me. Especially because I'd never had many role models on stage or in the media. There aren't many people with disabilities who play the lead in romantic comedies or whatever. So as a teen I spent a lot of time figuring out my body, both on and off the stage, what it could do and not do. I spent a lot of time wondering where I belonged and what was possible. My relationship with my first boyfriend had lots of firsts. He was my first kiss and my first sexual experience. It was my first time being physical with a boy, and I was doing it while I was out of my chair."

During Ali's junior year of high school, her parents go through a divorce. Her father moves down the street to live with Ali's grandma. Ali isn't happy about the divorce. "I was sixteen and feisty and angry," Ali says today. "My parents asked us who we wanted to live with, and I said, 'I will not pick!' So I lived half-time at both places. During that time, I discovered I had a bit of a wild streak, and I really liked feeling wild. I was never too crazy, never drank too much. Mostly, I discov-ered through theater that I could feel wild and free. I could sing any-thing and express anything with my voice. Whenever I was singing, I felt free."

After high school graduation, Ali goes to New York University and studies at NYU's Tisch School of the Arts, one of the nation's leading institutions for theater, dance, writing, design, and art. Ali describes her time at Tisch as "amazing but also challenging." She's a musical theater major, and as part of her core curriculum she must take dance classes, which initially are a challenge. But the school administrators and professors work with her to figure out a solution: she dances in her chair. When she graduates with her degree, she accepts her diploma at Yankee Stadium, is congratulated in person by then New York senator Hillary Clinton, and feels a strong sense of accomplishment in her achievement. Ali has made history. She becomes the first person in a wheelchair to earn a degree in fine arts from NYU-Tisch.

After university, Ali lands an agent and starts going to theater auditions, but the way forward is difficult. "The feedback I got from a lot of people was 'You're so talented; we just don't know what to do with you.' After hearing that several times, I was like 'Don't say that.' But I knew it was my challenge to figure out. Other people might not know what to do with me, so *I* need to know what to do with me. I was going to have to shape my career for myself. It's what every artist has to do. Sometimes people don't give you the answers. You have to go find the answers."

2

A New Direction Forward

Even then the way forward isn't easy. Ali lives in Manhattan with one of her best friends. She tries to get several things going with her career, but nothing is landing. Finally she calls her dad and asks, "What am I supposed to do? I have no purpose. No direction." Her father says, "Maybe you need to write your own show."

So Ali does just that. She writes and creates a one-woman show, and performs it in New Jersey and New York City. She's on her way.

Earlier, she worked with the ABC Diversity Showcase, an arm of the television conglomerate that seeks to discover and develop more diverse talent for TV and film. In meetings with casting people in Los Angeles, Ali auditions for FOX's hit TV show *Glee*, a comedy-drama TV series about a high school choir traversing the choir competition circuit. She hears that Ryan Murphy "loved" her audition performance, but waits and waits and doesn't get cast on the show. At this time she is living in Los Angeles and auditioning for other roles but mostly feels discouraged.

"I felt stuck during that season," she says today. "Brakes on. Stairs in front of me. Just defeated. Like I've spent a lot of time trying to figure this out, but I don't belong anywhere. I spent a lot of time just trying to fill the time, to do something every day to create movement. I knew I couldn't wait around for *Glee*."

So Ali moves back to New York. Then along comes *The Glee Project*, a reality TV series in which contestants compete to land a role in

Glee. At first she thinks she doesn't want to be on reality TV. She knows that participants don't have much say over how their story arcs are edited, and she worries about how she might be portrayed. But she auditions along with 44,000 other hopefuls, and she is one of the lucky fourteen chosen to be on *The Glee Project*'s second season. She competes as part of the reality TV show, doesn't end up winning the spot on *Glee*, but enjoys the process, and along the way she falls in love again—this time with a girl, another cast member on the show.

"She was androgynous and supertalented," Ali says. "I'd never had feelings for a girl before, but I felt so safe with her. I felt myself."

Ryan Murphy appreciates Ali's performance in *The Glee Project* so much that he ends up putting Ali into one episode of *Glee* anyway. "That gave me tons of exposure," she says. "I was on when the show was at its peak. *Glee* was a movement, and millions of people watched it every week. It was a huge break for me, and I'm still recognized on the street from *Glee*, which feels crazy."

After *Glee*, Ali's career gains more speed. She moves back to Los Angeles and lands a role in the revival of *Spring Awakening*, a frank and edgy rock musical about teen sexuality set in late-nineteenth-century Germany. About half the cast is hearing impaired, and for her role, she learns American Sign Language and meets a number of other highly talented diversity actors.

"The first week of the show, I didn't invite anyone to come see it," she says. "I was so nervous about how people would receive it, because it was so different. But people ended up loving the show."

The show's run is extended several times. Then the show is moved to a larger theater in Beverly Hills. For the first time, Ali thinks the show might actually go somewhere, maybe even Broadway. Ali is living with her girlfriend in LA. They break up, and then the show closes. Ali is devastated by the breakup and feels unsure about where she's headed next.

Ali travels to South Africa to work on a theater arts program with women and children who are HIV positive. While there, she receives an email from the producers of *Spring Awakening*. At first she can't believe what she reads. The email says the show has been picked up again. And this time the show is going all the way to . . . wait for it . . . *Broadway!*

"I cried and laughed," she says. "I just couldn't keep it together. I was so beyond excited. I'd been wanting to be on Broadway since back when I'd been in *Annie*. This was my dream come true."

Ali returns from South Africa, moves to New York, and starts rehearsals. The show opens several months later, in September 2015. Ali makes history again, this time as the first person in a wheelchair to appear on Broadway. Ever.

The show's a success, and soon Ali begins dating a boy named David she met back at Tisch. "It's the best relationship of my life," Ali says. "I'm so very happy."

Spring Awakening closes, but Ali's career continues forward at full speed. Since then, she's started her own theater company with her partner, David, called ATTENTION Theatre. She filmed a new TV show on ABC called *Ten Days in the Valley* and has written another one-woman show. In addition, Ali speaks nationally, inspiring and educating people about disability and overcoming obstacles.

"Every day is a new adventure," she says with a smile.

What kind of perspective does she have now about life in a wheelchair and about facing obstacles in general?

"I've always tried to take tough things and turn them into something good," she says. "My motto is 'Turn your limitations into your opportunities.' For a long time I thought being in a wheelchair was going to hold me back. But being in a wheelchair has actually set me free. My challenges have made me unique, memorable, passionate, angry, aware, excited, motivated, and so full of life. My chair has allowed me to find my calling and even allowed me to change the world as the first person in a wheelchair on Broadway. Yes, it's hard work every day. The reality of not being able to feel all of your body is really wild. That's hard. It's hard work to navigate New York City in a wheelchair by yourself. It's hard work to have people looking at you all the time and to learn how to deal with that. It's hard to take an airplane by yourself when you're in a wheelchair—and it's superhard if you need to use the restroom on the plane, because somebody has to carry you into the bathroom, which is intense. But I do all that. You just have to give yourself over to whatever challenges are in front of you, and it can be scary and hard. But no matter what your limitations are, your dreams can come true. I know that might sound corny, but that's been my experience."

What does Ali hope for next? "I'd love to get married someday and have a baby," she says. "And I'd love to be on Broadway again. Having a positive mind-set is so much of the whole game. You're never going to be able to fully control the things that happen to you. But you have one hundred percent control over your response."

Ali has a mantra she lives by: $E + R = O$. It stands for the Events of your life, plus your Response, equals the Outcome. "That equation is my story. I couldn't control being in that accident when I was two. But my response has been fully in my control. I turned negatives to positives. And my life today, a life I love, is the outcome."

3

Never Say "Can't"

Sharlee explains: We love Ali's motivational statement, "Turn your limitations into opportunities." It's the essence of flipping negatives to positives, one of the core skills that make up the Stuff. This skill can be discovered within you and developed. When you're under the duress of trauma or struggle, or facing severe obstacles in your quest for a dream, you may feel that the things that block your way are going to stop you. But you can succeed. Even if you experience a temporary setback, you are likely to emerge stronger, especially if you learn to flip negatives to positives.

Does it make sense to reframe negatives as positives? And if so, how is this done?

As people, we pretty much fall into two groups: optimists and pessimists, those who see the glass as half-full and those who see the glass as half-empty. Flipping negatives to positives involves taking our eyes off the half-empty portion of the glass and focusing on the half-full part. Yet even more, it's the developable skill of recognizing the opportunity offered by the half-empty portion. If you see a void in your life, learn to see that void as an opportunity. The half-empty portion is not a hindrance or a negative but an open doorway where good things can come in. Within the half-empty portion, great possibility awaits.

Two leading advocates of positive psychology say, "Good can triumph over bad, and often does, by force of numbers. We just need a lot more good to overcome the bad."[2] As an example, they point to re-search done by J. M. Gottman about how to predict divorce. Gott-man claimed that a marriage or intimate relationship will survive only if a couple has at least five times as many positive interactions as neg-ative ones. The numbers are key. He emphasized that although the amount of positivity needed may seem overwhelming at first, mar-riages that are happy and survive for decades do so because the cou-ples express affection five times as often as they express anger.[3]

The point? Learn to focus on the positives. Think about good things. Focus on the successes, however small; the progress, however slow; the things that work, however few; the encouragements, how-ever infrequent. You can overpower negative thoughts with the sheer force of numbers of positive thoughts. You can flip negative to posi-tive.

This applies to many areas besides relationships. For instance, when we were children, my mother never allowed me or my brother, Derek, to use the word *can't*. If we ever said "can't," she would gasp as if we had said a curse word and snap back, "If you say you *can't*, then you *won't*! There is nothing that you cannot do!" As adults, we still do not use that word, and today as a mother, I don't allow my five-year-old to use it. That's definitely one way positive thinking can be used.

Terry Waite, a hostage negotiator for the archbishop of Canter-bury, tested this aspect of the Stuff. He went to Beirut, Lebanon, in the 1980s to help negotiate the release of Western hostages from the hands of Hezbollah. In 1987, he was taken hostage himself and held under extreme conditions for five years. During that time, he was subject to solitary confinement and was often blindfolded, forbidden to speak or use his voice, chained, beaten, and exposed to mock execution. After his release, discussing how he had coped, he said, "Suffering is universal; you attempt to subvert it so that it does not have a destructive, negative effect. You turn it around so that it becomes a creative, positive force."[4]

Did you catch the line? "You turn it around." That's what it means to flip a negative to a positive.

Waite continues, "I was determined as much as I could not to take the experience as a negative, but as an opportunity to get to know myself better. It was almost a form of self-analysis. You inevitably discover both sides of personality—the light and the dark. When I [finally] came out of captivity, I slipped into my pocket my blindfold and a small piece of magnifying glass which had been given to me so I could read when eventually I was allowed books. They'd been the only possessions I had."[5]

Upon his return home, Waite placed both items on his desk and wrote a bestselling memoir of his experience; when he was finished, he handed over the two items to the university he worked for to remind people that hostages can be freed, that good can overcome evil, that light can overcome the dark.

Now, that's a man who has the Stuff.

Think of the act of positive thinking as you might imagine a shattered vase. At first it looks completely broken. Maybe this is how you feel when something unfortunate happens to you. Yet you have several choices: you can try to put the pieces back together exactly as they were; you can sweep up the pieces and drop them into the trash; or you can pick up the pieces and use them to make something new, perhaps a colorful mosaic. Dr. Stephen Joseph, a psychologist, provides this illustration and adds, "Those who try to put their lives back together exactly as they were remain fractured and vulnerable. But those who accept the breakage and build themselves anew become more resilient and open to new ways of living."[6]

Of course, this action doesn't deny or in any way minimize the fact that you've experienced grief or loss. But it focuses on moving forward more meaningfully in the light of what happened.

You flip negatives to positives. You use negative situations in your life to motivate you, even to help dictate what type of life you want to lead.

4

Dispatches from the Pediatric Ward

harlee explains: When I was going through my cancer treatments, I experienced a moment similar to that of Ali Stroker when she participated in the fund-raising theater production for children with muscular dystrophy. The experience made Ali see that other people could be worse off than she was. It prompted gratefulness for the abilities she did have. And ultimately her acts of service helped instill a sense of empowerment and increased confidence. It proved to be a two-way street. The children helped her, and she helped them.

In my situation, my initial chemo treatments were held in an open room with other adults, just like Christine Magnus Moore experienced. The room was huge, and my parents were there with me. That was at the height of Derek's fame with the New York Yankees, and for a while my parents were shown on TV, sitting at the games, almost every day. When I went to my first chemo treatment, we quickly learned that the attention given to us by people at the hospital was too much. The attention was mostly good—they just wanted to congratulate us or say how much they adored Derek. But we also saw how the attention was going to cause more problems than good—for my family, for me, but, most important, for the other patients. We'd made a decision as a family to keep things about my cancer quiet so I could go through my treatments without having to worry about anything else. So the hospital decided to take precautions and moved me to a private room on the pediatrics floor; I believe this was also out of respect for the other families who just wanted to spend time with their loved ones during their difficult time.

I don't know if you've ever seen the pediatrics floor in a hospital. Some of the children have been there for a long time, and in my case, this pediatric floor was completely decked out with hospital rooms that seemed to have been turned into mini-apartments so parents could stay there while they cared for their children. All the doors were colorfully decorated, there were signs up on all the walls with positive quotes, and painted on the walls were murals of animals and the sea. One morning I came in and saw parents walking around in pajamas and socks, their hair a mess, because they'd spent the night there, yet the parents were smiling and laughing with their kids, and the kids were laughing and enjoying the time they spent playing with their parents and being positive—and this thought hit me: *Sharlee, how dare you have a bad attitude?*

I mean, here I was: I could have my chemo treatment and then go home, and then fly back to college in Atlanta the next day. And sure, I'd be sick and it was no fun. But so many of these children were dealing with far harsher things. I remember feeling angry that children would have to go through such difficult experiences. I felt a tremendous sense of injustice. I was tapping into the reality that the world isn't always a fair place; something's broken here. Yet the realization built a greater sense of compassion into me. I became determined not to complain when it was time to fly back for treatments every other week. I was going to get through my sickness, and I was going to continue to feel compassion for others and help out wherever I could, something that's been a part of my life ever since.

That was my tipping point, my own moment of self-reflection. Yes, I was facing an obstacle, but yes, I could have had it worse. And I was going to use the inspiration I saw in those families to buoy my own sense of resilience. I would smile back to them and talk to them, and I even decided to name my IV pole "Ivy," just as the kids named theirs. This all helped me go forward.

I had to face reality, of course, and this factors into developing this part of the Stuff. Yes, I still had cancer. That was my reality. And positivity couldn't cancel that out. But I thought about how maybe it's possible and healthy to embrace both optimism and pessimism, blending negatives and positives together into healthy realism. The attitude of the children on that pediatric floor showed me that joy, love, strength, and determination are things that no one can take away from you. Those children inspired me. I wanted to be more like them, approaching life in a similar way.

I saw that cancer was an obstacle that also held out possibility. Over time, I learned I could actually embrace cancer in the sense that I could make it my personal badge of honor. Overcoming that challenge was the one thing that was *only* mine. For years I had grown up with comparisons—lots of siblings experience this, but when your older brother is Derek Jeter, the comparisons only intensify. People said things to me like "Oh, you're such a good softball player, you must get that from your brother" or "Your brother did so well in this class and was one of my top students—I'm not sure why it's such a struggle for you." But with cancer, for the first time ever I experienced a challenge where I wasn't compared to Derek, and Derek couldn't make it better for me or make it go away. It was my own mountain to climb. I needed to control my mind-set, and I determined that I was going to beat the cancer. It was still an obstacle— that was my reality. Yet it became my badge of honor; that's how I learned to be optimistic.

Sophia Chou, an organizational psychology researcher at National Taiwan University, noticed after several years of working in the business world that some people who were both optimistic and realistic were also successful. She gave a series of personality surveys to some two hundred college and graduate students, testing their outlooks on optimism. Her data showed that the optimists fell into two camps whom she called *realists* and *idealists*.

The idealists were people who saw life in a Pollyanna-ish sort of way. Life for them was almost too good, Chou reported. It wasn't based in reality. It was too good to be true.

The realists chose to value accuracy in addition to positivity. They also got better grades than the idealists, maybe because they knew— realistically—that they had to work hard to get those grades. Yet the realists were not on the whole unhappy or negative people.

Chou, who presented her research at the American Psychological Association's annual meeting in 2013, found that the realistic optimists had more self-control and perceived control of others, and she called that a key to making realistic optimism work. For example, when the realistic optimists faced a problem, they seldom claimed they had no choice. Instead they were creative, coming up with plans A, B, and C. It seems that having a healthy outlook involves having a clear-eyed view of reality but knowing what you can control, and then getting on with solving the problem.[7]

To me, that reinforces the fact that flipping negatives to positives is not mere whistling in the dark. No one is kidding themselves here. Obstacles are obstacles. Cancer is cancer. Yet there are always reasons to be positive if we look for them, and doing so seems to create more positivity and a greater likelihood of success. This is realistic optimism, not looking at the world through rose-colored glasses, not chasing illusions. It's simply choosing to focus on the positives.

5

_____

Fifty Cents and a Hot Dog Truck

S*ampson explains:* Much of my growing-up time was an exercise in flipping negatives to positives, although some of the flipping didn't happen until later on. I remember one day when I was twelve years old. I had come home from school and it was near dinnertime, but we had hardly any food in the house. It must have been near the end of the month, because Mom could always find ways to stretch her meager income. But somehow we had a day or two to go, and the fridge and cupboards were bare except for a small hunk of surplus cheese, which we got free from the government.

A hot dog truck parked in our neighborhood every day from about 10:00 a.m. until 6:00 p.m., and kids and grown-ups would buy hot dogs, sodas, and candy from the truck. It was right before 6:00 p.m., almost closing time. Mom tapped me on the shoulder and said, "Here's fifty cents. Go to the hot dog truck and ask to buy whatever buns he has left over."

I didn't want to do it. I felt embarrassed. But she said, "Go. Just go." So I obeyed her, went outside, waited until no one was around, and walked up to the guy's truck. He knew who I was and who my mom and brothers were. Dad had moved out by then.

I talked as fast as I could. "Listen. I have fifty cents. Do you have any buns left over for sale?" I felt very uncomfortable. Fifty cents wouldn't buy even one hot dog, much less feed an entire family.

He looked at me, paused, then nodded and said, "Okay." He knew what was happening and wasn't going to shame me. He handed me a package of buns. Six total. He put them in a brown paper sack, and I paid him the fifty cents and carried them home. Mom toasted the cheese that we had in our fridge on them, and that was our dinner that night.

What happened the next night? I don't remember. But somehow my family got along. Growing up, there were plenty of meals where we ate just fine: hamburgers, chicken, spaghetti. But then there were also plenty of meals like this, meals that shook me to the core, meals that made me realize that this was a tough place to be in.

I didn't disparage my mother for this, not at all. She was doing everything she could to help us kids along, and she was doing so many things right. This was at the height of the crack epidemic, and plenty of mothers and fathers were hooked and suffering. Plenty of children were raising themselves. But Mom didn't do drugs. She was still in our lives, still caring for us, still making sure we got by.

Meals like those became some of the negative experiences that helped propel me forward. Those meager meals lit a fire in me. I felt my embarrassment, and I owned it. I felt my sense of discomfort, and along the way I sensed I could do something more with my life. I made a quiet vow that grew over time. Perhaps I didn't even articulate it to myself until a few years later, but the vow was this: when I became an adult, I wasn't going to be caught in the same position. Those situations became my motivation.

Today, as a medical doctor, I continue to use the practice of flipping negatives to positives, although the circumstances have changed. I don't battle economic difficulties anymore, but I give seminars across the country and regularly face the challenges of public speaking. I've learned to turn any pretalk jitters into forward momentum. If ever I feel anxious, I use my nerves to feel more alert and to better tune in to my audience's needs. I know to channel the concern I feel into giving the absolute best talk I can give.

Similarly, with the patients I care for, I regularly see people's health improve when they focus on the positives. Medically, we know that the opposite is true, that "individuals who have suffered a major upheaval, such as the death of a spouse or a divorce, are more vulnerable to a variety of major and minor illnesses."[8] But this can be buffered by such things as a social support network, a hardy disposition, and understanding and assimilating the trauma, which in turn relieves the physical illnesses.

Yes, it requires work to do the heavy lifting of flipping negatives into positives, yet some of the tips offered by experts are disarmingly simple. These include:

- **Writing about it.** This is recognized as one of the best ways to understand and assimilate negative life events. In a recent study, fifty healthy college students were told to write for twenty minutes a day for four days, half the group about trivial topics and half about personal traumas. They had blood tests before and after, with follow-up health assessments. Afterward, the students who wrote about their personal traumas tested healthier.[9] It's not about grammar or spelling; it's about getting your thoughts and feelings out.

- **Expressing gratitude.** Gratefulness is a choice, and seeing the positive invokes gratitude. Negativity is released, along with any pessimism you might be holding on to.[10]

- **Staying away from "all-or-nothing" thinking.** Shift from black-and-white thinking to somewhere in the gray zone, where you'll find fresh perspective.

- **Trying not to take everything personally.** Not everything is about you. Adopting this perspective helps us look at circumstances more objectively.

- **Celebrating.** May we never dismiss good things or take them for granted, even if they are small. It's important to celebrate whenever you recognize a blessing.[11]

Setbacks can be turned around and leveraged into advantages. Our call is to be eternal optimists—realistic, but not idealistic, in our positivity. Obstacles or fear can be seen through new eyes, and in the end they can become assets, needful parts of our journeys.

We're nearly at the end of the book, yet there's one more trait of the Stuff that we can discover and develop. It's what we've seen time and time again in people who have the Stuff. Success for these individuals isn't strictly about making it through their own tough times; it's about extending a hand to others and thereby making themselves that much stronger.

CHAPTER TWELVE

Be a Giver

For it is in giving that we receive.
—Saint Francis of Assisi

1
———

A Sense of Something Beyond Us

Deval Patrick grows up in the shadows of the projects in the late 1950s and early 1960s, living in his grandparents' two-bedroom tenement on Chicago's South Side. His grandparents sleep in one bedroom. Deval sleeps in the other, along with his sister and mother, who's sometimes on welfare. Dad is long gone. In their bedroom is a set of bunk beds, and the trio rotates each night from the top bunk to the bottom bunk to the floor and back again. There's a window to the outside world in the bedroom that looks out about eight feet to an air shaft and the bricks of the neighboring building.

The community itself was deeply segregated, Deval says, looking back. "A handful of doctors, nurses, and teachers lived there, among many blue-collar laborers who worked in the stockyards. Lucky ones had jobs at the US Steel plant. There were lots of broken homes, but many families were intact, too. Financially, most people just got by. When I was younger, it seemed a place of relational and community riches, but the atmosphere changed as I grew up. My grandparents talked about when they were younger and it was too hot in the summer to be in the house, they'd go over to Washington Park and sleep outside. Lots of people did. By the time I left Chicago, nobody did that anymore."

Deval's earliest schooling experiences were mostly troublesome. "I went to a big, broken, crowded, underfunded, underresourced public school on the South Side," he says. "I can't remember when I didn't love to read, but I didn't own a book of my own until age thirteen, through a program called Better Chance."

Yet a few bright lights shine in the educational system. Deval's sixth-grade teacher is Mrs. Eddie Quaintance, and he describes her influence: "There were thirty-five to forty children in her classroom, all of us from similar neighborhoods where everything was broken— broken sidewalks, broken playgrounds. But she was the first person who helped us imagine what it might be like to be a student and citizen of the world. For a kid from the South Side of Chicago, that's huge. She taught us to count and say greetings in German. She took us to an opera—the first I'd ever seen; I had no idea what they were singing about, but it was magical. She took us to a movie that was just out, *The Sound of Music*, and taught us about modern European history. She was a legendary teacher who could command the room and our attention."

Deval's other big positive influence as a child is his church. His grandmother cooks a Southern country breakfast each Sunday morning—biscuits, grits, country ham, sausage—but Deval and his sister aren't allowed to eat breakfast unless they go to church.

"It was called the Cosmopolitan Community Church," Deval says today, "and it was an unusual type of church for that community. The pastor, Dr. Mary Evans, was a woman of great faith, and the sanctuary was always prayerful, solemn, and quiet, not the joyful and loud black church you might imagine. The church people had a sense of generational responsibility, and if a boy started squirming or talking to his neighbor, then one of the elderly ladies would shoot you a look that meant you needed to get it together. I knew these ladies from the neighborhood, too, because it was that type of community. They all had calamity in their own lives, yet they always had a hug and a word of encouragement for the kids in church. All sorts of societal expectations said we as kids would not do right or accomplish big things, but these elderly ladies constantly encouraged us, and I felt very lifted up. I was sometimes in church against my will, yet I'm so glad today that we went. There are so many ways in which that experience resonates in my life today. That's part of what made our community rich: the faith component along with the education component, working hand in glove to create a longing in our hearts, a sense of something beyond us."

Deval's first job is making snow cones when he's just a boy. Three doors down lives a fireman who owns an old jeep refitted with an ice crusher and syrup holders. They go to various neighborhoods on hot summer days, the fireman driving, Deval scooping up cones and collecting sticky money. Deval can't see his future in the job, but it gives him a taste of interacting with the public, a skill he'll use often later in life.

As Deval grows older, the community begins to fray. In his teens, he lives through the collective anguish of the Woodlawn riots and the riots following the Democratic National Convention of 1968. Some of the angst is about the Vietnam War; some of it is racial. And then gangs begin to organize. Two rival gangs, the Black Stone Rangers (later called the Black P. Stone Nation) and the Disciples, begin to recruit teens. Deval's mother is terrified by this, and one summer sends Deval and his sister to Camp Beechwood in Michigan. This is Deval's first time away from home, and he initially doesn't want to go, yet his mother insists. The first thing he has to do at the camp is take a swimming test, something foreign to him. But eventually he settles in, has a wonderful camp experience, and begs to go again the following summer.

Deval's mother is a firm believer in the power of education. She learns of and applies to a program called A Better Chance, and through it Deval secures a full scholarship to Milton Academy, a prestigious preparatory school in Massachusetts. It's a complete countercultural experience for Deval, going to a boarding school with a dress code. When the clothing list arrives at home, his grandparents see *jacket* on the list and buy him a windbreaker. Only when Deval sees other boys at school putting on blue blazers and tweed coats for class does he realize what *jacket* means in this culture.

At first Deval feels like a fish out of water at Milton. After sporting events on Wednesdays and Saturdays, there's a tea, poured by the students' white-gloved mothers. Boys are expected to participate in sports, shower and change clothes, then come to the tea in suits and ties and converse with the guests. Day students arrive at Milton in chauffeured cars with liveried drivers. He has classmates whose last names are on the buildings. "It was a very foreign place to me at first," Deval says.

But it's not all bad news. At Milton, he has his own bed every night—something he's never had before. He has his own bureau, his own desk. And his window looks out over half a mile of lawn framed by large, stately trees and ivy-covered brick buildings. He doesn't have enough clothes to fill the bureau, but for the first time in his life he begins to see how opportunity can extend to anybody, even him.

"My feelings about Milton were complicated," he says today. "Milton is a different culture, an unfamiliar setting without my usual supports. I don't speak the same language, and there's a code I haven't broken yet. But there's also a big sense of excitement."

Racial tensions hit close to home. One of the Milton treats is that the boys are permitted a burger run every now and then if the dining hall food is particularly bad. The boys prevail on the housemaster to take orders, have a student phone the order in, then have a staff member drive a selected boy to the nearest fast-food joint to pick up food for all.

Deval is assigned the job one evening. He's fifteen, in his second year at school. He takes orders, phones the nearest hamburger stand in Dorchester, and heads over to the restaurant with the floor master, Mr. Evans, a tall, thin, bespectacled history professor in his early thirties.

When Deval and Mr. Evans pull into the restaurant parking lot, they see a group of older teenagers, town kids. It's 1971, and Deval is sporting an Afro. As soon as he steps out of the car, the racial slurs begin. "They were shouting 'N-this' and 'Monkey-that,'" Deval says today. "One kid takes his cigarette butt and tries to flick it into my hair. We say nothing to the crowd of kids but go inside and collect our order. While we're inside, the kids outside start to pound on these big plate-glass windows, shouting all manner of unpleasantness. It feels like things could become really dangerous at any second. The manager is so freaked out. He's in a hurry to get the order to us and get us out. He doesn't want any trouble. So Mr. Evans and I collect our order, head back outside, load up in the car with all the food, and pull out. He and I ride most of the way back to school in total silence. I've experienced this type of thing before, but I can see how shaken he is, so I end up trying to comfort him, saying 'You know, Mr. Evans, it's okay.' Of course, it really *wasn't* okay. But we were safe. We weren't hurt. We'd displayed our own version of poise under fire. Yet in retrospect, I could have used some comforting myself."

It's not the only incident of racism Deval encounters in the small town of Milton, where the school by the same name is located. "If a black kid was in town, walking to the corner store, we'd be stopped by police and asked to show identification, something that white kids were never asked to do," he says today.

"One day at Milton we were going to do a reading of a play in class," he adds. "One character was black and called a 'nigger' within the play's dialogue. There was one other black kid in the class besides me, and the professor looked at us and said with a smile, 'Which one of you two niggers wants to play the nigger?' I think he was trying to be familiar and funny, but it was neither familiar nor funny. There was nervous laughter and shock from the other students, and I think the teacher was instantly aware that he'd said too much, although neither I nor the other black kid had the presence of mind to call him out. We both just sat there stunned."

2

The Power of Common Cause

D eval finds an enjoyable niche at Milton by running cross-country. He also learns how to be real. "My new friends at Milton were not so interested in my life back on the South Side of Chicago as my friends at home were not so interested in my new life at Milton," Deval says. "So I needed to figure out how to be who I was all the time and not worry about my setting. I needed to be clear about who I was, what I believed, how I behaved, and then just be that person all the time. I figured that the people who liked or loved me for who I truly was would reveal themselves. And the folks who liked or loved me only for who they thought I ought to be would drift away. It was an early lesson in personal integrity. You have to find your True North, and then live by it."

Historically, Milton students are prepared to go to Harvard after they graduate, and most Milton students do so, including Deval. "No one in my family had ever been to college," he says. "But they believed in the power of education. They believed I'd be saved by *education itself*, and it wasn't dependent on a particular school. I didn't fully appreciate that until many years later. Nobody in my family knew how to apply for college or get ready for it, and when my acceptance letter arrived, I called home and said, 'Grandma, I got into Harvard!' She was overcome, just yelling and screaming, so excited for me, and then she paused and said, 'Now, where is that, anyway?' Her response devastated me. How could she not know about Harvard? But years later, with new perspective, I see that she was excited not about the prestige but the opportunity. It wasn't that her grandson was going to Harvard that made the big impression on her. It was that her grandson was going to college."

Harvard isn't academically easy. Milton was a rigorous academic environment, and Deval is used to getting good grades, but when he writes his first Harvard paper, it comes back with a big red C on top. "I realized I needed to find another gear here," he says. "Succeeding at Harvard would mean longer hours and saying no to social stuff and paying attention to study habits."

Deval finds his groove and graduates with honors from Harvard, then from Harvard Law School. Mrs. Eddie Quaintance, his favorite sixth-grade teacher, is in the audience at both events, cheering him on. Deval clerks for a federal judge in Los Angeles, where he meets Diane, the woman who later becomes his wife; then they move to New York, where Deval joins the NAACP Legal Defense Fund. They marry in 1984 and are still married today, going strong.

Deval succeeds as an attorney and sues Bill Clinton over the issue of easier access to voter registration when Clinton is governor of Arkansas. "I actually think that Governor Clinton wanted the access to be easier," Deval says. "It was controlled by the county clerks back then, who weren't making access easy. The problem was this: Say you live in one county and work in the next county, and maybe you start work at eight a.m. and don't return home until six p.m. In some instances, clerks offered the opportunity to register to vote only between ten a.m. and noon and between one and three p.m. They were unwilling to make registration more convenient, and that was particularly difficult for the working poor. If you can't get registered, you can't vote. There was no same-day registration or registration by mail back then."

The terms of the settlement become the bones of what's now called the "motor-voter law," which President Clinton signs in his first term of office. Deval later joins a Boston law firm and becomes a partner at age thirty-four. Later, Clinton nominates Deval to be US assistant attorney general.

In 2005, at age forty-nine, Deval begins his run for governor of Massachusetts. He's motivated by two reasons. "One is [a distaste for] short-term thinking," he says today. "We govern from news cycle to news cycle, not generation to generation. I felt we needed to get back to this concept of community responsibility, and make hard choices in our time to benefit the generation to come. The other motivating factor was to see if it's possible to run for office and really stand for something, really put convictions on the line, even if they'd cost you the election. I believe as a citizen that's the type of real leadership we're hungry for. So I ran, willing to lose, with an optimistic, forward-looking agenda."

Deval begins his campaign with no money and only 2 percent name recognition. He must beat an entrenched Democratic candidate in the primary and an equally entrenched Republican in the general election. Yet his campaign gains momentum and begins to soar. The general election sees record turnout, and he wins the governorship. He's the only African American ever to serve as governor of Massachusetts and holds the office from 2007 to 2015.

"We were able to get a lot of good stuff done," he says, looking back. "Massachusetts became the first in America in health care, student achievement, entrepreneurial activity, veterans' services, and energy efficiency. We had the highest bond rating in the history of the commonwealth and a twenty-five-year high in employment. We didn't get it all right by any means, but we did a lot of good. We made some hard choices, and not everybody got what they wanted. But it was about everybody getting a little and giving a little, and I think the public respects principle. They don't agree with every decision, but they respect authentic principle, and that's what we were trying to display."

On April 15, 2013, Deval is scheduled to crown the female winner of the Boston Marathon, while Boston's mayor is set to crown the male winner, but the mayor is sick in the hospital. Deval goes to see him early that morning, and the mayor asks if he will do both honors. It's a stunningly beautiful day in Boston, warm, friendly, with the atmosphere of a block party. Visitors and competitors from all over the world are in Boston for the race.

Deval crowns both winners, finishing his official duties just before noon. He leaves the scene of the marathon, gets in a workout, has his hair cut, then plans to putter in his garden for the rest of the day. He's on his way home on the Southeast Expressway when his youngest daughter, who lives in the city's South End, calls. "Dad, I just heard a big boom. Everybody's running. What's going on?!"

"Maybe some sort of celebratory cannon," he says. "I don't know. Just stay out of the way."

He hangs up, and his phone rings again. It's the state's emergency management person, who was at the finish line when two terrorist bombs went off. He describes the scene as a "wreck and a mess" and says he's "never seen anything like it."

The state trooper who's driving Deval immediately announces that he's taking Deval to an emergency bunker fifteen miles out of town, but Deval tells him to turn the car around and head back to the scene of the bombing.

"To head out to the bunker felt like running away," Deval says today. "And that's not what my instincts said to do. This wasn't something we could manage at a distance. The evidence was there at the finish line. I wanted to deploy people and give instructions within reasonable proximity."

He sets up a command center a block away from the first bomb scene. By the time he arrives, many of his staff and most agency heads are there. President Obama calls. The head of the Red Cross calls. Deval calls the mayor at the hospital. "Then we had to get organized," Deval says, "and I knew from my time in the Justice Department that if we didn't designate one agency to lead the criminal investigation, then we'd be stepping all over ourselves. I convened the heads of the FBI, Secret Service, Bureau of Alcohol, Tobacco, and Firearms, Boston police, state police, transit police, National Guard, fire marshal, and others in one room and said, 'Look, there's something for everybody to do.' And in fairly short order, we settled on the FBI being in charge, and then I looked every agency head in the eye and said, 'You okay with this?' and went right around the circle. Everybody said yes. The FBI took charge, and the team stuck together and ended up doing an extraordinary job, basically finding two needles in a haystack."

Eventually two suspects are fingered: Chechen American brothers, extremists. One brother soon dies. He's shot in a gun battle with police and then is run over by the car driven by his escaping brother. The other brother is caught several hours later, hiding in a boat in a backyard. He's arrested, and later convicted of more than thirty charges and sentenced to death.

The bombs planted and detonated at the Boston Marathon by the two brothers initially kill three people—Krystle Campbell, Lu Lingzi, and eight-year-old Martin Richard[1]—and wound some 264 others. At least 14 people have limbs amputated. MIT police officer Sean Collier is killed four days later, shot by one of the terrorists on MIT's campus while sitting in his patrol car, bringing the total to four. Police officer Dennis Simmonds dies on April 10, 2014, a year after the bombing, and state examiners recognize his death as the result of head injuries caused by the shootout. Five people in total are killed.[2]

Referring to the day of the blast, Deval says today, "The acts of kindness performed by Boston-area citizens were extraordinary. So many people came out of their homes along the race course and sheltered runners, helping them connect with family and friends at the finish line. So many people helped down at the blast sites. Those acts of kindness spawned other acts of kindness all across the region, and they were just as important to the overall recovery as anything else."

Deval describes his job after the bombings as "a servant role, providing direction, insight, even encouragement. During crisis management, we're all on the same team. We're definitely not going to pit one agency against another. We've got a problem to solve. Here we go."

Today, at age sixty, now out of public office, Deval is preparing for more years of service. He's back in the business world, launching an investment fund for companies that promote positive social or environmental impact. Rumors of a run at the presidency have been heard, although he isn't talking yet.

"I'm not at the end of my journey," he says. "And I'm not trying to regain my youth. I don't want to become a valedictorian in my last thirty years of life for what happened in the previous sixty. I believe in the power of optimism. In these deeply cynical times, it's harder and harder for people to accept optimism. But we can still shape our own futures. I believe my grandmother was right when she said, 'Hope for the best. And work for it.' Meaning, set your sights high, but don't leave your future to chance. You have to apply yourself and encourage others and lean on others and let them lean on you. I believe in the power of common cause. As people, as a country, there's much more we have in common with each other than what divides us. This is the only nation in human history organized not around geography or religion or language or common culture but around a handful of civic ideals. We've defined those ideals over time as opportunity, equality, fairness, freedom. That's what makes us the envy of the world. It's not how much money or how many weapons we have. That's why people risk their lives trying to get here, legally or illegally. Our ideals—that's our real power in the world. If we squander those ideals, that's what makes us weaker."

3
———

Antiques Stores and That Restless Feeling:

THE SUSAN SCOTT KRABACHER STORY

Susan Scott Krabacher's eyes are glued to the eyes of the little boy on the TV screen.

It's 1994, and the little boy is sleeping in a sewer in Mongolia because it's the warmest place at night on the streets where he lives. He's just eaten a rat because he's hungry and there's no other food available. He's an orphan, and his older brother looks after him. The little boy is featured on one of those late-night infomercials about starving children, and Susie recognizes the look of absolute desperation in his eyes—a look of defeat, sadness, terror, shame, and worthlessness—and Susie wonders where she's seen that look before.

Susie's watching TV in her home in Aspen, Colorado, the home she shares with her new husband, Joe, a successful attorney, and she wants to flip to some other channel, but something about the infomercial prompts her to stay put. Susie and Joe are young, hip socialites with no children, and Susie tells herself, *You really should get to bed* and *Surely somebody will do something about those children in the sewer!* But she cannot take her eyes off the boy's.

Susie's day job is running an antiques shop selling expensive old furniture to wealthy Aspenites. The antiques store is a failure because Susie self-admittedly stinks at running a store, but she doesn't know what else to do with her time. Mostly she's listless, searching for purpose, she admits today. She's thrown her new life into Joe, and she adores being a housewife, despite her restlessness. Every night, she creates incredible multicourse dinners. Four courses minimum; five on average. Each day she spends hours fixing her makeup and putting together sexy ensembles so Joe never sees the same outfit twice. Yet ultimately she's bored. She tans and waxes and runs and diets and spends hours at the hair salon and gym. She thinks the best way to move forward is by becoming the perfect cook. Perfect wife. Perfect human. But she's hitting the wall, becoming unglued, because there's still something hollow inside her. She yearns to do something more with her life. She just doesn't know what.

Then it hits her—why she recognizes the look of desperation in the sewer boy's eyes. It's because she would have seen the same look in her own eyes when she was five years old and looked into a mirror.

Her mind flashes back to the childhood she endured in rural Alabama. Back to her schizophrenic mother, violent and abusive. Back to being called a "wicked, evil child" at age four and then being spanked because she got her dress dirty. The words choked in her throat when she tried to explain to her parents why: earlier that day, her grandfather had taken her out to a dry creek bed, made her lie down on the ground, and raped her. That same childhood horror happened again and again from age four to eight. She remembers the whippings, the hurting, the screaming, the confusion, the loneliness, the abuse.

"I told no one," she says today. "I was too scared. This was my life. My childhood. I felt totally isolated."

Susie stares at the TV, transfixed, and feels united with the boy in his despair. She wonders what part of his body got the last bruise. She wonders who yelled at him last. She wonders what it's like to lift a dead rat to your lips—to chew and swallow and somehow be thankful because at least you've survived another day. She doesn't know what to do for the boy, but she knows she has to help. Period. This is her lightbulb moment.

There's a number at the bottom of the screen and she moves to scribble it down on a scrap of paper, but the commercial is over and the number is lost. She has no training as a humanitarian. She's smart as a tack but dropped out of school in tenth grade because life at home was so hard; her only solution was to get a job so she could get away. She's never even thought of herself as a particularly upright or altruistic person. When a string of low-paying jobs fell through, she made money modeling. One thing led to another, and she was discovered by a photographer with connections. Susie wound up modeling for *Playboy* and landed the coveted centerfold slot: Miss May 1983. She felt conflicted by modeling nude, she says today. It went against her principles and conscience, but at last she had money of her own—enough to stay out of her parents' house; enough to fill the desolation in her heart. Or so she thought.

With her modeling money in hand, Susie dated celebrities and lived at Hugh Hefner's mansion and took vacations in Acapulco and appeared on TV and signed autographs on calendars and T-shirts, beer mugs and baseball caps. She partied hard and snorted cocaine and got married and divorced and moved to Aspen, and when her money ran out she worked at the only job she could find. Cleaning houses.

Then she met and married Joe, and at last life started to come together for her, she says today. For real. For good. With Joe she is loved and financially secure and not being abused and not compromising her values. Her life is now truly blessed. But she still feels restless, purposeless. She keeps on wondering if maybe there's something *more*.

"The abuses in my childhood had caused tremendous shame and embarrassment," she says today. "I felt like my power had been stripped from me, and it all just hurt. When something traumatic and horrible happens, some people go out and become so strong that they can literally change the world. Other people shrivel up and die—and I was doing that in Aspen. I was protected by beautiful things, and I thought these things were keeping my soul content and docile. Yet part of me was in utter rage that these abuses had happened to me as a child. I felt so marginalized. I felt like nobody—including me—was ever going to do anything about it. Then I saw the documentary, and it hit me like a grenade: *Holy smokes, that poor child, I just want to help him. This is the one thing I can do.*"

The next morning, she calls an organization that works in Mongolia, but a representative only encourages her to send a check. Susie wants to actually meet the children she saw on-screen. She wants to hold them, hug them, tell them that they're stronger than they feel. She wants to let them know that children can survive crises, however horrible, and that somehow, some way, it's going to be okay.

"Would it work if I went to Mongolia and met your staff and the children you help and volunteered for a couple of weeks?" she asks. Nope. She calls organization after organization, but the response is the same. No one bites at the idea.

A week or so later, a friend convinces her that although Mongolia has pockets of desperation, the country that needs the most immediate attention is actually Haiti, and if she truly wants to help poverty-stricken children, she should go there.

Susie researches the country. Located five hundred miles off the coast of Florida and bordered by the Dominican Republic, Haiti is a beautiful Caribbean island nation filled with vibrant, industrious people with a rich culture and heritage. For a brief window of time in the 1970s, Haiti became a popular tourist destination for cruise ships. But an AIDS scare in the 1980s, combined with a series of hurricanes and floods, uncontrolled deforestation, and a twenty-nine-year run of alleged corrupt governing by the controversial father-and-son dictators François "Papa Doc" Duvalier and Jean-Claude "Baby Doc" Duvalier, all helped run Haiti's economy into the ground. Haiti was now the poorest country in the Western Hemisphere.

Hearing all of this, Susie feels a strange draw toward the devastated land. She can't quite articulate why, but she knows she has to go see the country for herself. She must meet the people. She must get to know their names.

"Okay," Susie says. "I'll go."

Her decision is straightforward. Susie gets on a plane to Haiti, lands in Port-au-Prince, the capital, hails a cab, and asks to be taken to the poorest section of the city. The taxi driver takes Susie to Cité Soleil, lets her out, and drives away. It's considered the worst slum in Haiti. Many of the houses in Cité Soleil are just cinder-block shanties with roofs of rusty tin, wood, or cardboard. Susie starts walking from shack to shack in an attempt to meet people. She realizes she must be a strange sight in this environment—a tall, blond woman wearing a long white sundress. A group of children gathers around, pointing and giggling. Finally a group of adults gathers.

"Are you with the government?" a man asks.

"No," she says. "I want to know how to help."

"We need food!" comes a shout. Several other voices agree.

It's that simple. Susie promises to return with food.

But before she leaves, she has one request. A dry swallow goes down her throat and she states her intention, just as she practiced it earlier: "I need a place to sleep tonight. Can someone help me?"

4

———

"In This World, You Were Loved"

A few laughs. A few jeers. There are no hotels for tourists in Cité Soleil. No comfy bed-and-breakfasts. No expensive inns. Nothing close to that sort of thing.

But then somebody glimpses the promise that Susie is offering. A man named Marcelon agrees to take Susie back to the shanty he calls home. He lives with his wife and five children, his grandmother, seven cousins, and a friend. His shack is about the size of a garden shed. Dusk falls, and Susie follows Marcelon to the shack. It's already filled with dozing bodies. Marcelon introduces her, and a few people inch apart so there's enough room for one more body on the dirt floor. Susie lies down and closes her eyes. She knows she's not experiencing the full reality of what it's like to live in an impoverished country, but she wants to feel a closer identification with the people, not just swoop in and out. She wants to place herself among the people she feels drawn to empower. She wants a fuller understanding of what it feels like to have nothing.

When she wakes in the morning, all the people in the shack are gone except one little girl who sits nearby, stroking Susie's hair. Susie is covered in itchy red bumps. Something bit her repeatedly during the night. Fleas. Maybe lice.

Yet Susie remains undaunted. She realizes she hasn't looked in a mirror for more than twenty-four hours, and this is a first. Something selfless has stirred inside her soul, and all she can think about is going home so she can sell her furniture store and raise money to come back to Haiti and do whatever good she can do. From this point onward, her life will never be the same.

More than twenty-five years have passed since Susie first spent the night in a shack in Cité Soleil. She describes her life today as rich—incredibly rich—but in a way you might never imagine. She lives in a world far from the glitter she once knew. She and Joe founded an organization called HaitiChildren that's now grown to give long-term help to more than five thousand people annually. The organization provides feeding programs, clean-water programs, medical care, schools, and orphanages in Haiti and specializes in helping the most vulnerable and destitute segment of the population: abandoned and abused children, many of them with special needs.

For all Susie's troubles, the former model has contracted lice, scabies, mange, and dengue fever and been treated for encephalitis. In her first eighteen months in the most dangerous areas of Haiti, Susie saw twelve children shot and killed by gang violence. In the years since then, she's lost many people she's worked with, helped, cared for, loved, and adored.

Every time she closes the lid of a coffin, she first slips a note inside. The note reads, "In this world, you were loved."

Susie and Joe draw no salaries for their work with HaitiChildren, and they've contributed more than $1 million of their own money to the organization. They don't consider it a charity. It's an organization that empowers people. Some two hundred Haitian nationals work for HaitiChildren, and Susie and Joe want to see the nation become 100 percent independent and sustainable. They know it's possible someday because they see hope and action in the people they meet.

And Susie's life has become rich because she knows she's not only helping others, she's helping herself. She's gripped by these children in pain because she knows firsthand what childhood pain feels like, and she wants it to stop—for one, then another, then another. In helping others, she describes how she's found what she never found by living the high life. Her emptiness is now filled. She's finally helping the little girl from Alabama who was once so deeply hurt herself.

"People ask me all the time if it was difficult to start HaitiChildren," she says. "No, it wasn't difficult. People are hungry. That can be easily solved. People need clean water to drink. That's not an insurmountable problem. Abandoned babies need to be taken care of. Children need to be educated. Medical care needs to be given. These are all obstacles that can be overcome. Sure, I was naive when I first started. I had no idea what I was getting myself into, but helping people seemed like such a piece of cake in my head. How did I start? I just started. I went to Haiti and talked with people. I kept going back and developed contacts in Haiti and met the heads of gangs in Cité Soleil and let them take ownership of what I did. I raised funds back in Aspen and constantly kept telling the story of what I encountered in Haiti. The rest is history."

5

The Necessity of Giving Back

(SHARLEE AND SAMPSON)

W e love the stories of Deval Patrick and Susan Scott Krabacher, because both show inspiring people who give back.

Deval overcame many obstacles in his childhood years and then as an adult entered a life of public service. As a boy and teen, he learned the power of a strong community from his schools and church, and then he relied on this power to become a leader who could positively impact many other people and help hold the city of Boston together during a time of crisis.

Susie self-admittedly didn't have her life together, yet she started to give *anyway*—and the giving actually helped heal her. She describes her life in Aspen in 1994 as an unfulfilled time. Although she had money and security and even love, her inner void and unhealed wounds were still there. Similarly, we might think we're not in a position to give back, but Susie's story shows that giving, *even while we are in a position of growth and development*, is actually part of the process. By helping others, Susie was able to help herself.

This understanding is so key for all of us. The action of altruism is something we all need to discover and develop in our own lives. People with the Stuff give back to others, but giving doesn't happen only after success is in the bag. When we discover and develop the Stuff, we learn to give all along the way, through the ups and downs of our own journey to success, both when we have much to give and when we have little to give. We become people with giving hearts.

The research is clear: we may worry that giving will drag us down, but the opposite is true. Giving back boosts our happiness, refreshes us, and gives us a shot in the arm to carry on. Not only is giving a good thing to do *after* we overcome obstacles—it's a good thing to do *in the process of* overcoming obstacles. The more we help others, the happier and more resilient we become. The more value we create for others, the more value we assign to ourselves; in other words, giving enhances our self-esteem and boosts our sense of purpose.[3]

And a sense of purpose is pure fuel.

Stephen Post of the Department of Bioethics at Case Western Reserve University in Ohio compiled a study with the telling title "Altruism, Happiness, and Health: It's Good to Be Good." He found that "a strong correlation exists between the well-being, happiness, health, and longevity of people who are emotionally and behaviorally compassionate."[4] As long as people are not overloaded with giving tasks, givers actually live longer. It works like this: The giving that people do out of kindness and charitable impulses produces positive emotions. Those emotions do wonderful things within our bodies. In a famous study in the 1990s, psychologists were intrigued by the neurological impacts of people who give back. They studied nuns and Alzheimer's disease, and the nuns who displayed a high degree of positive emotion lived on average a decade longer than others in the study and were able to ward off dementia more effectively.[5]

Positive emotions actually get down to work at the cellular level to give us longer life. Studies show that the more positive emotions we have, the healthier our DNA will be and the longer our cells will live—giving us as much as an entire decade more of life.[6] It's much harder to get caught up in the stressful emotions of sadness, fear, anxiety, and hostility if we're expressing love and care to other people.[7]

6
———

A Sense of Purpose Is Pure Fuel

Charlee explains: Some people think that the only way they can give back is financially, but giving back is not just about money. Giving back is about discovering what you are passionate about, what you enjoy, and what your gifts are—and then living in light of helping others succeed with your gifts and passions.

Ask yourself: What's the best way I can help others? Maybe it's volunteering at your local library or being a mentor or volunteer coach for a kids' baseball team. We all have something to give, and the decision of how best to initiate the process is up to each person.

The ability to give is something dear to both Sampson and me, and it's brought another level of fulfillment to our lives as well as to the lives of the students we help in our foundations. Since its inception in 2000, the Three Doctors Foundation has proved successful in many ways, and in a previous chapter, you heard what Sampson's foundation does to mentor students and provide free health initiatives—programs that continue today. Another initiative helps students learn how to use positive peer pressure and form their own "pacts."

Recently, a group of four young high school students in Alabama, inspired by Sampson, George, and Rameck, made their own pact to hold one another accountable and help one another succeed. The pact held true; all four subsequently received full-ride scholarships, three to the University of Alabama and one to Auburn University.

Four more youths have since joined the same pact. Sampson's organization brought all eight students to New Jersey to honor them at the Three Doctors' annual fund-raiser.

In the organization I lead, the Turn 2 Foundation, we've been working since 1996 to help youth avoid drug and alcohol addiction and "Turn 2" healthy lifestyles. We also help develop a new generation of leaders by encouraging mentoring and community service and rewarding academic and behavioral excellence. And the results have proved fruitful.

One of our core programs is Jeter's Leaders. We studied 228 of the students who'd been in our program, all of whom had gone on to graduate from the program. The 228 students represented sixteen years of programming. When they enter our program, more than eight out of ten students are facing significant risk factors at home, in peer groups, or at school.[8] As we work with our students, we help them develop a sense of responsibility to themselves, their families, their schools, and their communities—in great part by giving back. Among other things, they give back through mentoring, role modeling, peer-to-peer counseling, and community service programs. We're proud that in the past twelve years, 100 percent of our participants have graduated from high school and gone to college—and even more rewarding is to see that more than 75 percent of Jeter's Leaders report experiencing significant transformational benefits. They're more confident and resilient, which helps them do better in school, prepare for success in college and careers, and act as ambassadors and role models in the community.

Ultimately, we help our students become high achievers and discover who they're destined to become. We give our students a sense of purpose—and the stats don't lie: since 1996, 87 percent of Jeter's Leaders alumni have immediately enrolled in postsecondary education—significantly higher than the national average of 66 percent—and 91 percent of alumni dedicate their time to volunteering, compared to a national average of only 25 percent.[9]

Let's face it: none of us lives successfully on our own. We all receive help. And when we in turn help others, we're involved in shaping their vision of what it means to give back. This creates a ripple effect. By paying it forward, the ripples keep spreading. Using the Stuff means we are givers—and the giving helps us as much as it helps others.

All we need to do now is put together a plan of action.

You've Already Got What It Takes

1

———

Take One Step Forward—Right Now, Today

(SHARLEE AND SAMPSON)

What will you do today, as soon as you finish this book? We hope, very simply, that you will take one positive step toward your goal. Start by doing one thing—right now, today—that leads toward overcoming your obstacle and living your maximized life.

Make that phone call.

Fill out that application.

Start that conversation.

Apply for that class.

Send that email.

Schedule that appointment.

Get up and go for a walk.

Choose to hope.

Create your mantra.

Catch your negative chatter and reframe it.

Decide you will be open to being inspired.

Do whatever is necessary to step toward your goal. Make one decision that brings you closer to your maximized life. We don't presume that the one thing you do today will completely change your life or help you entirely overcome your obstacle or reach your goal. Yet that one step can be the most important step of your journey. That one step is the spark that will lead to the bonfire of good things to come. Just launch!

We have never intended to offer you a magic formula or a one-size-fits-all plan for overcoming obstacles. As we said in the beginning, life is too nuanced and messy for that, and we respect your ability to engage in an honest journey of discovery for yourself. Our hope all along has been that you will observe, interpret, and apply the principles shown in this book so you can discover and develop the Stuff within yourself—and then use the Stuff not only to face and overcome life's challenges but also to take advantage of life's many opportunities. Throughout the pages of this book, we've tried to highlight some tools to help you live your absolutely best possible life—not a life where you're stuck in a rut or held back by fear, but a life where you're entering into all the good opportunities offered by your destiny.

As we've seen, you already have the Stuff within you—the grittiness, resilience, and unshakable inner strength that all people are born with. Yet the Stuff lies latent and untapped within too many of us. Our inner engines must be started, fine-tuned, and regularly fed fuel. That's what our examination of the elements of the Stuff has been about. We must hit a gong that's already ringing—none of the participants described themselves as "experts" in overcoming obstacles, and all of them exhibited these traits largely without being aware of them. This is simply another indication that these traits are inherent. We all have the Stuff.

When we personally started this journey, we started it simply as a conversation on an airplane. We went looking for a thing that we didn't even have a name for at first. We traveled the nation, had a lot of fun moments along the way, dug into research, and ended up meeting some extraordinary "ordinary" people whose stories blew us away. Happily, we connected immediately with the people we spoke with, and it felt as though we'd known them for years. It was refreshing and exciting to speak the common language of overcoming challenges. We met people just like you and us, people who have chosen to hope, created motivational statements, launched, developed their teams, pushed their limits, refused to give in to fear, refocused their rage, leaned into hard work, stayed open to unforeseen possibilities, and embraced the power of giving. Our lives were changed in this process, too. As we put these last few pages of thoughts down on paper, we feel inspired, grateful, and motivated to keep pressing forward with our own goals. We find ourselves overflowing with ideas we want to share, with future projects we want to create and implement, with steps of personal and professional growth we want to take. We're excited for the next step in our own journeys, and we want to keep growing as individuals and helping other people wherever we can.

We hope you're feeling similarly empowered in your own life. By using the Stuff, you can resolve to go forward. Facing challenges won't be easy. But the challenges in front of you now do not need to become your final destiny. Great opportunities await, and we trust by now you've seen in the lives of others and in our discussions the skills and actions you need to move forward in your own journey. You can develop the Stuff for yourself, then pull out the Stuff and use it for greater strength and benefit whenever you wish.

The power and the beauty of the Stuff is that it's not something that only a few people have. This is not a message that's confined to a certain age group or demographic. The Stuff is for everybody, everywhere. Each person can harness the strength that's already inside of him or her. Why? Because the Stuff is a universal language. We hope you've noticed that there is a strong diversity of voices in this book and that the people featured are from different races, religions, socioeconomic levels, skill sets, and orientations. Nobody is exactly the same, and everybody has a different past, present, and future. Yet we are all joined together by the elements of the Stuff. And we all use the Stuff in different ways. The way you use your Stuff will look different from how we use the Stuff, so our big encouragement for you is to figure out how the Stuff works best for you.

You might start your journey by gathering your team around you. Or you might dig deeper into pushing limits in ways other people don't. You might be motivated more by your mantra, you might lean into hope more than someone else, or you might mix up the sequence of any of the elements so they fit your life best. That's the beauty of this journey: your challenges and successes won't look exactly like anyone else's, and that's all okay. The individuality of each person's journey is part of what makes the Stuff so amazing.

Throughout our journey we've seen this diversity and uniqueness lived out. As we put this book together, both of us found we were taking this journey in more ways than one. We were creating this book by interviewing people and doing new research, and much of the process and content was new to us. We were reliving and codifying our own personal stories and experiences, recognizing and naming the traits and actions we'd used to overcome obstacles. We were also remembering and gleaning the findings from our teaching and work over the past several years—and we found that much of that content related to the Stuff, too. Everything came together synergistically. The research and stories correlated with many of our past seminars and work. We found we'd actually been teaching various components of the Stuff for years, even though we didn't have a name for it at first. For instance, teamwork is a huge part of the Turn 2 Foundation's teaching, and altruism is a huge part of Sampson's lectures.

During our personal journeys, we have seen results of the Stuff lived out in other people's lives in many different and unique ways:

- We learned about a retiree who was able to get onto an airplane and fly across the country to attend the funeral of his beloved sister. That might sound like a straightforward thing to do, but it had been many years since he'd flown. He had hip problems and heart problems, and prior to the trip he had been concerned that he wouldn't be able to sleep very well in a hotel room in the destination city. But after hearing some of the stories we featured in this book, he was able to summon the fortitude within himself and take the trip he very much wanted to. As he said afterward, "Hey, Sean Swarner was able to climb Mount Everest with only one functioning lung. When I heard about that, I told myself I could take this trip."

- A woman we know graduated from college as a psychology major even though her real passions were sports and fashion. She landed a coveted job at ESPN—the dream job of so many people—and thrived there, even though she felt deep within herself that she wasn't growing the way she knew she should. So at a time when the job market was tight, and against the advice of those who knew her well, she quit her job and launched out on her own. She started a sports, fashion, and culture blog and began teaching college courses on sports marketing, participating in numerous panel discussions, and hosting seminars to help others who were interested in the field. For a while the going was extremely difficult. Money was tight, and she pruned away all the spending she could. Yet she stuck with her dream and succeeded. Today her blog and career are a success, and she's being pursued by major companies, asking her to work for them. Most important, she's fulfilled and happy. We're in awe that she walked away from a dream job in order to pursue what she truly wanted to do. That's the power of the Stuff.

- A teenage boy was doing drugs and failing high school. He was moody and reclusive, and all he wanted to do was sleep. At age sixteen, he was arrested for drug possession. But while still in high school, he entered the Derek Jeter Academy at Phoenix House, a teen rehabilitation facility in Tampa, Florida. He succeeded, beat his addictions, and eventually won a college scholarship. He's now starting his studies at the University of Central Florida, looking forward to a bright future.

- A woman always wanted to be a doctor but didn't think she had what it took. She studied a different academic field in college and finished her degree but knew something in her life was still unresolved. She attended a panel where Sampson spoke and was inspired to go after her dream. She went back to college and took all the prerequisite courses for medical school. With those completed, she applied to medical schools but didn't get accepted. So she applied internationally and was accepted by a Cuban medical school. She didn't know any Spanish and didn't know the Cuban culture, but she packed up anyway and moved to Cuba. On her first day there, she started medical and language studies at the same time—an extremely difficult thing to do, as medical studies use virtually another entire language in and of themselves. She finished medical school five years later and came back to the United States to begin her residency, which she wanted to do in emergency medicine, one of the top three most competitive residencies to get into. Her medical studies in Cuba proved to have been robust, and she beat the odds to land a residency in emergency medicine in the United States. Today she's a practicing physician. She achieved her goal out of hope, sheer will, and persistence. She created her own pathway, and it worked for her.

- A middle-aged woman in a wheelchair was able to learn how to drive a car with hand controls. She'd been in a wheelchair since age twenty and had convinced herself that people in wheelchairs don't drive. Yet when she heard of the elements in this book, she knew that her initial choice wasn't her final destiny. She learned to drive again and said her life has taken on greater independence, thanks to her new ability to get around by herself.

That's only a fraction of many positive results we've seen. How will your success story read?

2
_____

How Overcoming Obstacles Can Bring About Growth

We don't know what you're going through. Maybe you're a high school or college student and looking to define the rest of your life. Maybe you're a millennial or middle-aged adult and looking to leave a rough relationship, or you want a new career. Maybe you're in your final quarter of life and looking for a new sense of purpose. Or perhaps you are undergoing a season of trauma, an extremely difficult and devastating time of life. Maybe the obstacle you're facing seems overwhelming or even insurmountable. Maybe it seems as though you can't go forward. Please draw your team around you. Don't walk the road alone. Keep hoping, keep persevering, keep pressing forward!

While researching this book, we came across encouraging studies on posttraumatic growth (PTG).[1] Their conclusions are basically that people can be changed by their struggles in good ways[2]—and this is a theme that's been underscored and developed all throughout this book. The hopeful news is that up to 90 percent of the people studied[3,4] reported positive outcomes. Thanks to their struggles, they now enjoy some or all of the following benefits:

- A greater appreciation of life

- Closer relationships

- An awareness of new possibilities

- Increased personal strength

- Positive spiritual changes[5]

That's a big encouragement for all of us not to give up. What makes the difference? Essentially, the change in outcomes boils down to a positive mind-set—although it's a bit more nuanced, which we hope we've explained in previous chapters. If you can reevaluate a situation after experiencing trauma, look past the pain, and find the positive elements of the experience, you are better positioned to grow from it. That doesn't mean you rewrite your history, make up things that never happened, or merely put a happy spin on your situation.

Rather, you reinterpret the facts in light of strategic positivity. You look for possible good to come from a situation, then make changes and grow from there.[6] That's how obstacles can be redefined and re-purposed so they produce a positive outcome. The obstacles themselves don't need to be your final destiny. You never need to be stuck.

Consider any of the people featured in this book, and you'll find this switch to be evident. Conventional wisdom and stereotypes would say that Sean Swarner should be dead from cancer, Mindee Hardin should be bankrupt—or at the very least angry and bitter because of the raw business deal she received—and Susan Scott Krabacher should be stymied by her childhood abuse.

We might think that burn victim John O'Leary would pine for the life he might have had or that Rich Ruffalo would have long since quit teaching and engaging in sports because he went blind or that the O'Neill family would have simply accepted their daughter's difficult diagnosis or that Traci Micheline would be locked in grief.

From the type of abuse Wess Stafford had received as a boy, nobody would blink if he'd ended up in jail. Debra Peppers might have stayed an addict. Austin Hatch might never have walked or played basketball again. Christine Magnus Moore might have remained closed off from the world. Martha Hawkins might still be in a mental hospital. Mercy Alexander might be bitter and angry. Ali Stroker could have told herself that people in wheelchairs don't appear on Broadway. And Deval Patrick could easily have joined a street gang rather than pushing on to become the first African American governor of Massachusetts.

Yet today all the people featured in this book are doing well, and their lives have been redefined in positive ways by the obstacles they overcame and the trauma they endured.

Sean's motivation statement, *"This* is the best day ever," came about only *because* he knew firsthand the fragility of life.

Mindee Hardin developed a more balanced life and a closer relationship with her children *after* and *because of* experiencing the pain of a collapsed business and a failed marriage.

Susan Scott Krabacher was empowered to help impoverished Haitian children because *she knew firsthand* what it felt like to suffer as a child.

And on and on and on and on. All these people redefined what was possible for them. Life initially dealt them a bad hand, but they discarded the cards they could, built a workable hand, and went on to win. That's why we told you their stories. We hope that we've shed light on the fact that if everyone lived in this space, drawing on the Stuff daily, all our lives would be different. Our workplaces would be different. Our homes would be different. Our communities would be different. People everywhere would be more accomplished and more fulfilled. In a word—happier.

We wanted to show you that nobody needs to settle for less or accept defeat. Circumstances can indeed be changed, and people can move past current situations. We are all able to live our maximized lives. Sure, we will all be faced with life situations that are unexpected, uncontrollable, and unimaginable. We may be faced with something we aren't expecting that rocks us to our core. The outward circumstances of some situations won't change. That's true. But our attitudes, our perspectives, how we live in light of the situations that come our way, and in many cases the outcomes—these are what can be changed.

One way we can sift through the practical outworking of this principle is shown in the writings of the philosopher Reinhold

Niebuhr and adopted as the mantra of Alcoholics Anonymous: "God, grant me the serenity to accept the things I cannot change, the courage to change the things I can, and the wisdom to know the difference."[7] May all of us learn to do this as we continue to journey forward.

3
—————

Never Give Up

A legend is told about a hearty band of travelers on a long journey. As they headed toward their destiny, they came to a huge mountain. The massive obstacle, the mightiest snowcapped peak in the whole mountain range, blocked their way. They tried hiking up the mountain, but the way was too steep; they couldn't go over it. They looked for an alternate route to take around it, but the other possible routes were too long. Meanwhile, the mountain threw every kind of storm at them until at last they had to retreat.

There, near the base of the mountain, they sat in silence for a day and a night, feeling stymied by their obstacle, heartbroken.

They felt as though *the mountain had won.*

But as they sat there, the weary band made an important discovery: the ground all around them was surprisingly pliable.

They started digging, and then dug some more. They dug a hole wide enough to fit a person through, and kept digging. They brought in beams to shore up a tunnel. As they kept digging, they discovered the remnants of another tunnel that had been built by some travelers before them, which they followed for a while. They kept digging and going forward. Their quest took hope and teamwork and launching and turning a devastating negative into a positive and a lot of hard work. In time they emerged on the other side of the mountain—the victors, stronger and better for the challenge. They could move forward with their journey and complete their quest. And that's your encouragement, too: *Your mountain doesn't need to win!*

You might try and not succeed at first. You might need to sit in silence at the base of your mountain for a time, contemplating what move to make next. You might need to go under your mountain. You might need to go over it or around it or tunnel through it. And the victory most likely won't happen instantly. But in the end you'll succeed, because you have the Stuff within you, and now you've seen how it can be discovered, developed, and applied.

Ask yourself: Why do we encourage you to take simply *one step* forward today? Why not a full leap that would get you to the goal right now?

It's because the process of tapping into the Stuff can be learned, but it *can't be hurried.* Yes, we encourage you to press forward with all you have, but we also encourage you to be gracious with yourself. Recognize that significant change toward good seldom happens overnight. This knowledge helps take the pressure off. It lets us breathe as we wrestle with our obstacle. It allows us to be patient with ourselves. We can relax even, grieve our losses if needed, and feel our pain as we move on toward our growth and opportunity.

Your invitation now is to use the Stuff in your own life—in big ways, in small ways, in good ways, in mighty ways, in considerate ways. Use it individually, make it your own. Use the Stuff to live your maximized life, and use the Stuff to help others reach their maximized life, too. Use the Stuff to reach goals, to overcome fears, to get unstuck, to help and heal, to promote empathy, kindness, compassion, confidence, and strength. Live the Stuff, love the Stuff, breathe the Stuff, ingest the Stuff, trust the process of the Stuff—and now go out and blaze your path forward.

Use the Stuff to change this world for the better.

And never give up.

For more information about our participants, see:

Mindee Hardin
juiceboxconsulting.com

Martha Hawkins
marthasplacebuffet.com

Susan Scott Krabacher
haitichildren.org

Christine Magnus Moore
bothsidesofthebedside.com

John O'Leary
johnolearyinspires.com

Glenn and Cara O'Neill
curesff.org

Debra Peppers
pepperseed.org

Rich Ruffalo
richruffalo.com

Wess Stafford
compassion.com

Ali Stroker
alistroker.com

Sean Swarner
seanswarner.com

Acknowledgments

First of all, we would like to thank Marcus Brotherton, our amazing collaborator on this project. Your unique ability to capture the pure essence of each story is truly inspiring to witness. Thank you to Derek Jeter and Jeter Publishing for believing in our vision and giving us the opportunity to share these amazing stories of triumph and inspiration. Thank you to Casey Close, Maureen Cavanagh, Gary Hoenig, and Alana Segars for believing in the initial project we brought to you almost three years ago. Your encouragement and genuine excitement for this book are what solidified our passion to push forward. Thank you to David Oxfeld and Stirling Eads for all your support, hard work, and feedback.

Thank you to Dr. Charles Jeter, Dr. Evelyn Montañez, Diane Marquess, and Dr. Dennis Hunyadi, our amazing group of psychologists and social workers who lent their expertise to the project. It was important to us that the information we provided to our readers was not only inspiring but also well researched, and your commitment and dedication made that possible.

To our agents at Aevitas Creative Management, Todd Shuster, Jenn Gates, and Laura Nolan. Thank you for believing in this vision from day one and helping us stay true to our overall mission while offering much-needed guidance along the way. We want to thank Simon & Schuster, Gallery Books, Jennifer Bergstrom, Louise Burke, our editor Adam Wilson, Jennifer Robinson, Liz Perl, and Laura Waters for all your dedication to making this book come to fruition and for always making our input and questions a priority as we moved through this process. We appreciate the platform you have provided to us so the world can experience *the Stuff*.

Thank you to our public-relations and marketing team, Lori van Arsdale and Rebecca Horn, for helping us create The Stuff Movement and spread the word to people everywhere.

A very special thank-you to our scheduler, travel agent, photographer, videographer, joke teller, and "fixer," Johanna Desrosiers, who at times wanted to strangle both of us but handled all logistics like a champ and with a smile on her face. Your hard work did not go unnoticed, and we appreciate you keeping us in line and dealing with us while we went on the road to meet all the participants in this book.

There were so many people who assisted us along the way, and without them this book would not be what it is today. Thank you to Terry Prince, Jaymee Messler, Sam Maller, Tom Booth, Dennis Chominsky, Jenn Allocco, and Lemar Charles. For those of you we may not have named, please know we hold you close in our hearts and pray you understand what you mean to us. Without your support, thoughts, and presence, this project would not have been possible.

Thank you to everyone who has joined The Stuff Movement and shared your stories of triumph and overcoming. In doing so, you have allowed the world to be inspired by your journey and you give hope to so many others.

Last, but definitely not least, we would like to thank all of those who lent their story to this book. Without you, there would be no book. We are very humbled that you have trusted us to tell your amazing stories and honored to have had the opportunity to meet and learn from each of you and your families. We hope that we have done your story justice and that we will help you on your mission to impact the lives of countless others who will be just as inspired by your Stuff as we are. THANK YOU!

Sharlee's Personal Acknowledgments

First and foremost, I'd like to thank my son, Jalen. Mommy is so proud and blessed to have you!!! You have made motherhood so easy. You allowed me to work late and still come home to your smiling, happy face. You are my reason for absolutely everything. I love you!

I would like to thank all of those who worked so hard to make this project come to fruition and those individuals who trusted us with their stories. Thank you for your time and for believing in our vision.

To my coauthor, Sampson, thanks for trusting me enough to work on such an amazing movement and book project together. You've dedicated your life to inspiring and helping others, especially young people, which is what I most admire about you. Knowing you over the years has only driven me to want to do more and more. For the record, I told you from day one that I'd have your back and do everything in my power to get this message out there. Hate to say I told ya so! Thanks for the laughter and the talks of encouragement. Till the wheels fall off, Sammy . . . I had to call you that one time. I am sorry!

To my dad, this book would not have been possible if it wasn't for you. You read every single word along the way, offering countless hours of your time to give advice, input, and encouragement. You tell me you are proud of me almost every single day, and that alone has had such an amazing impact on my life. You always lift me up but are more than willing to kick me in the butt when I need it most, and for that I am forever grateful. You are my sounding board, my shoulder, my counselor (and I know that is the toughest job, especially when I believe I am the one with the PhD), my mentor, my friend, and the love of my life. I will always strive to make you proud.

To my mom, the Queen of our Castle, I love you! Thank you for all the advice, love, encouragement, and honesty over the years. Thanks for giving me the encouragement I needed to commit to a book like this and for always supporting me and making sure I always had someone to turn to when I needed it. You, too, spent late nights reading every chapter, and for this I thank you! Thanks for telling me when I had booked the wrong flights for Sampson and myself, whether it was the wrong airport or the wrong time—you always knew how to let me know it was probably my fault we were in a predicament. Without you, Lola, my participation in this book would not have been possible.

Derek, my best friend and brother, I would need an entire book to express my appreciation for you. Thanks for believing in me and for always having my back. You always made sure that I had a big brother to look up to who was worthy of emulation. Mostly, I thank you for making me work for everything I've accomplished in my life. You gave me many opportunities but made me work for everything, allowing me to discover what I am truly capable of. Thank you for trusting me, holding me accountable, making fun of me, loving me, and being the best brother in the entire world. I love you, and I thank you from the bottom of my heart! To my sister-in-law, Hannah, and my beautiful, perfect niece, Bella Raine, I love you both!

To G'Ma, who always had a home filled with children, love, and laughter. Your faith and love have been an example to all those you've come in contact with. To my late grandfather, Sonny, thank you for teaching me the true meaning of hard work and tough love. You are truly missed.

To my grandmother Lugenia Jeter, whom I never had the pleasure of meeting. Please know that your presence was always a part of my life because my dad always told me stories about you. I hope that my mission to help others has made you proud. And I only hope to one day have the impact on my son's life that you have had on yours.

Charmine, you are a true gift from God. Without you, I would not have been able to work late, travel, focus on this book, and KNOW that my son was being cared for like he is one of your own. Your spirit is contagious, and your presence allowed me to accomplish this goal. For this, I thank you, and I promise, Charmine, "I am just getting on the Brooklyn Bridge and will be home in a few minutes!"

To my baby cousin Catherine for always having my back and helping me out when I needed it. To Julie, thank you for everything. I will always be your Princess! To Aunt Fran for always telling me that because I am a math major, I am brilliant and that only you, Jalen, and I can understand some of the complexities of this mathematical world. To Aunt Dimp, thank you for giving me my attitude and the belief that I am usually right about just about everything, and when I am wrong, it's okay, as long as I look cute doing it! To my friend Kimmy, who showed me that it's possible to juggle motherhood, an amazing career, and being a wife (I'm still working on that one, though). You inspire me! To Preem, thanks for always holding me down and being a great father to our son.

To my oncologist, Dr. Stephen Nimer, I thank you for telling my parents that I was capable of handling treatments and college. You believed in my abilities, even before I did. For this, I will forever be in debt to you!

To Britney Mayfield and Nneka Frye. While I was going through treatments, you were my family, my rocks, and my shoulders while at

Spelman College. Thanks for studying with me, staying up late with me, hanging with me when everyone else was having fun. You two never ever left my side, and for this I'll always hold you close to my heart. To Mariah, who stayed by my side throughout my treatment, checking on me, supporting me, and being the sister I so needed through my tough times. You helped me get through the most difficult stage of my life, and I will never forget that. Shana Renee, Melissa Feliciano, Vince McMillon, Abbie Maikoski, Tre' Fellings, Angie Henry, and all my friends who supported me through my battle with cancer and who hung out with me at a time when I know it wasn't exciting, you know who you are. I thank you.

To Deborah Tymon, who was such an amazing friend and role model to me over the years. To my big brother, Gerald Williams, just know that I LOVE YOU! And to Lisa Evers, Doug Biro, Roxanne Wilder, Alana Segars, Caitlin Brinkman, Danielle Rich, Nina Greenberg, Chick Lee, Pete Falcone, Dede Agar, Mike Evans, James Cruz, Amber Sabathia, and all of you who have been such amazing friends and supporters along the way, please know you are in my heart. I appreciate you and I thank you!

To my Turn 2 Foundation staff—the hardest-working staff I know—thank you for stepping up, allowing me to take the time to write this book. And to my Jeter's Leaders and Alumni, I am so proud of all of you and your mission to promote social change and be role models in your community. You are a true example of the Stuff at its finest.

Keep on pushin'!

—Sharlee

Sampson's Personal Acknowledgments

The thought of this book was sparked from a conversation—30,000 feet high in the air—with my friend and coauthor, Sharlee Jeter. As we returned home from a talk for the Turn 2 Foundation baseball clinic, who would have thought the journey to the Stuff and The Stuff Movement would have been born. God indeed is the greatest, and to him goes the glory. Every day I am blessed and thankful for life. To the readers of this book, I am encouraged and hopeful you will find the message to be one that resonates within you, and that you feel the same inspiration and sense of discovery I felt as I listened to the stories shared.

To our Stuff team, again I say thank you for your time, belief, and commitment to this project. Countless hours in meetings, on the phone, and emailing have resulted in something I hope will inspire so many as it has inspired me.

We owe endless thanks to every person who shared their story. Thank you for entrusting us with your testimony and sharing your inspiration to all readers. It is my hope for those who read your story that they too will find the power and courage in your words as well as the same sense of unveiling the Stuff within them.

To my family and friends, without you life's meaning would be called into question. Thank you for loving, supporting, and being a constant force in my world. Because of you, I am a better person. To my mother, you have always been the rock in my world. Words could never express the magnitude of love and appreciation I have for you. Your infectious testimony, strength, and relentless attitude toward life have given me the wind underneath my wings to challenge myself to rise higher than ever dreamt possible. Even now, at this stage of life, I look for your approval and acceptance in all I do. To Melissa and our two boys, Jaxson and Luke, thank you three for being my heart and soul. Your presence gives meaning to my every day and delivers inner peace and clarity to life. My siblings, Kenny, Rose, Andre, and Carlton, and my uncles, aunts, nieces, nephews, cousins, and family, I love you all. Thank you for your unwavering support. I live for special moments and the holidays because I know we will once again gather and spend time with one another. To my sister Fellease in heaven, I think about you and miss you every day. To my father, Kenneth Davis, I wish you were here to meet your grandkids. I hope I am making you proud. I miss you, Pop. To Betty, Jay, and Angela, thank you for always being there and being a presence in our lives.

To my circle of friends, mentors, and relatives, I say thank you. I feel bad for beginning to name you for fear of leaving many out, but to Carla Dickson, Dr. Linda Hsu, Dr. Duane Dyson, Dr. Marc Borenstein, Dr. Nathan Doctry, Dr. Lee Leak, Darrell Terry, Camille, Reggie Brown, Sabu, Dax, Nnamdi, Melba, Will, Lawrence, Al-Tereek, Serron, Hassan, Rabu, Maria, Derrick, Carole Jackson, Mary Ann, Frankie, Thelma, Cynthia, Lisa, Clarise, Trina, Renee, Valerie, Angelo, Edwin, Orlando, Cee, Mrs. Richardson, Melanie, Stephen and Paul, thank you for shaping my world.

Dr. Rameck Hunt and Dr. George Jenkins, my brothers, who together are the Three Doctors. Our pact began in high school and has not only transformed *our* lives but helped to inspire so many others. I am eternally grateful to have you in my life and thankful to be on this journey together. To all who have embraced our pact, I say thank you. It is you who inspire us, and we are honored and privileged to be able to spread the message of hope, inspiration, education, mentoring, health, and leadership. To the hundreds of high schools, colleges, graduate programs, special groups, community programs, and corporations that I have had the honor to address, I want to thank you for embracing our message. Windy White, your leadership and dedication have allowed our dream of the Three Doctors Foundation to remain alive and well. Thank you for your service. To Donna, Yolanda Blaize, Gail, Sherifa, Maurice, Lloyd, Nicholl, Janell, Carla, Yolanda Mendez, and Michelle, I thank each of you for your volunteerism over the years in elevating the foundation to serve its purpose in giving back. Your dedication to philanthropy is something to marvel at and aspire to duplicate. Special thanks to Jim Sinegal, Art Jackson, Jim Craigie, and Tracee Walls for your consistent support of the Three Doctors Foundation.

To my sister, coauthor, and friend, Sharlee Jeter, thank you for sharing in the vision and putting so much energy, effort, belief, and dedication into this book. You have quarterbacked this project from the beginning and have been the engine to keep it moving. I imagine that your efforts to touch lives and your vigilance in giving back can be exhausting at times, but I've yet to see you waver or give in. You are the Stuff, as we all are, and it is a joy to witness your ability to unknowingly wear it proudly and boldly in your everyday world. To your family, Dr. and Mrs. Jeter, Derek, Hannah, and circle of relatives and friends, thank you for the constant support in helping to bring this project to life. Your presence and focus on excellence don't go unnoticed.

To Cindy Speigel, Lisa Frazier Page, Joann Davis, Linda Lowenthal, and my extended literary family, thank you for always believing and helping to shape my messages in an engaging and powerful narrative. Your expertise always inspires me to aim higher in delivering the best. Thank you!

Lastly, there are many more to whom I am forever indebted, those who have stood with me throughout this journey. I am lucky to call you friend, teacher, mentor, and family. I am thankful to all of you. And please forgive me if I failed to mention you, but do know I hold you in my heart and hope you know what you mean to me.

Let's all tap in and live our Stuff!

—Sampson

Notes

CHAPTER **ONE**

The Question Everybody Asks

1   H. Crichton-Miller, "Fortitude in War," *Mental Health* 1, no. 3 (July 1940): 65–69.

2   James Clear, "The Science of Developing Mental Toughness in Your Health, Work, and Life," http://jamesclear.com /mental-toughness.

CHAPTER **TWO**

Choose to Hope

1   Margarita Tartakovsky, review of Shane J. Lopez, *Making Hope Happen: Create the Future You Want for Yourself and Others* (New York: Simon & Schuster, 2013), 21, https://psychcentral.com /blog/archives/2013/03/21/the-psychology-of-hope.

2   Dale Archer, "The Power of Hope—Reading Between the (Head) Lines," *Psychology Today*, July 31, 2013, https://www.psychology today.com/blog/reading-between-the-headlines/201307 /the-power-hope.

3 Liz Day, Katie Hanson, John Maltby, Carmel Proctor, and Alex Wood, "Hope Uniquely Predicts Objective Achievement Above Intelligence, Personality, and Previous Academic Achievement," *Journal of Research in Personality* 44, no. 4 (August 2010): 550–53, http://www.sciencedirect.com/science/article/pii/S00926566 1000067X.

4 Kirsten Weir, "Mission Impossible," *Science Watch* 44, no. 9 (October 2013): 42, http://www.apa.org/monitor/2013/10 /mission-impossible.aspx.

5 Lopez, *Making Hope Happen.*

6 Susie S. Sympson, "Rediscovering Hope: Understanding and Working with Survivors of Trauma," in C. R. Snyder, ed., *Handbook of Hope: Theory, Measures and Applications* (San Diego: Academic Press, 2000), 3–21 (or see http://www.sciencedirect.com /science/article/pii/B9780126540505500038).

CHAPTER **THREE**

Forge Your Motivation Statement

1 Travis Mills, *Tough as They Come* (New York: Convergent Books, 2015), 218.

2 Phil Hansen, *Embrace the Shake*, TED 2013, filmed February 2013, https://www.ted.com/talks/phil_hansen_embrace_the_shake.

3 Derrick Coleman, Jr., *No Excuses: Growing Up Deaf and Achieving My Super Bowl Dreams* (New York: Simon & Schuster, 2015), 248.

4   Winston Churchill, "Blood, Toil, Tears and Sweat," May 13, 1940, http://www.winstonchurchill.org/resources/speeches/1940-the -finest-hour/blood-toil-tears-and-sweat.

5   Winston Churchill, "We Shall Fight on the Beaches," June 4, 1940, http://www.winstonchurchill.org/resources/speeches/1940-the -finest-hour/128-we-shall-fight-on-the-beaches.

6   The Ministry of Information—Britain's Wartime Propaganda Ministry, http://www.ministry-of-information.com/ministry/keep -calm-and-carry-on.

7   Aviva Berkovich-Ohana, Meytal Wilf, Roni Kahana, Amos Arieli, and Rafael Malach, "Repetitive Speech Elicits Widespread Deactivation in the Human Cortex: The 'Mantra' Effect?," *Brain and Behavior* 5, no. 7 (July 2015), http://onlinelibrary.wiley.com/wol1 /doi/10.1002/brb3.346/full.

8   Twyla Tharp, *The Creative Habit* (New York: Simon & Schuster, 2006).

CHAPTER **FOUR**
You Must Launch

1   Gregg Krech, "Taking Action: Finishing the Unfinished (and Unstarted)," March 2017, http://www.todoinstitute.org/taking action.html?gclid=CImTxtrxsNICFZCcfgodUkYPTw.

2   Dan Ariely and Klaus Wertenbroch, "Procrastination, Deadlines, and Performance: Self-Control by Precommitment," *Psychologi-*

cal Science 13, no. 3 (May 1, 2002): 219–24. http://web.mit.edu /ariely/www/MIT/Papers/deadlines.pdf.

3 Ibid.

4 Bruce A. Fernie, Marcantonio M. Spada, Ana V. Nikčević, George A. Georgiou, and Giovanni B. Moneta, "Metacognitive Beliefs About Procrastination: Development and Concurrent Validity of a Self-Report Questionnaire," *Journal of Cognitive Psychotherapy: An International Quarterly* 23, no. 4 (2009): 283–93, DOI: 10.189/0889-8391.23.4.283. http://citeseerx.ist.psu.edu /viewdoc/download?doi=10.1.1.457.1365&rep=rep1&type=pdf.

5 We're thankful to author and speaker Michael Hyatt for his teaching on this topic. See Michael Hyatt, "7 Steps to Launching Your Next Big Project," Your Virtual Mentor, https://michaelhyatt.com /7-steps-to-launching-your-next-big-project.html.

CHAPTER FIVE

Develop Your Team

1 A standard American football field is 1.32 acres, including the end zones: https://www.reference.com/sports-active-lifestyle /many-acres-football-field-a20196b5a2b4acc8.

2 Pando Populus, https://pandopopulus.com/pando-the-tree/.

3 Utah Education Network, "SciTech Now Report on Pando Aspen to Air on UEN-TV Feb. 29," http://www.uen.org/news/article.php ?id=689.

4   John Mathieu, M. Travis Maynard, Tammy Rapp, and Lucy Gilson, "Team Effectiveness 1997–2007: A Review of Recent Advancements and a Glimpse into the Future," *Journal of Management* 34, no. 3 (June 2008): 410–76, DOI: 10.1177/0149206308316061, https://www.researchgate.net/profile/Tammy-Rapp/publication 220041231-Team-Effectiveness-1997-2007-A-Review-of -Recent-Advancements-and-a-Glimpse-into-the-Future/links /55cOce2b08ae092e9667018c.pdf.

5   Denise A. Bonebright, "Perspectives—40 Years of Storming: A Historical Review of Tuckman's Model of Small Group Development," *Human Resource Development International* 13, no. 1 (February 17, 2010): 111–20, http://www.tandfonline.com/doi/ref /10.1080/13678861003589099?scroll=top. (Note: accessing full article requires payment.)

6   Ibid.

7   Brad Sugars, "Building Your Support Team," *Entrepreneur*, July 23, 2007, https://www.entrepreneur.com/article/182012.

8   Lambeth Hochwald, "Family Lives in Self-Imposed Exile in Hopes of Saving Daughter," Yahoo! News, October 29, 2014, https://www.yahoo.com/news/family-lives-in-self-imposed-exile -in-hopes-of-saving-101273473712.html.

CHAPTER **SIX**
Push Your Limits

1 Dennis Mulgannon, answer to "What's the origin of the phrase 'raise the bar'?," September 2, 2015, https://www.quora.com /whats-the-origin-of-the-phrase-raise-the-bar.

2 Auren Hoffman, "Why You Should Never, Ever Stop Challenging Conventional Wisdom," *Inc.*, May 26, 2017, https://www .inc.com/quora/why-you-should-never-ever-stop-challenging -conventional-wisdom.html.

3 Dr. Evelyn Montañez, a psychologist, therapist, and social worker who works with the Turn 2 Foundation and New York–Presbyterian Hospital, noted that a number of people, when facing an obstacle, imagine their present or future without the adversity—and that this technique of visualization can be very beneficial and can further empower people. Visualization can be limited to one season or be ongoing, for however long it is needed.

4 Matt Mayberry, former linebacker with the Chicago Bears and current motivational speaker, says, "All top performers, regardless of profession, know the importance of picturing themselves succeeding in their minds before they actually do in reality." He cites the boxing legend Muhammad Ali, the actor Jim Carrey, and the athlete Michael Jordan as using visualization techniques. "The Extraordinary Power of Visualizing Success," *Entrepreneur*, January 30, 2015, https://www.entrepreneur.com/article/242373.

CHAPTER **SEVEN**

Refuse to Give In to Fear

1 Alan Ewert, "Fear and Anxiety in Environmental Education Programs," *The Journal of Environmental Education* 18, no. 1 (1986): 33–39, DOI: 10.1080/00958964.1986.9942729, http://www .tandfonline.com/doi/abs/10.1080/00958964.1986.9942729.

2 T. Michelle Magyar and Melissa A. Chase, "Psychological Strategies Used by Competitive Gymnasts to Overcome the Fear of Injury," *Technique* 16, no. 10 (November–December 1996), https:// www.usagym.org/pages/home/publications/technique/1996/10 /fear.pdf.

3 Noam Shpancer, "Overcoming Fear: The Only Way Out Is Through," *Psychology Today*, September 20, 2010, https://www .psychologytoday.com/blog/insight-therapy/201009/overcoming -fear-the-only-way-out-is-through.

4 Mark Tyrrell, "5 Sure-fire Ways to Overcome Fear and Anxiety Today," Uncommon Help, http://www.uncommonhelp.me/articles /overcome-fear-and-anxiety/.

CHAPTER **EIGHT**

Focus Your Rage

1 Intense anger, such as Wess Stafford felt when he refused to drop the candle, has been known to cause intense physiological responses, including so-called out-of-body experiences, the "phenomenon whereby the center of consciousness appears to occupy

temporarily a position spatially remote from a body." Psychologists have researched these experiences for more than a hundred years and remain stymied by what actually happens. The British researchers Dr. David Wilde and Dr. C. D. Murray note, "That an out-of-body experience does occur is without doubt. Whether or not the event is a literal separation of something from the physical body or an elaborate hallucination is a matter for further investigation." Harvey J. Irwin and Caroline A. Watt, "Out-of-Body Experiences," in *An Introduction to Parapsychology*, 5th rev. ed. (Jefferson, NC: McFarland Co. Inc., 2007),173–91.

2 Geoffrey B. Stearns, Pamela G. Dunn, Marcus R. Earle, Lois J. Edmund, and Chilton Knudsen, *Mamou—Final Report of the Independent Commission of Inquiry*, November 15, 1997, http://www.mksafetynet.org/content/mamou-final-report-independent-commission-inquiry.

3 Arun Gandhi, *The Gift of Anger: And Other Lessons from My Grandfather Mahatma Gandhi* (New York: Simon & Schuster, 2017), 29–31.

4 Marcelle Pick, "Harnessing the Power of Anger," April 4, 2017, https://www.marcellepick.com/harnessing-power-anger/.

5 "Making Anger Your Ally," http://www.dummies.com/health/mental-health/making-anger-your-ally/.

6 Lindsay Broder, "Before You Send That Angry Email, Read This," *Entrepreneur*, February 25, 2014, https://www.entrepreneur.com/article/231734.

7   Nicholas A. Cummings and Janet L. Cummings, *Refocused Psychotherapy as the First Line Intervention in Behavioral Health* (New York: Routledge, 2013), 45.

8   In a study of fear of terrorism that took place after the 9/11 attacks, those who felt anger tended to expect fewer attacks in the future; those who felt fear were more pessimistic and expected more future attacks. In other words, the angrier a person was, the more optimistic he or she became. Jennifer S. Lerner, Roxana M. Gonzalez, Deborah A. Small, and Baruch Fischhoff, "Effects of Fear and Anger on Perceived Risks of Terrorism: A National Field Experiment," *Psychological Science*, March 1, 2003, http://journals.sagepub.com/doi/abs/10.1111/1467-9280.01433.

9   Paul J. Silvia, "Looking Past Pleasure: Anger, Confusion, Disgust, Pride, Surprise, and Other Universal Aesthetic Emotions," *Psychology of Aesthetics, Creativity, and the Arts* 3, no. 1 (2009): 48–51, DOI: 10.1037/a0014632, https://libres.uncg.edu/ir/uncg/f/P_Silvia_Looking_2009.pdf.

10 "The Upside of Anger: 6 Psychological Benefits of Getting Mad," *Psyblog*, March 6, 2012, http://www.spring.org.uk/2012/03/the-upside-of-anger-6-psychological-benefits-of-getting-mad.php.

11 Ibid.

12 Ibid.

13 Ibid.

14   Mayo Clinic Staff, "Anger Management: 10 Tips to Tame Your Temper," Mayo Clinic, http://www.mayoclinic.org/healthy-lifestyle /adult-health/in-depth/anger-management/art-20045434?pg.

CHAPTER **NINE**

Lean Into Hard Work

1   Colin Powell, *It Worked for Me: In Life and Leadership* (New York: Harper Perennial, 2014), https://www.values.com/inspirational -quotes/6860-there-are-no-secrets-to-success.

2   Estée Lauder, *Estée: A Success Story* (New York: Random House, 1985), http://www.1000ventures.com/business_guide /cs_entrepreneurs_lauder.html.

3   David Z. Hambrick and Elizabeth J. Meinz, "Limits on the Predictive Power of Domain-Specific Experience and Knowledge in Skilled Performance," *Current Directions in Psychological Science* 20, no. 5 (2011): 275–79, http://journals.sagepub.com/doi /10.1177/0963721411422061.

4   John B. Watson, *Behaviorism* (New York: Norton, 1970), 212.

5   Hambrick and Meinz, "Limits on the Predictive Power of Domain -Specific Experience and Knowledge in Skilled Performance."

6   Gerardo Lopez, "The Value of Hard Work: Lessons on Parent Involvement from an (Im)migrant Household," *Harvard Educational Review* 71, no. 3 (September 2001): 416–38, http://

hepgjournals.org/doi/abs/10.17763/haer.71.3.43x7k542x
023767u?code=hepg-site.

7 Clayton R. Critcher and Melissa J. Ferguson, "'Whether I Like
It or Not, It's Important': Implicit Importance of Means Predicts
Self-Regulatory Persistence and Success," *Journal of Personality and Social Psychology* 110, no. 6 (2016): 818–39. http://haas
.berkeley.edu/behavioral_lab/images/Critcher2016.

8 Carol S. Dweck, *Mindset: The New Psychology of Success* (New York:
Random House, 2006), https://www.fastcompany.com/3039181/
why-determination-matters-more-than-smarts-in-getting-ahead.

9 Jayaram V, "The Power of Determination," in *Think Success:
Essays on Self-help* (PureLife Vision Books, 2014), http://www
.hinduwebsite.com/selfdevt/determination.asp.

10 Lonnie W. Aarssen and Laura Crimi, "Legacy, Leisure and
the 'Work Hard—Play Hard' Hypothesis," *The Open Psychology Journal* 9 (2016): 7–24, https://pdfs.semanticscholar
.org/fb71/7c9fd758c4bcec79c7861e8f98498324ab72.pdf?
_ga=2.17782905.155875094.1506620053-909806038
.1506620053.

CHAPTER **TEN**

Stay Open to Unforeseen Inspiration

1 William Wordsworth, "Surprised by Joy," Poetry Foundation,
https://www.poetryfoundation.org/poems/50285/surprised-by-joy.

2   C. S. Lewis, *The Essential C. S. Lewis*, ed. Lyle W. Dorsett (New York: Simon & Schuster, 1996), 26.

3   Steven J. Rubenzer and Thomas R. Faschingbauer, *Personality, Character, and Leadership in the White House: Psychologists Assess the Presidents* (Dulles, VA: Brassey's, 2004), 12.

4   Ciro Conversano, Alessandro Rotondo, Elena Lensi, Olivia Della Vista, Francesca Arpone, and Mario Antonio Reda, "Optimism and Its Impact on Mental and Physical Well-Being," *Clinical Practice & Epidemiology in Mental Health* 6 (2010): 25–29, DOI: 10.2174/1745017901006010025, https://www.ncbi.nlm.nih.gov/pmc/articles/PMC2894461/.

5   2 Corinthians 1:3–4.

CHAPTER **ELEVEN**

Flip Negatives to Positives

1   "More than Forty Years of Progress for Child Passenger Protection: A Chronicle of Child Passenger Safety Advances in the USA, 1965–2009," compiled by Deborah D. Stewart, updated February 2009, Safe Ride News, http://www.saferidenews.com/srndnn/LinkClick.aspx?fileticket=NIPfcuqNL1U%3d&tabid=375.

2   Dean Keith Simonton and Roy F. Baumeister, "Positive Psychology at the Summit," *Review of General Psychology* 9, no. 2 (2005): 100, http://citeseerx.ist.psu.edu/viewdoc/download?doi=10.1.1.602.1519&rep=rep1&type=pdf.

3 J. M. Gottman, *What Predicts Divorce?* (Hillsdale, NJ: Erlbaum, 1994).

4 Terry Waite, *Taken on Trust* (London: Hodder & Stoughton, 2010; originally published 1993), cited by Stephen Joseph, Post-traumatic Growth, https://www.psychologytoday.com/blog/what -doesnt-kill-us/201402/posttraumatic-growth.

5 Peter Stanford, "Terry Waite: 'I Spent Five Years as a Hostage in Beirut—But I Never Cried,'" *The Telegraph*, September 3, 2016, http://www.telegraph.co.uk/men/thinking-man/terry-waite-i -spent-five-years-as-a-hostage-in-beirut---but-i-ne/.

6 Stephen Joseph, "What Doesn't Kill Us . . ." *The Psychologist* 25 (November 2012): 816–19. https://thepsychologist.bps.org.uk /volume-25/edition-11/what-doesnt-kill-us.

7 Tia Ghose, "Realistic Optimists May Have More Success and Happiness, Study Suggests," *Huffington Post*, Aug. 24, 2013, http://www.huffingtonpost.com/2013/08/26/realistic-optimists_n _3816827.html.

8 James W. Pennebaker, Janice K. Kiecolt-Glaser, and Ronald Gla-ser, "Disclosure of Traumas and Immune Function: Health Im-plications for Psychotherapy," *Journal of Consulting and Clinical Psychology* 56, no. 2 (1988): 239–45.

9 Ibid.

10 Michael Jacobs, "Become More Positive with These 5 Tips," *Entrepreneur*, https://www.entrepreneur.com/article/230613.

11   Alex Blackwell, "10 Steps for Transforming Negative Thoughts into Positive Beliefs," *The BridgeMaker*, November 13, 2008, http://www.thebridgemaker.com/10-steps-for-transforming -negative-thoughts-into-positive-beliefs/.

CHAPTER TWELVE
Be a Giver

1   "Boston Marathon Bombing Victims," http://www.cbsnews.com /pictures/boston-marathon-bombing-victims/.

2   Garrett Quinn, "Late Boston Officer's Death Tied to Attack by Boston Marathon Bombers," May 28, 2015, http://www.masslive .com/news/boston/index.ssf/2015/05/late_boston_cop_named _fifth_bo.html.

3   A. A. Sappington, John Bryant, and Connie Oden, "An Experimental Investigation of Victor Frankl's Theory of Meaningfulness in Life," *International Forum for Logotherapy* 13, no. 2 (1990): 125–30, http://psycnet.apa.org/psycinfo/1991-18399-001.

4   Stephen G. Post, "Altruism, Happiness, and Health: It's Good to Be Good," *International Journal of Behavioral Medicine* 12, no. 2 (2005): 66, http://citeseerx.ist.psu.edu/viewdoc/download ?doi=10.1.1.485.8406&rep=rep1&type=pdf.

5   Deborah D. Danner, David A. Showdon, and Wallace V. Friesen, "Positive Emotions in Early Life and Longevity: Findings from the Nun Study," *Journal of Personality and Social Psychology* 80,

no. 5 (2001): 804–13, https://www.apa.org/pubs/journals/releases
/psp805804.pdf.

6 Elissa S. Epel, Elizabeth H. Blackburn, Jue Lin, Firdaus S. Dhabhar, Nancy E. Adler, Jason D. Morrow, and Richard M. Cawthorn, "Accelerated Telomere Shortening in Response to Life Stress," *Proceedings of the National Academy of Sciences of the United States of America* 101, no. 49 (2004): 17312–15.

7 Norman B. Anderson, *Emotional Longevity: What REALLY Determines How Long You Live* (New York: Viking, 2003).

8 Susanna Brinkerhoff Zens and Robert Brinkerhoff, "The Jeter's Leaders Program Evaluation, Executive Summary," April 2004, 20.

9 Ibid., 18.

POSTSCRIPT
You've Already Got What It Takes

1 "*Posttraumatic growth* (PTG) refers to the transformative process that can lead to positive changes after dealing with a traumatic event." H. Kampman, K. Hefferon, M. Wilson, and J. Beale, "'I Can Do Things Now That People Thought Were Impossible, Actually, Things That I Thought Were Impossible': A Meta-synthesis of the Qualitative Findings on Posttraumatic Growth and Severe Physical Injury," *Canadian Psychology/Psychologie canadienne* 56, no. 3 (2015): 283–94, http://psycnet.apa.org/journals/cap/56/3/283/?_ga=1.117073153.602173466.1477499312.

2 *The Handbook of Posttraumatic Growth: Research and Practice,* ed. Lawrence G. Calhoun and Richard G. Tedeschi (New York: Psychology Press, 2014).

3 The traumas Jenna Van Slyke, researcher for the Naval Center for Combat & Operational Stress Control, researched were defined as events that deeply change a person's "fundamental schemas, beliefs, and goals, as well as the ability to manage emotional distress, and . . . profoundly [affect] the individual's life narratives." See Jenna Van Slyke, "Post-traumatic Growth," Naval Center for Combat & Operational Stress Control, https:// pdfs.semanticscholar.org/b2aa/8aed76f97e16d36c1450f50 fc66784f4f010.pdf.

4 See Jill E. Bormann, S. R. Thorp, Julie L. Wetherell, Shahrokh Colshan, and Ariel J. Lang, "Meditation-Based Mantram Intervention for Veterans with Posttraumatic Stress Disorder: A Randomized Trial," *Psychological Trauma: Theory, Research, Practice, and Policy* 5, no. 3 (2013): 259–67, http://psycnet.apa.org/record /2012-06372-001.

5 Laura A. King and Joshua A. Hicks, "Detecting and Constructing Meaning in Life Events," *The Journal of Positive Psychology* 4, no. 5: 317–30, http://www.tandfonline.com/doi/abs/ 10.1080/17439760902992316?src=recsys&journalCode =rpos20.

6 Gabriele Prati and Luca Pietrantoni, "Optimism, Social Support, and Coping Strategies as Factors Contributing to Posttraumatic Growth: A Meta-analysis," *Journal of Loss and Trauma*

14, no. 5 (2009): 364–88, http://www.tandfonline.com/doi/full /10.1080/15325020902724271.

7   Fred R. Shapiro, "Who Wrote the Serenity Prayer?," *The Chronicle of Higher Education*, April 28, 2014, http://www.chronicle .com/article/Who-Wrote-the-Serenity-Prayer-/146159/.

About the Authors

Dr. Sampson Davis is an emergency-room physician, public speaker, philanthropist, and *New York Times* bestselling author.

He was raised as the fifth of six children in Newark, one of New Jersey's poorest cities. As a child, Dr. Davis grew up in cramped living quarters, surrounded by fragmented families, crime, and drugs. Still, he was a good student, able to strike the fragile balance between being smart and socially acceptable on the streets. It was that skill, he says, that was most crucial to his survival.

While attending University High in Newark, he met Rameck Hunt and George Jenkins, two fellow students, and they made a promise to one another to become doctors. Today, all three have fulfilled their pact. In 2000, during their residency, Drs. Davis, Hunt, and Jenkins felt the burning need to give back, and together they created the Three Doctors Foundation (www.threedoctorsfoundation.org). The nonprofit organization offers a series of free public programs focused on health, education, leadership, and mentoring.

Dr. Davis has appeared on numerous talk and radio shows, including *Oprah*, *Today*, *The View*, and *The Tavis Smiley Show*, as well as in print publications, including *Reader's Digest, O Magazine, People, The Washington Post, The New York Times, USA Today, Vibe,* and *Black Enterprise.* Oprah Winfrey delivered her highest honor to Dr. Davis, calling the Three Doctors "The Premiere Role Models of the World."

Dr. Davis has coauthored many *New York Times* bestselling books. His titles include *The Pact, We Beat the Street, The Bond,* and *Living and Dying in Brick City: An ER Doctor Returns Home.* In 2000, he was honored with the *Essence* Lifetime Achievement Award and was named one of the publication's forty most inspirational African Americans in the country. He is the youngest physician to receive the National Medical Association's highest honor, the Scroll of Merit, and was honored on national television at the 2009 BET Awards.

Dr. Davis is committed to making a deep and positive impact on the world and is determined to inspire others to find the Stuff within themselves. Dr. Davis is the father of two boys and resides with his family in his home state of New Jersey.

Sharlee Jeter is the president of the Turn 2 Foundation, which was established by her brother, baseball legend Derek Jeter. The Turn 2 Foundation creates and supports signature programs and activities that motivate young people to turn away from drugs and alcohol and "Turn 2" healthy lifestyles.

As president, Sharlee has developed innovative ways to build the organization, creating special fund-raising and programming events that further promote the foundation's mission and forging key branding opportunities and partnerships that have increased exposure and corporate support. She has helped the foundation successfully channel its fund-raising power into results, as demonstrated by its signature initiative, Jeter's Leaders, a leadership-development program for high school students. The program has seen 100 percent of its participants go to college upon graduating from the program since 2008 and has placed Leaders in 135 paid internships over the last five years.

Under her leadership, the foundation has increased its revenue and welcomed major new corporate partners. Working with organizations and individuals across the worlds of sports, business, and media, she has played a central role in elevating the profile of Turn 2, which is now among the most visible nonprofits in the United States.

Sharlee was raised in Kalamazoo, Michigan, and went on to receive a bachelor of science degree in mathematics from Spelman College in Atlanta in 2001. When she was diagnosed with Hodgkin's lymphoma in her senior year, giving in to cancer was never an option. She finished school while undergoing chemotherapy treatments and won her battle with cancer. She enjoys a successful career dedicated to improving the lives of youth and encouraging them to develop the Stuff within themselves. Sharlee lives in New York City with her son, Jalen.